Stay with me

The most creative hotel brands in the world

GINGKO PRESS

First Published in the
United States of America, 2017
Gingko Press, Inc.
1321 Fifth Street
Berkeley, CA 94710, USA
email: books@gingkopress.com

ISBN: 978-1-58423-572-9

Printed in China

Copyright © 2017 *Catherine Harvey*
Design & Text by *Catherine Harvey*
Foreword © 2017 *Steven Heller*
All Rights Reserved.

No part of this book may be reproduced or utilized
in any form or by any means, mechanical or electronic,
including, but not limited to photocopying, scanning
and recording by any information and retrieval system,
without permission in writing from the publisher.

Contents

4   Foreword STEVEN HELLER
6   Introduction CATHERINE HARVEY

America

13   NoMad Hotel NEW YORK, NEW YORK
20   Hôtel Americano NEW YORK, NEW YORK
29   The Standard, High Line NEW YORK, NEW YORK
37   Wythe Hotel NEW YORK, NEW YORK
44   Palihouse Santa Monica SANTA MONICA, CALIFORNIA
53   Hotel Lincoln CHICAGO, ILLINOIS

Europe

63   citizenM LONDON, ENGLAND
70   Claridge's LONDON, ENGLAND
78   The Ampersand Hotel LONDON, ENGLAND
86   The London Edition LONDON, ENGLAND
95   Hotel Wiesler GRAZ, AUSTRIA
102 Hotel Daniel VIENNA, AUSTRIA
111 Mama Shelter PARIS, FRANCE
118 Casa Camper BERLIN, GERMANY
127 Michelberger Hotel BERLIN, GERMANY
134 Hotel The Exchange AMSTERDAM, NETHERLANDS
142 The Student Hotel AMSTERDAM, NETHERLANDS
151 The Thief OSLO, NORWAY
159 Hotel OMM BARCELONA, SPAIN
166 Ett Hem STOCKHOLM, SWEDEN
175 Scandic Grand Central STOCKHOLM, SWEDEN

Asia

185 Lux Maldives MALDIVES
193 Bulgari Hotel BALI, INDONESIA
200 Nine Hours Hotel KYOTO, JAPAN
208 Wanderlust Hotel SINGAPORE

Oceania

218 QT Hotel SYDNEY, AUSTRALIA
227 Art Series Hotel Group AUSTRALIA
235 The Oyster Inn WAIHEKE, NEW ZEALAND

242 Photography Credits
243 Acknowledgements
244 Author

Foreword

Steven Heller

There was a time not long ago when the majority of hotels were branded in rudimentary ways: through matchbook covers, baggage labels and towel monograms. Unless it was an incredibly swanky grand hotel — like in the 1932 film starring Garbo, Barrymore and Crawford — the matchbooks usually looked nothing like the labels, and the labels might have an entirely different typography than the rest of the identity. That is probably because hotels, like restaurants and laundromats did not always hire graphic designers. Rather commercial art studios gave their clients what their printing vendors provided. Of course, this is an over-generalization; many hotels and even motels attempted to synchronize their typographic conceits. Yet it was more true than not during the 20s, 30s, 40s and even 50s before branding emerged as a strategic virtue.

I don't know who during the postwar era began the widespread practice of unifying hotel brand standards, but I bet it began with architects who realized the benefits of a singular design campaign that wed building and interior design to graphic and identity design, from signage to luggage tags. And let's not forget the staff uniforms emblazoned with a version of the logos that grace the entrances.

Perhaps the influence for this was luxury ocean liners, those mammoth sea-going hotels, which were branded to the hilt. Branding gave the customer a sense of belonging to an exclusive club (so did being in the middle of the ocean unable to leave). Branded objects were meant as souvenirs for passengers to whisk away and later serve as advertisements for the ship lines.

Hotel branding, which was yet to be labelled as such, had become *de rigeur* during the late 50s and 60s especially when mid century modern architects made mid-century modern hotels into total design experiences. Designers then as now focused on every strategic detail — no bed was left unturned and no pillow chocolate failed to include the hotel's name or trademark.

Little has changed since then. Hotels stake their success on having an excellent reputation. Before the age of digital rating apps, the reputation was represented by the brand and vice versa. And the brand encompassed every experiential virtue of the hotel. A palatial lobby suggested luxurious rooms. Even in the modern hotels, expanses of space implied supreme luxury. From the lighting to the furniture, to the carpets on the floor and the hangings on the wall, the brand story is a critical mass of props.

A hotel is a stage on which guests and staff play certain unpredictable and constant roles. Branding, however, is more than just the backdrop of this drama (or comedy, as the case may be). It is everything that is visible and invisible to the guest's eyes. It is the real, exaggerated or imagined legacy of the hotel. It is what goes on behind the check-in desk and inside the rooms. It is the amenities and the essentials. There are plenty of basic, economical hotels everywhere — being basic is also a brand. But this book is about the exemplary brands, those whose names and logos evoke desire and trigger awe; where the minute a guest walks through the door, they are completely enveloped in the arm's of the hotel's brand.

Introduction

Catherine Harvey

For the past ten years, I have had an inexplicable fascination with hotels. For me, they provide a unique combination of complete privacy and an escape from the everyday. In addition, the aesthetics of hotels appealed to my creative nature as I dissected interior design choices, along with which branded bathroom amenities they chose to align themselves with. It was through these observations, made over many years as a graphic designer, that I began to notice how hotels were branding themselves.

Branding basically assists the consumer, or guest in the case of hotels, to differentiate between one product or service based on a range of conscious, and sometimes unconscious, decisions. As the competition increases between choices, this brand comes to represent more than merely a product or service but also reflects the vision, philosophy, values and attitudes of the people who work for the company. Success is measured by the consumer's, or guest's, perception of the brand.

Hotels were once classified using stars — greater numbers of stars indicated greater luxury. However, this system changed depending on the part of the world you were in, and even today there remains no global rating standard. As such, many hotels have taken to self-classification, granting themselves even higher star ratings than five in an attempt to distinguish themselves from others.

The hotels that I chose for inclusion in this book were not based on the number of stars they actually had, or advertised to have, but through hours of research. The hotels that I believed were utilizing their branding to interact with their guests in unique ways, whether through tangible or intangible experiences, were the hotels that I chose to contact. Following this, I financed trips myself to stay in the majority of the hotels included in this publication, to experience each hotel in person and ensure that the integrity of the content for you, the reader, was assured.

There was an overwhelming response for incorporation into this book and, for this reason, I had the difficult task of deciding which hotels to include and which to omit. Some of the hotels that I visited went above and beyond for me; however, I took none of this into consideration when deciding which hotels were to be included.

Plenty of books and reviews on particular hotels already exist, but the authenticity of this particular book and its content is purely related to the branding of a hotel, and how it related to its overall experience. This book is, of course, not all-inclusive, with some establishments such as Ace Hotels (largely the creation of the late Alex Calderwood), declining to be included. I do believe, however, that contributions to the industry like Calderwood's have elevated the importance of branding in hotels almost as much as Ian Schrager contributed to the idea of 'lifestyle' branding for hotels in the 1980s.

All hotels fundamentally provide a room with a bed in exchange for payment. However, the evolution of this offering has seen a dramatic shift from a 'cookie cutter' approach of standardization (mostly as seen in large chains) to terms such as 'boutique' becoming ubiquitous within the industry.

Traditionally, hotel guests would check in at reception, where a staff member would give them their room key. The guest would then retreat to their room to work or rest, only emerging to come together with other guests for breakfast. Now, however, you can check yourself in online (room keys are often optional, with guests using their mobile phone or retina scans to gain access to their room), and hotels provide guests numerous spaces to work, play, or relax before they retreat to their room solely to sleep. The focus has shifted to spending less time in your hotel room and more time interacting with others. Along with these changes, hotel guests are now far more sophisticated. They want to engage with the hotel brand, and are paying more attention to how the hotel speaks to them and the services it offers, along with the traditional factors such as location and price.

Although hotels are usually chosen through images of their rooms, there's a new breed of hotel today that offers more than a place to sleep and instead becomes a destination in itself.

Rather than relying solely on one design team, hotels are now collaborating with a wide variety of architects, graphic designers, interior designers and artists to create an experience that is truly unique to a particular hotel. Now, more than ever, hotels are trying to connect with guests on an artistic, intellectual and emotional level. Personalized communications, rather than corporate processes, are becoming the norm amongst the hotels that understand their guest's needs.

In addition, hotels are now periodically reinventing themselves to ensure that their offerings remain unique, exciting and appealing to guests who frequent them regularly. Whether it is through the creation of self-sustaining rooftop gardens, embracing technological advances, curated art spaces or bringing the hotel's local neighborhood inside, hotels are now engaging with their guests in a manner and tone previously unseen.

This new 'language' of hotels creates a story and makes a connection with their guests. In the graphic design industry, I can't recall the amount of times that I have heard about the importance of applying an identity consistently across a range of collateral. This almost formulaic approach is common, and you will find yourself fighting many battles if you attempt to break this mould. The most unique brands, however, avoid this approach by utilizing subtle variations whilst avoiding the familiarity through repetition ethos. In particular, hotels have a unique position of being able to reinvent their story (so that it remains relevant) while removing themselves from branding that relies solely on repetition. Of course, this is no easy task and relies on a fine balancing act between many contributing factors.

One such factor is whether a hotel would like to appear as part of a chain so that guests recognize their other hotels or whether they prefer to appear as a standalone.

Indeed, today there are numerous high end hotels that appear to operate in isolation, while actually belonging to larger chains. Similarly, a considerable number of the large hotel chains are now opening more boutique offerings under a different brand to appeal to a more design conscious market. In addition, this balancing act continues as hotels have to decide whether they are firstly a hotel and secondly a brand or vice versa.

Hotels also, of course, cater to different types of guests, including business travellers, tourists, families and others seeking a luxury experience. Their success, as a brand, relies on their reputation, so much so that high-end fashion houses are now opening their own hotels to extend their brand. Quite a few hotels are also offering their own branded products (many within an on-premise store) so that you, the guest, can take a piece of the hotel with you.

There are many practical decisions to undertake when designing, building, and operating a hotel, from determining the size of each room in order to maximize the number of rooms offered, to evaluating prices guests will be willing to pay. Perhaps that is why the 'smaller' details, such as stationery, signage and other marketing collateral have been undervalued within hotels for so long. My hope is that this book demonstrates that these 'smaller' details are just as important as the size of a room, and could add even more to the overall experience of your stay. After all, a hotel is far more than just a place to sleep.

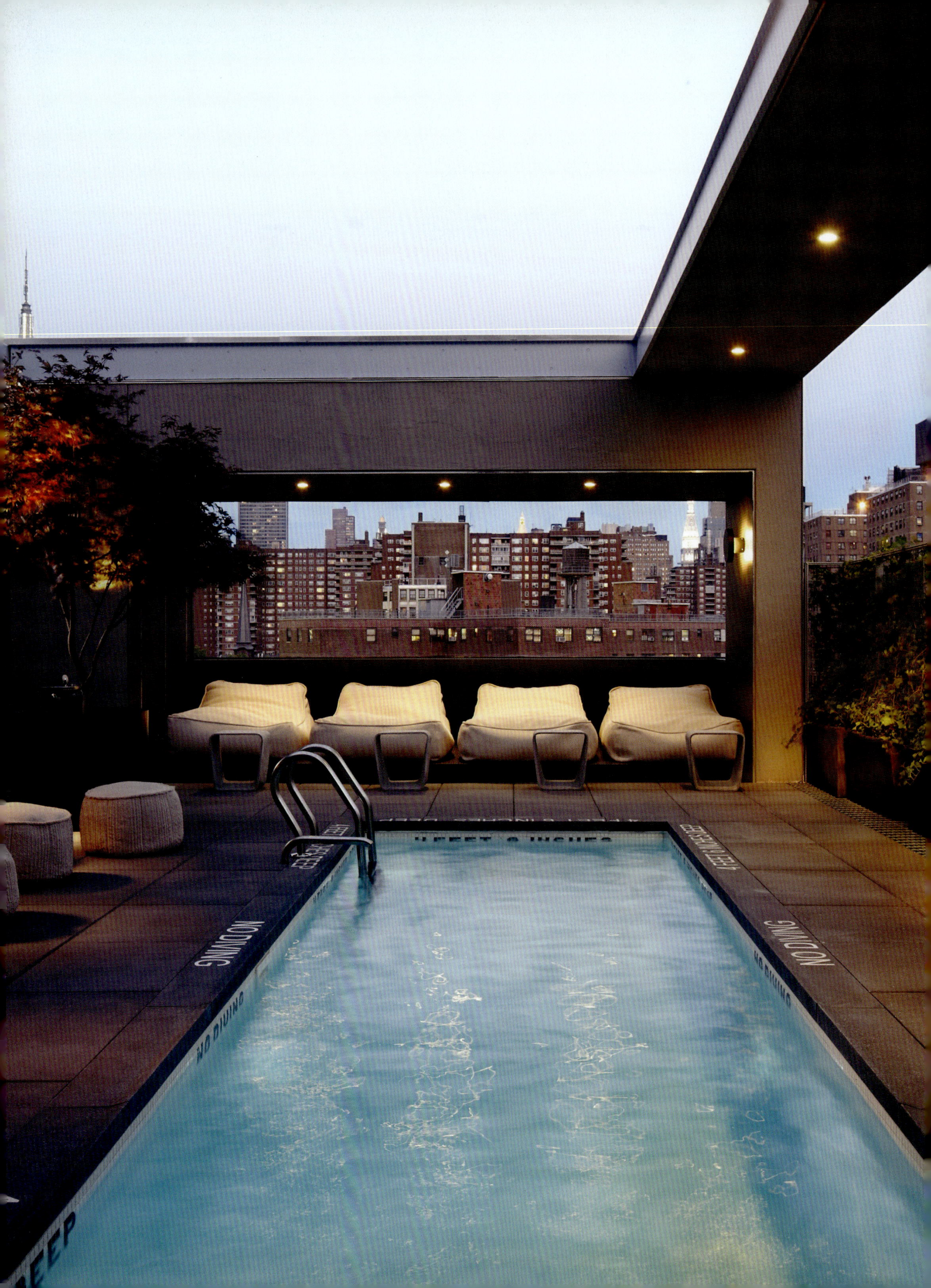
NO DIVING
NO DIVING

'Quality is never an accident.
It is always the result of intelligent effort.'

— John Ruskin

NoMad

1170 BROADWAY

HOTEL   NEW YORK

AMERICA | NEW YORK | THE NOMAD

The NoMad Manhattan, New York

ADDRESS | 1170 Broadway & 28th Street, New York, USA
ROOMS | 168, including 14 suites
OPENED | April 2012
ARCHITECT | Schickel & Ditmars (original building); Stonehill & Taylor (conversion)
INTERIOR DESIGN | Jacques Garcia
GRAPHIC DESIGN | be-poles

The NoMad Hotel (whose name comes from 'North of Madison Square Park') was originally built in 1903. Formerly the Beaux-Arts Johnstone Building, it has been restored to its original grandeur and transformed with layers of luxury.

French designer Jacques Garcia has ensured the hotel's opulence with the use of richly textured custom designed furniture and artwork. Inspired by Garcia's bedroom from his childhood, the rooms contain decadent features, including mahogany French writing desks, embossed leather headboards, velvet and damask patterned paravents, claw feet baths and reclaimed maple hardwood floors.

Completed with sophistication, elegance and charm, the hotel includes a large central atrium complete with a pyramidal glass roof, dining room, library, cocktail bar and rooftop. Following this, an exclusive private function area exists in the restored cupola that sits atop the roof's northwest corner.

Design studio be-poles developed the identity, along with the hotel's art program, based on the idea of the 'voyage.' With a variety of 19th century correspondence, 20th century travel collectibles and contemporary photography, the artwork within each guest room communicates a consistent story of a journey through time and space.

'Every guest room at the NoMad is complete with unique custom furnishings. Mahogany French writing desks, embossed leather headboards, velvet and damask patterned paravents, claw feet baths and reclaimed maple hardwood floors.'

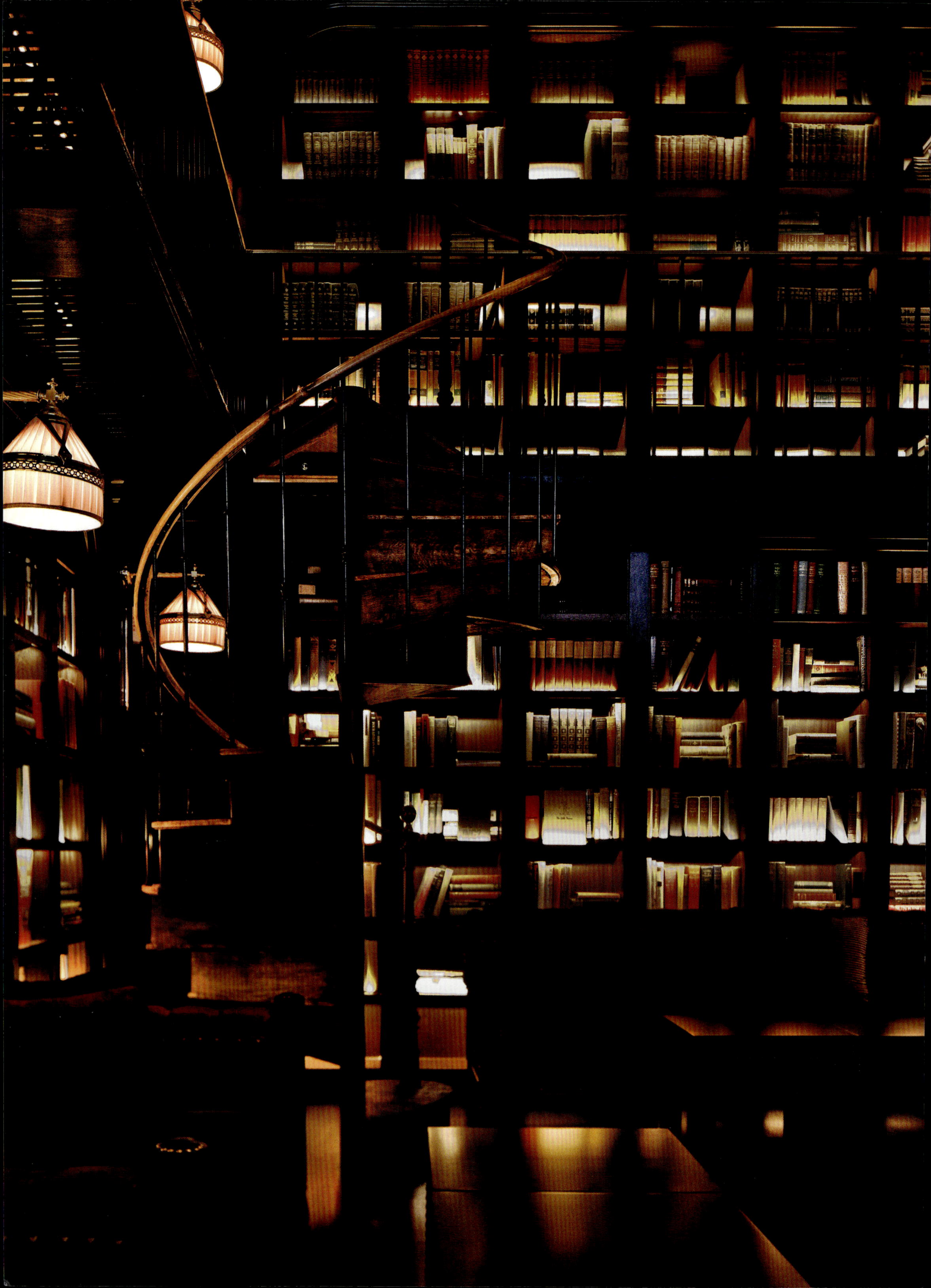

THE NOMAD

AMERICA | NEW YORK

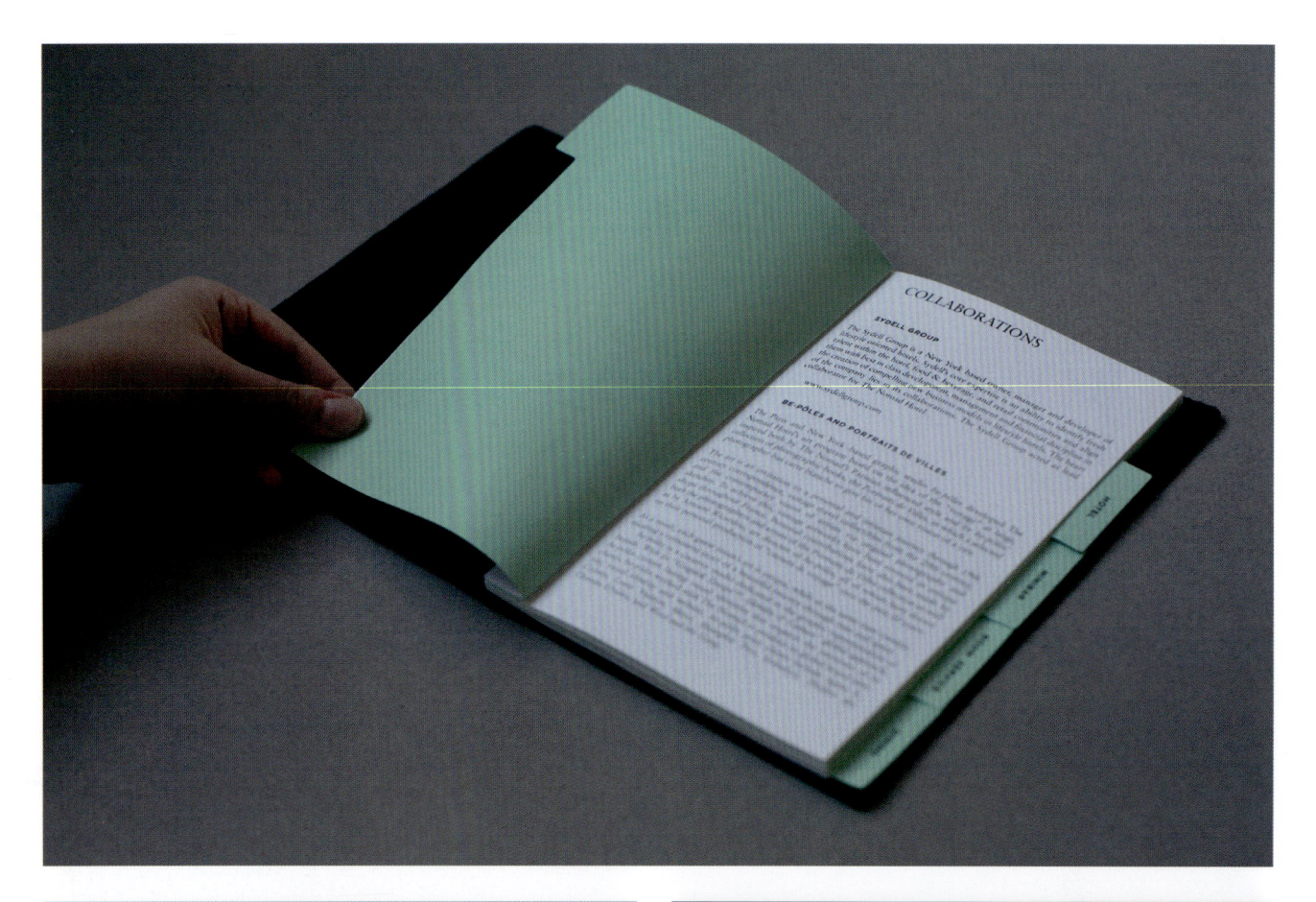

The identity, created with strong typography, is elegant and minimal. It is enhanced with gold foil and debossing to create a level of sophistication that reflects the hotel experience.

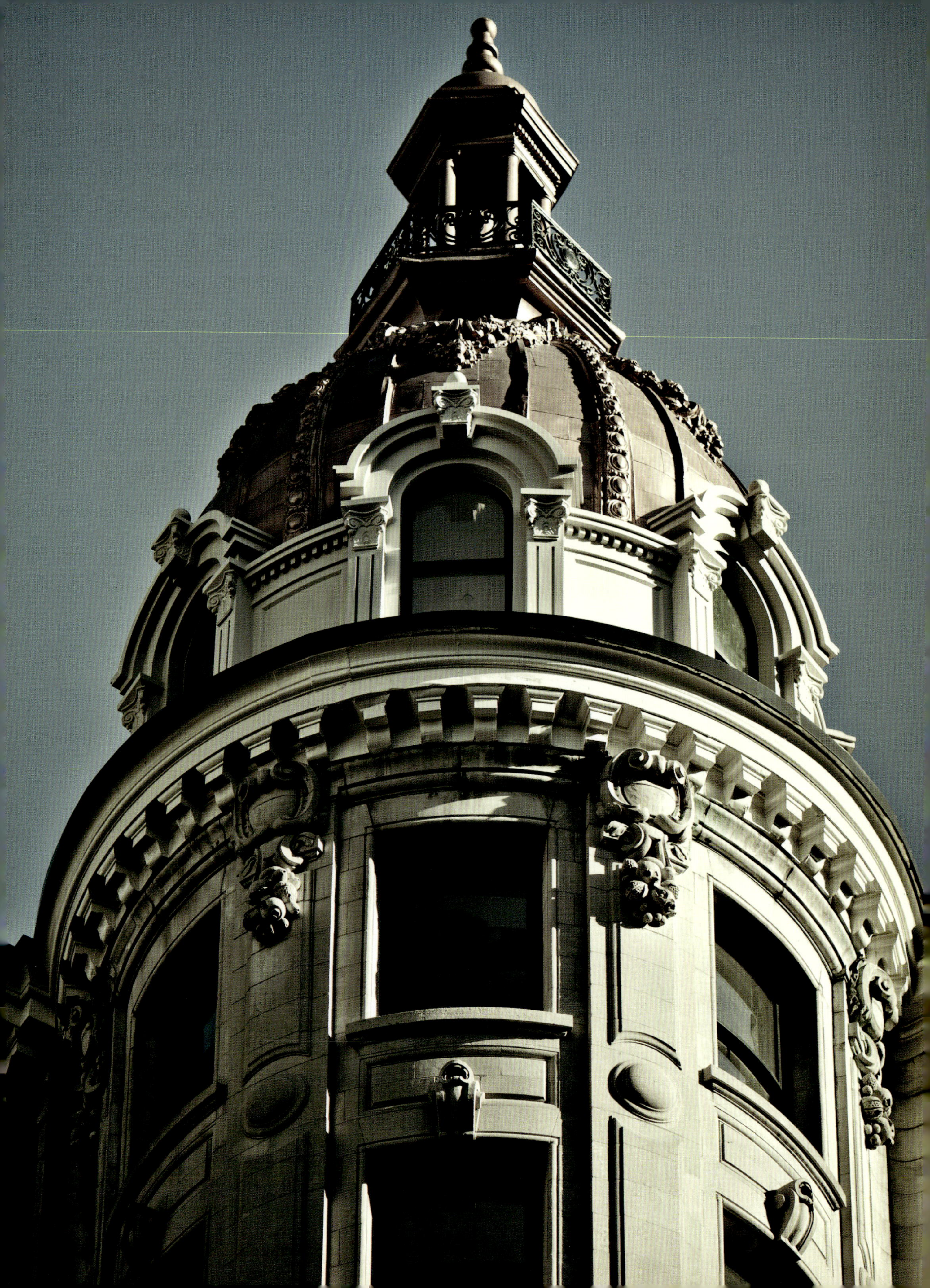

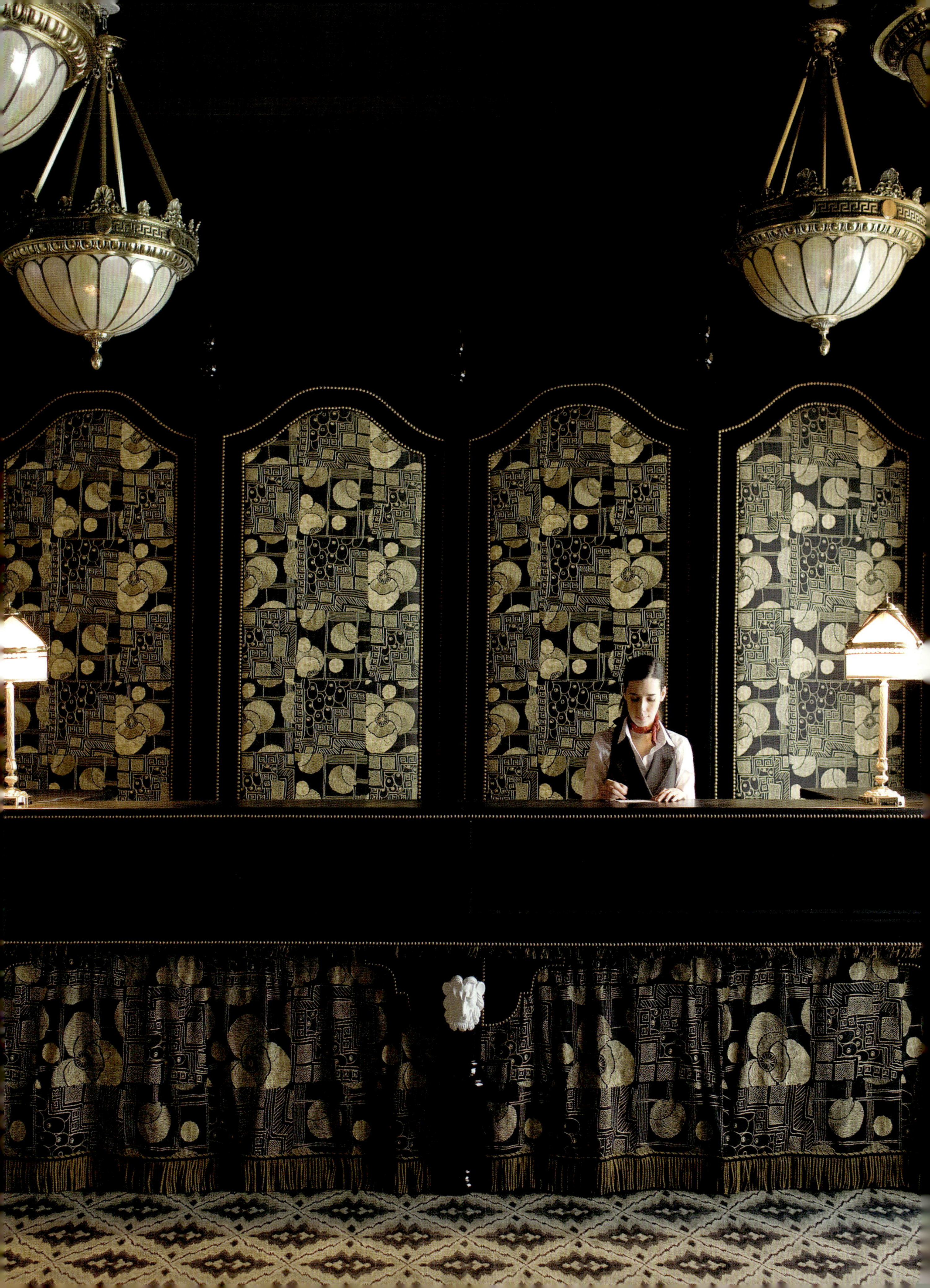

Hôtel Americano
Chelsea,
New York

ADDRESS | 518 West 27th Street, Chelsea, New York, USA
ROOMS | 56 guest rooms, suites and studios
OPENED | September 2011
ARCHITECT | Enrique Norten, TEN Arquitectos
INTERIOR DESIGN | MCH Arnaud Montigny and Gianni Lavacchini
GRAPHIC DESIGN | Pandiscio Co.

Hôtel Americano is located in the Chelsea neighbourhood alongside more than three hundred art galleries, the High Line and the Hudson River. The hotel is the first in America for owners Grupo Habita (who already own thirteen hotels in Mexico) and, as such, encompasses a variety of international influences.

Designed by Mexican architect Enrique Norten, the ten-story building is a glass structure encased in a metal mesh façade — an innovative use of salvaged conveyor belts. This structure not only captures the industrial spirit of the neighbourhood but provides a visual distinction amongst the surrounding buildings.

The rooms, by French designer Arnaud Montigny, are comprised of wooden platform beds (inspired by Japanese ryokans) to create an unexpected feature within a modern hotel. To enhance this modern experience, the hotel also provides an iPad with a preloaded selection of music to play from hidden speakers within each room.

Hôtel Americano's branding is purely black and white, consisting of a simplistic sans serif softened with a secondary italic typeface. The branding is modern and clean, reflecting the interior of the hotel itself. In addition, the technology for this hotel has been extended to include their own app that recommends experiences for guests either 'in' or 'out' of the hotel.

'The industrial-modernist structure, designed by Mexican architect Enrique Norten, captures the industrial spirit of the Chelsea neighbourhood.'

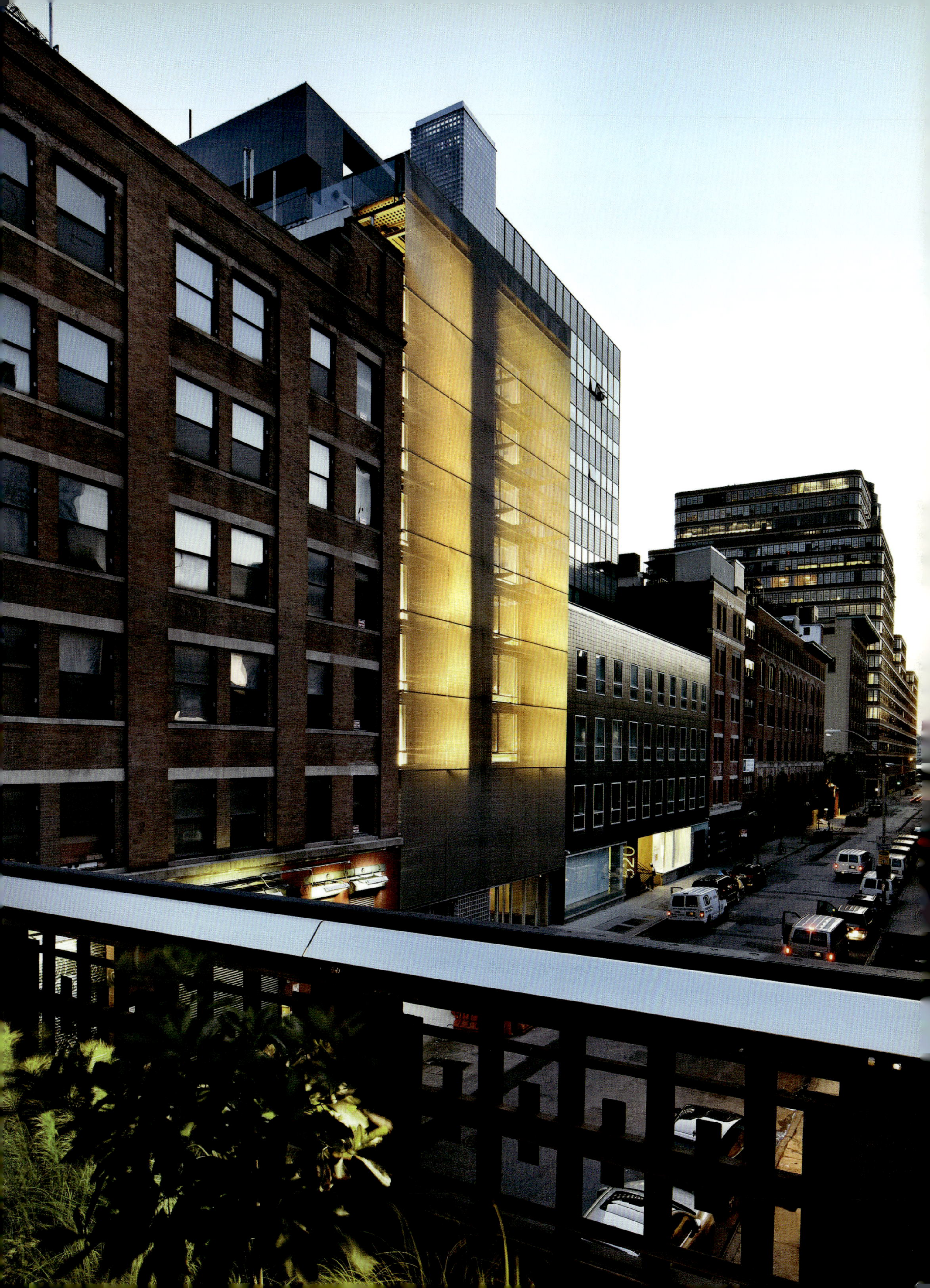

AMERICA | NEW YORK

HÔTEL
AMERICANO

HÔTEL AMERICANO

HÔTEL AMERICANO

CHELSEA NEW YORK

518 West 27th Street, New York NY 10001

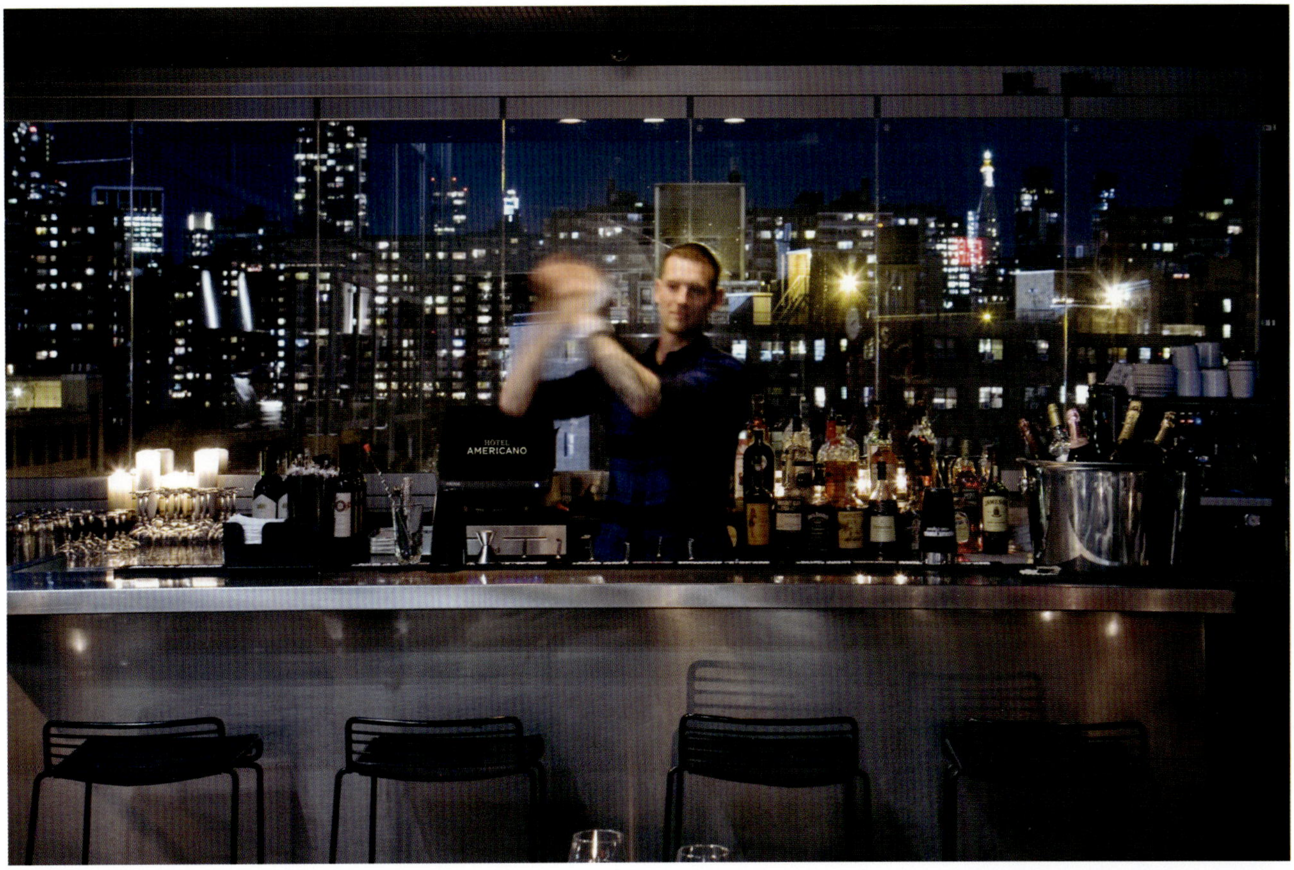
HÔTEL
AMERICANO

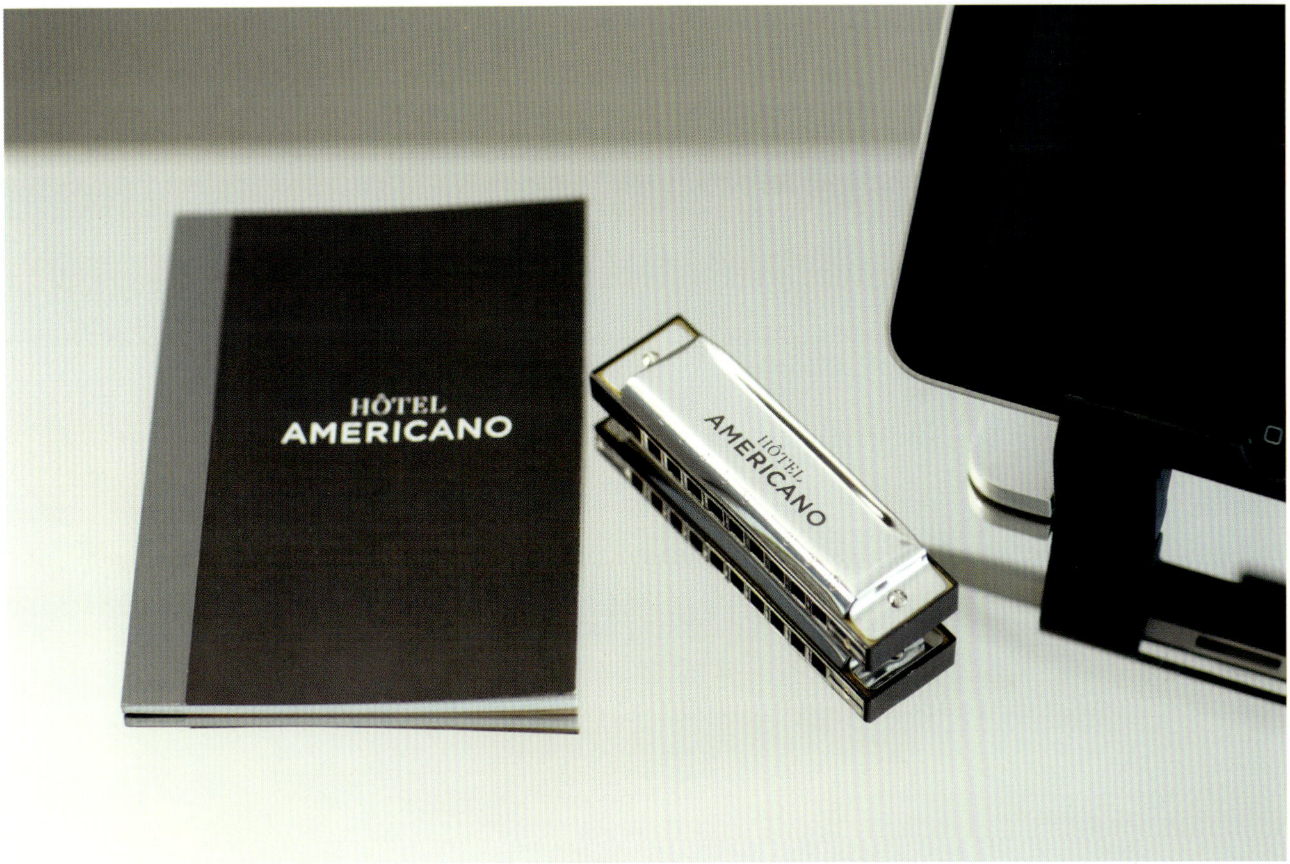
HÔTEL
AMERICANO
HÔTEL
AMERICANO

AMERICANO

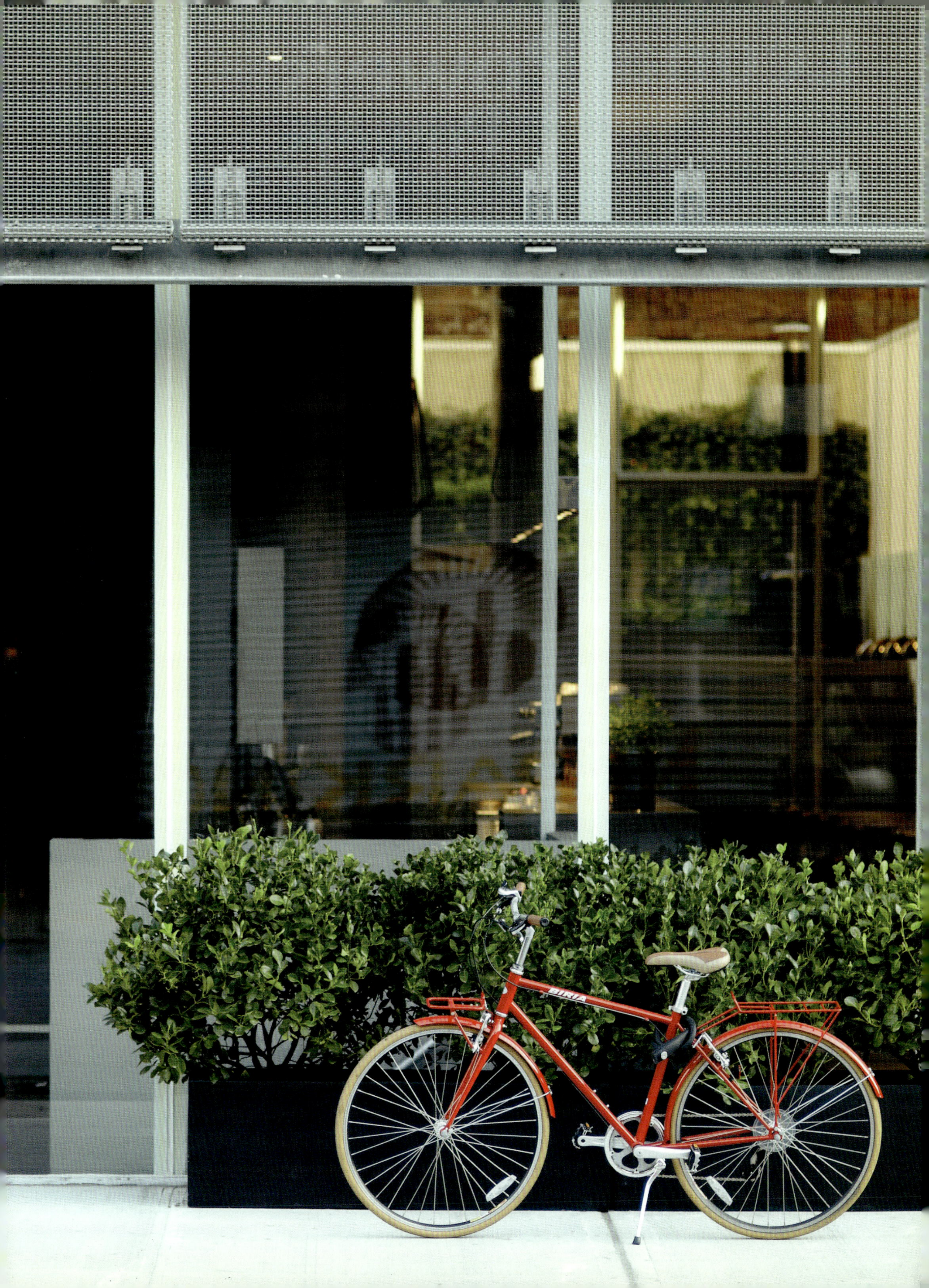
BIRIA

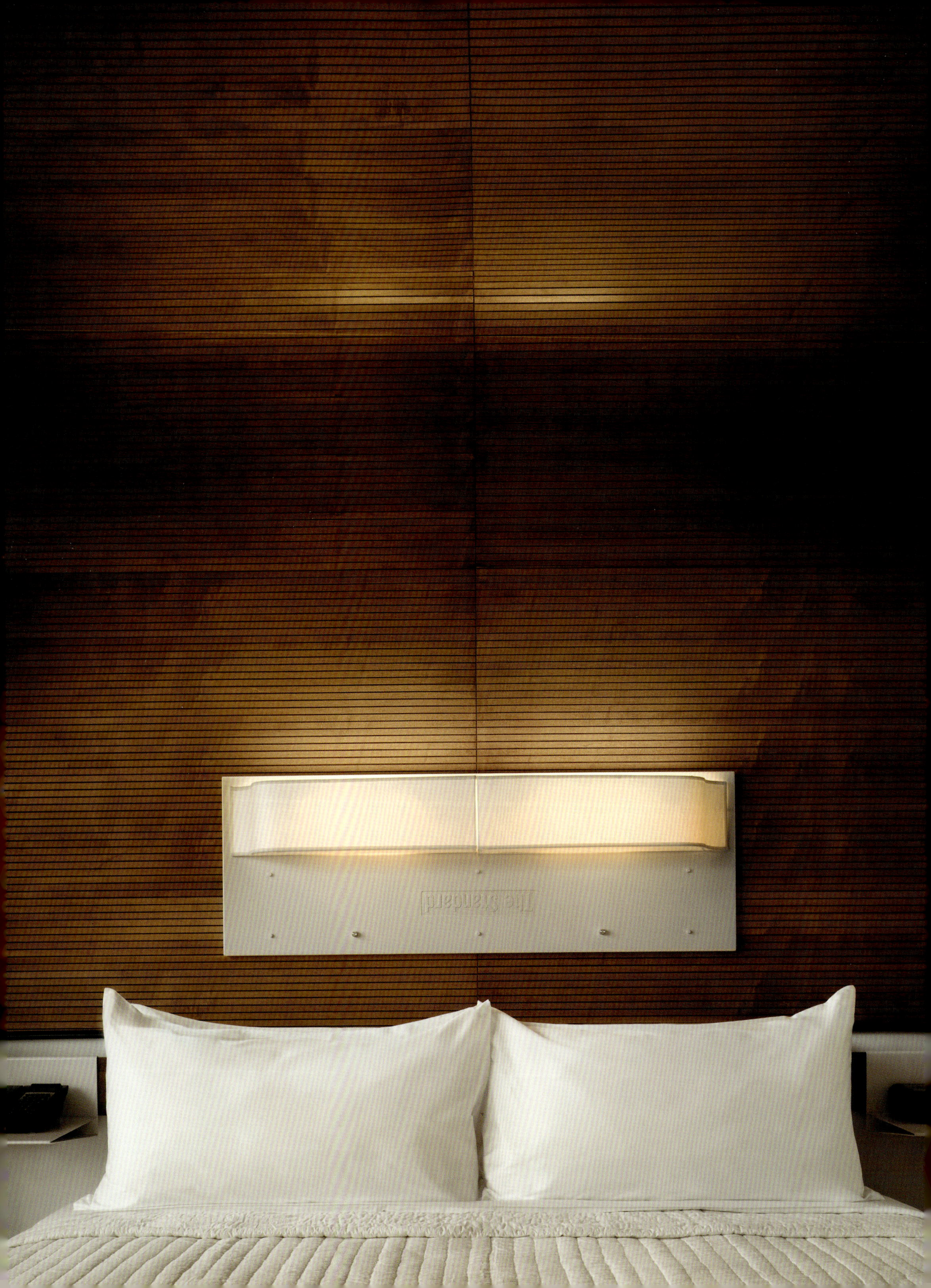

AMERICA | NEW YORK | THE STANDARD, HIGH LINE

The Standard High Line, New York

ADDRESS | 848 Washington Street, New York, USA
ROOMS | 337
OPENED | September 2008
ARCHITECT | Ennead Architects
INTERIOR DESIGN | Roman and Williams
GRAPHIC DESIGN | Internal Design Team

The Standard, High Line is a uniquely designed building by Ennead Architects located in the Meatpacking District of Manhattan.

Built above the High Line (the former elevated railroad that has now been developed into a linear public park), the eighteen floor, three hundred and thirty-seven room hotel proudly stands as a beacon of concrete and glass.

Owner Andre Balazs chooses site-specific hotel locations and once inside The Standard, High Line guests have access to breathtaking views of the Hudson River and the New York City skyline.

The iconic upside down logo appears throughout the hotel in multiple versions, including gold foil, embossed into leather and recessed into the building's entrance. Amenities within the room, including ear plugs, soap, cotton buds and bubble bath, are also branded and available to purchase in The Standard's on-premise store. This is where you can also find a selection of co-branded items between selected artists and the hotel.

The Standard, High Line has an irreverent yet playful sensibility which, together with its careful consideration for design and service, ensures a complete experience is created for their guests.

'The hotel's iconic upside down logo appears in many variations throughout the hotel — from traditional stationery and bathroom amenities to their own branded ATM.'

AMERICA | NEW YORK

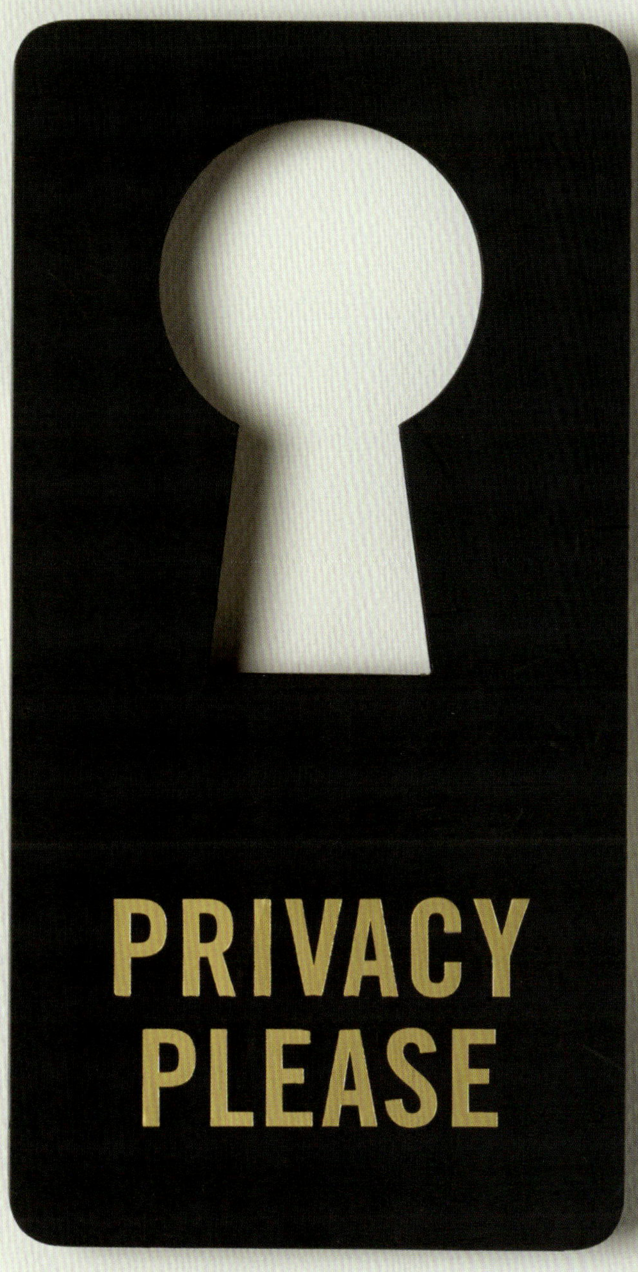
PRIVACY
PLEASE

H'
The Standard
1 RAZOR & BLADE
SHAVE CREAM
H'
SHAVE CREAM
60 mL. / 2.0 Fl. Oz.
The Standard
H'

THE STANDARD, HIGH LINE

AMERICA | NEW YORK

'A Year of Unusual Requests' Calendar, designed by KesselsKramer, shows a playful interpretation of customer feedback throughout the year.

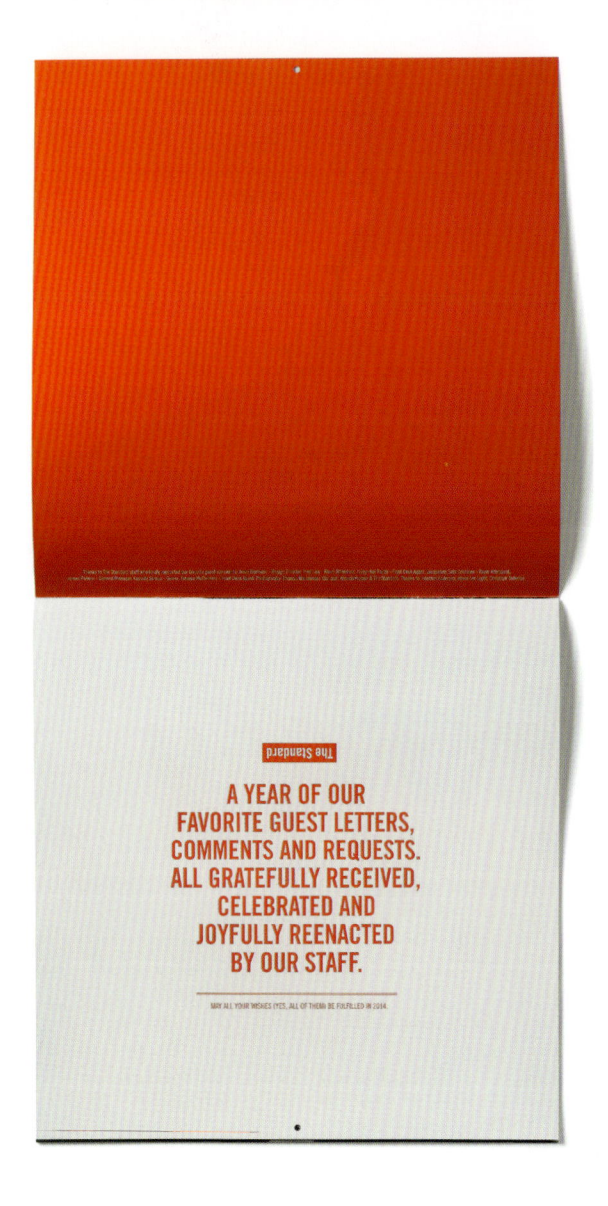

34

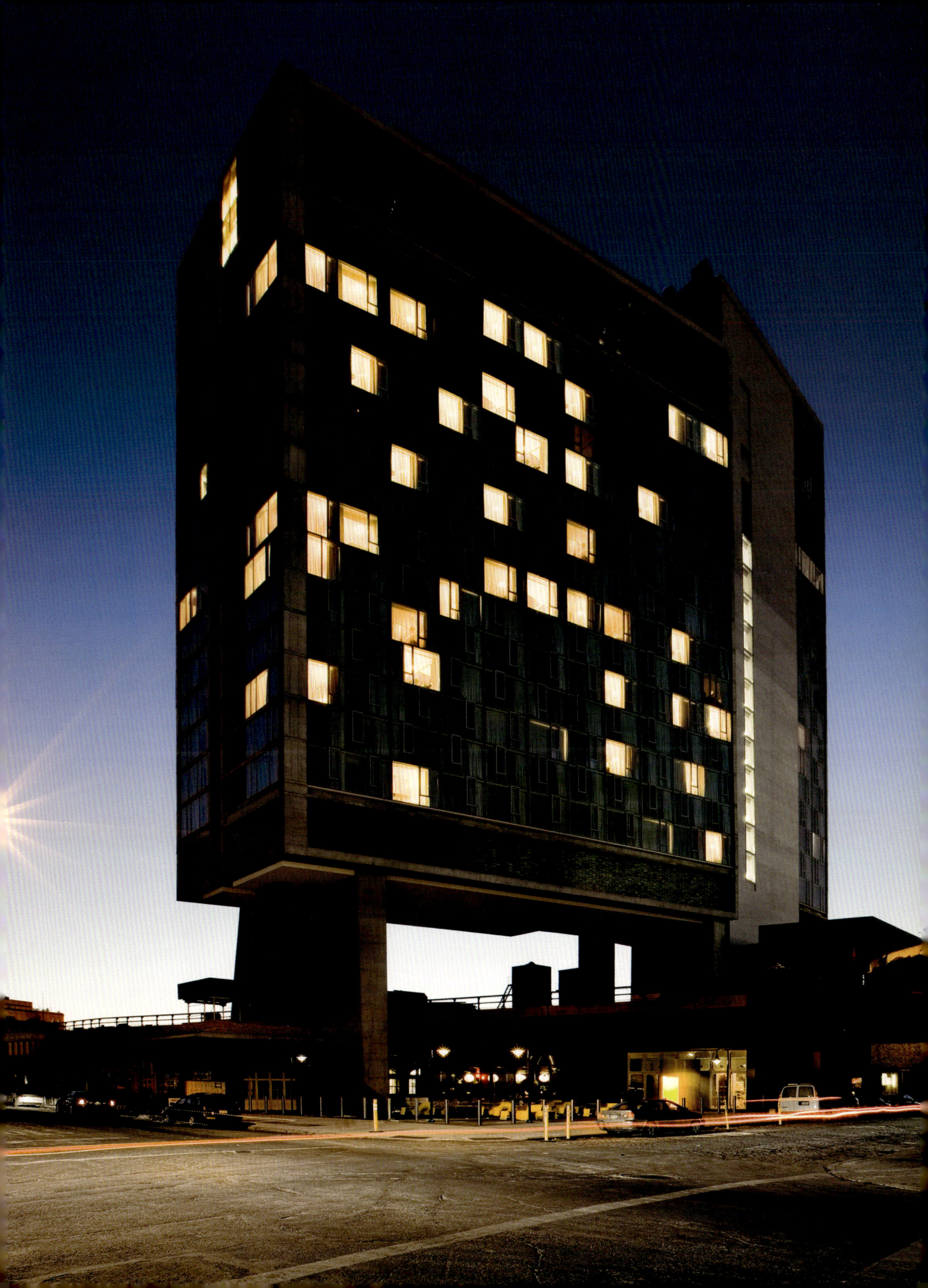

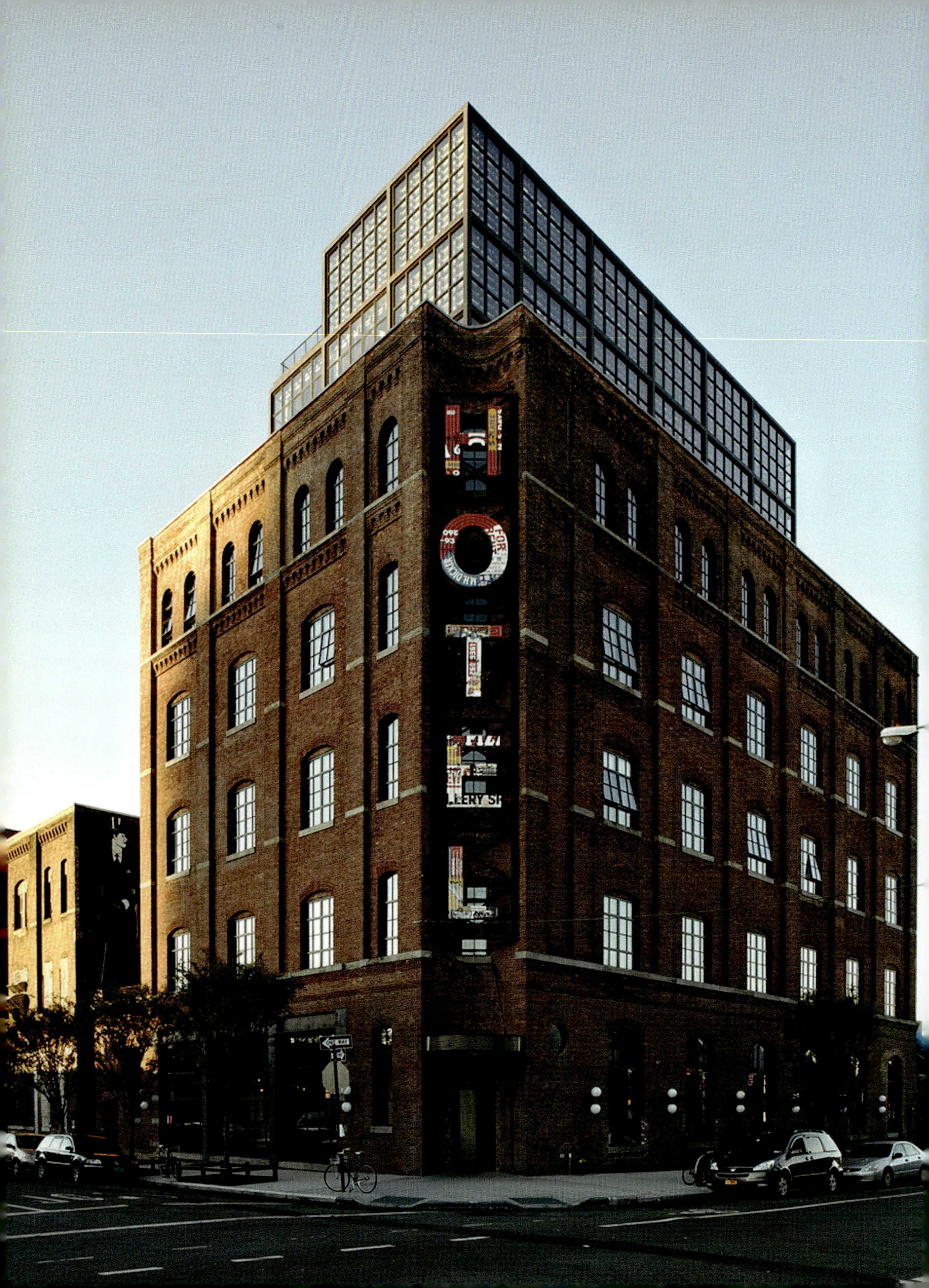
HOTEL

Wythe Hotel Brooklyn, New York

ADDRESS | 80 Wythe Ave, Brooklyn, New York, USA
ROOMS | 70
OPENED | May 2012
ARCHITECT | Morris Adjmi Architects (three-story addition)
INTERIOR DESIGN | Public spaces by Workstead; Restaurants by Andrew Tarlow, Guest rooms — a collaboration between Workstead, Andrew Tarlow, Peter Lawrence and Jed Walentas of Two Trees and architect Morris Adjmi.
GRAPHIC DESIGN | Derick Holt

The Wythe Hotel is an eight-story building on Williamburg's waterfront in Brooklyn. Originally built in 1901 as a cooperage that made barrels and casks, it has been meticulously converted into a historic, yet modern, hotel. The industrial character of the brick and wood combination (including its concave corner entrance, original pine beams, masonry, arched windows and cast iron columns) have all been preserved and now seamlessly integrate with the modern additions.

This includes the three-story glass and aluminium structure above the hotel that dramatically pulls the building into the present. Housing The Ides Bar, the 6th floor bar and terrace, this additional space has created arguably the best platform to view Manhattan at night.

The hotel exposes guests to the works of other artists not only within their on-site pop-up store but also from the exterior of the building. From the street, artist Tom Fruin's fifty-foot sign spells 'HOTEL' down the side of the building (made from salvaged New York street signs framed with neon red tubing), whilst the work of Steve Powers (aka ESPO) can be seen within certain hotel rooms as large hand-painted signs on exposed brick. Through this integration with artists, the Wythe Hotel showcases the eclectic nature of the Williamsburg neighbourhood.

> 'Originally built in 1901 as a cooperage that made barrels and casks, the building has been meticulously converted into a historic, yet modern, hotel. The Wythe Hotel's philosophy was to create a hotel that reflects the borough's creative spirit, history and vibrant energy.'

The main rooms on floors two to five are either Manhattan Kings or Brooklyn Queens, which denotes not only the size of the beds but the boroughs they face. Rooms feature thirteen-foot high original timber ceilings, oversized windows, heated polished concrete floors and bed frames made from recycled wood salvaged from the original building.

WYTHE HOTEL

The essence of the hotel has been captured in the branding with custom illustration and lettering that utilises a minimal colour palette primarily consisting of navy blue. Applied cohesively across all collateral, the graphic design has effectively added an additional layer to the success of the restoration.

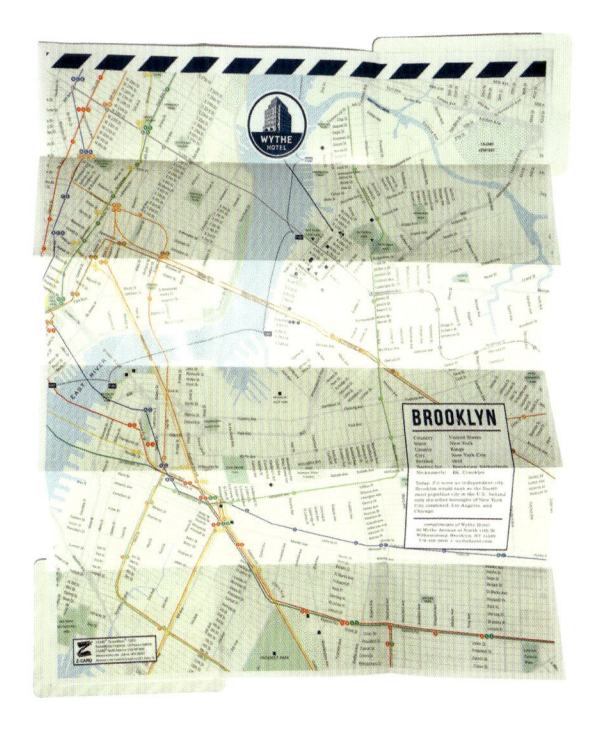

39

AMERICA | NEW YORK

The Ides Bar at the Wythe Hotel has the most stunning views of Manhattan and Brooklyn, all from the rooftop.

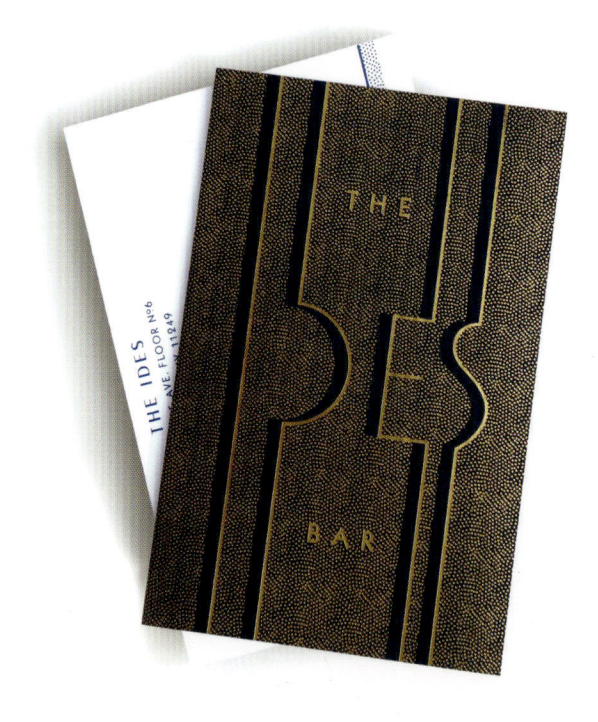

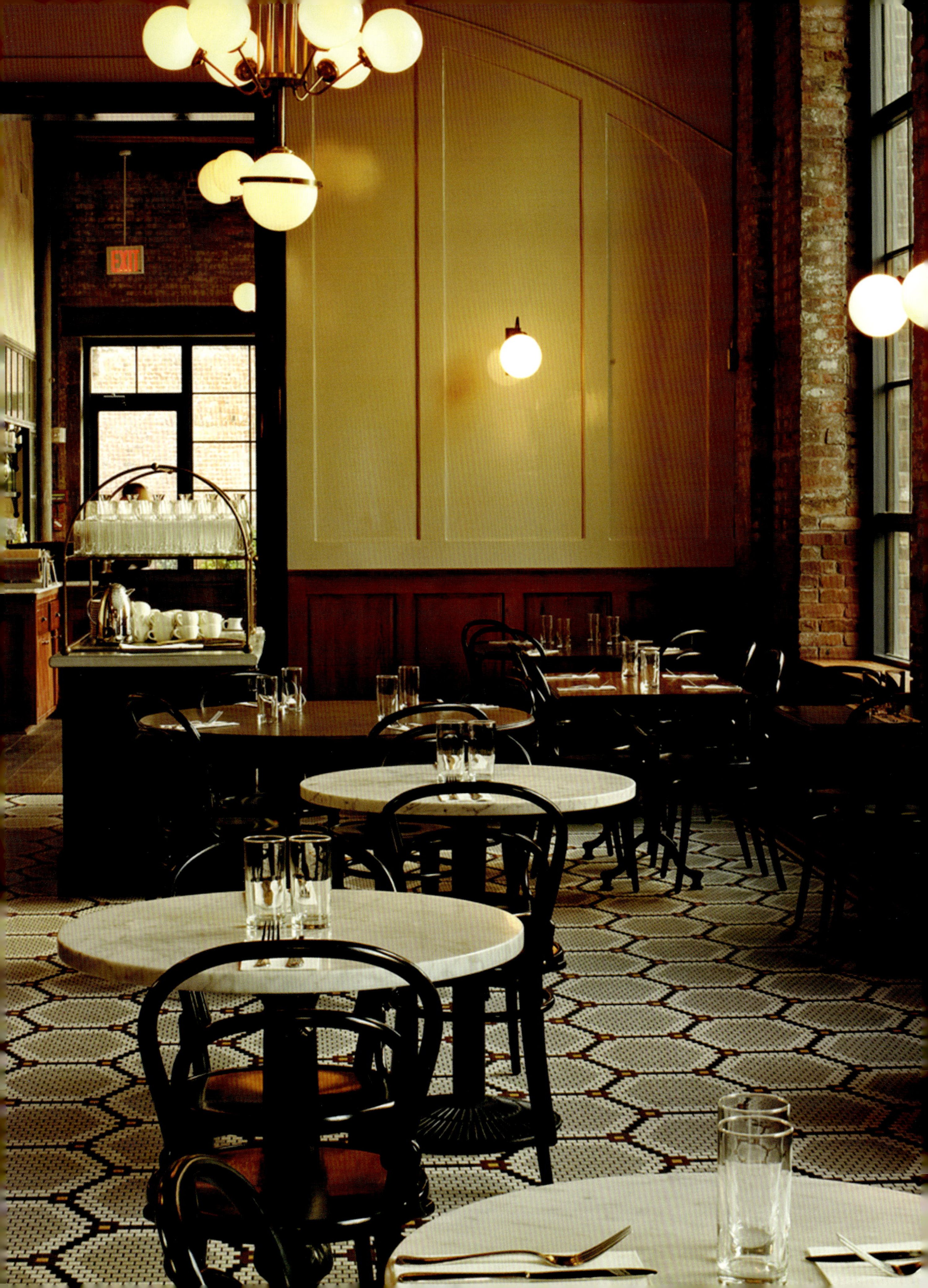

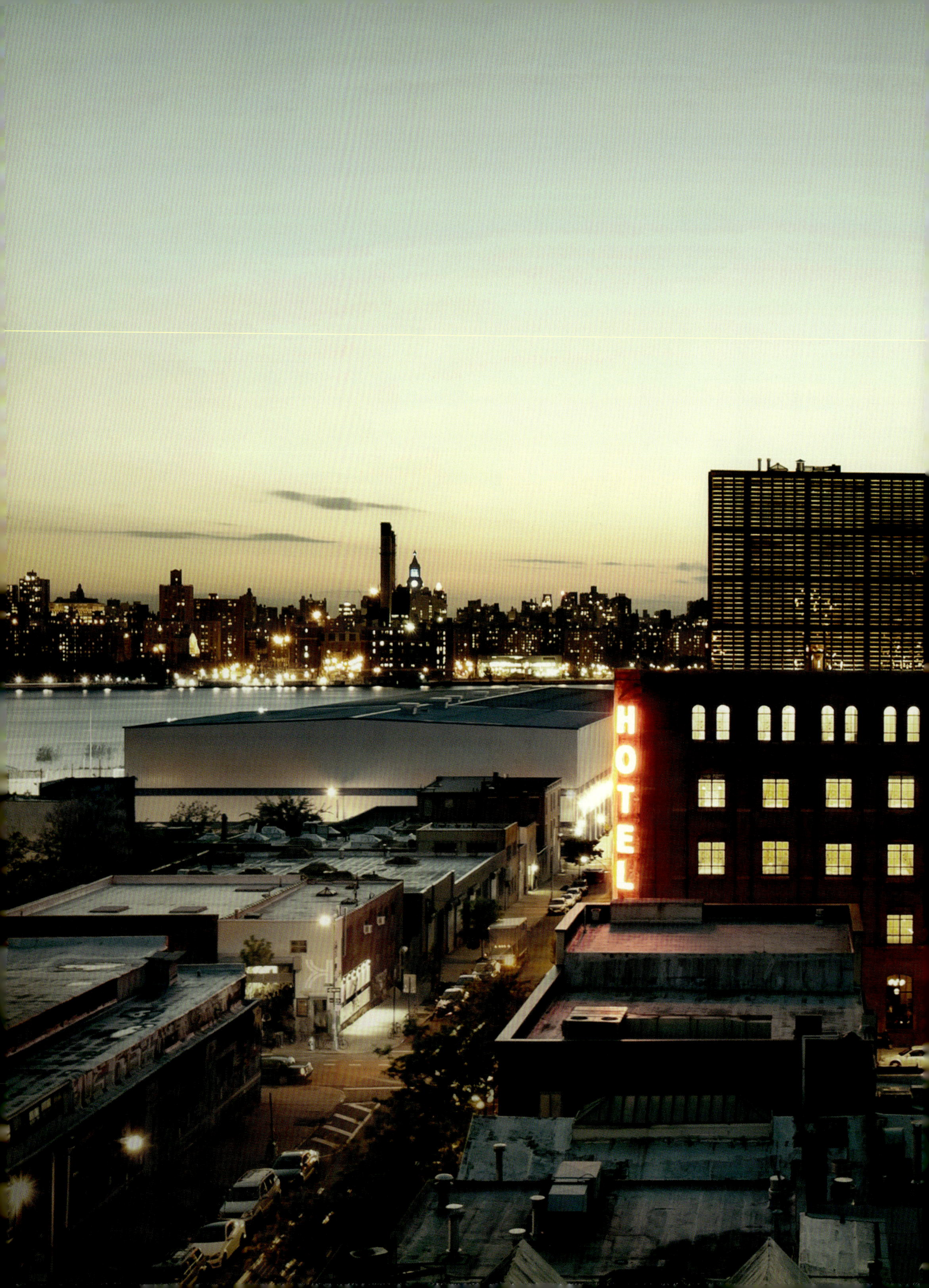
HOTEL

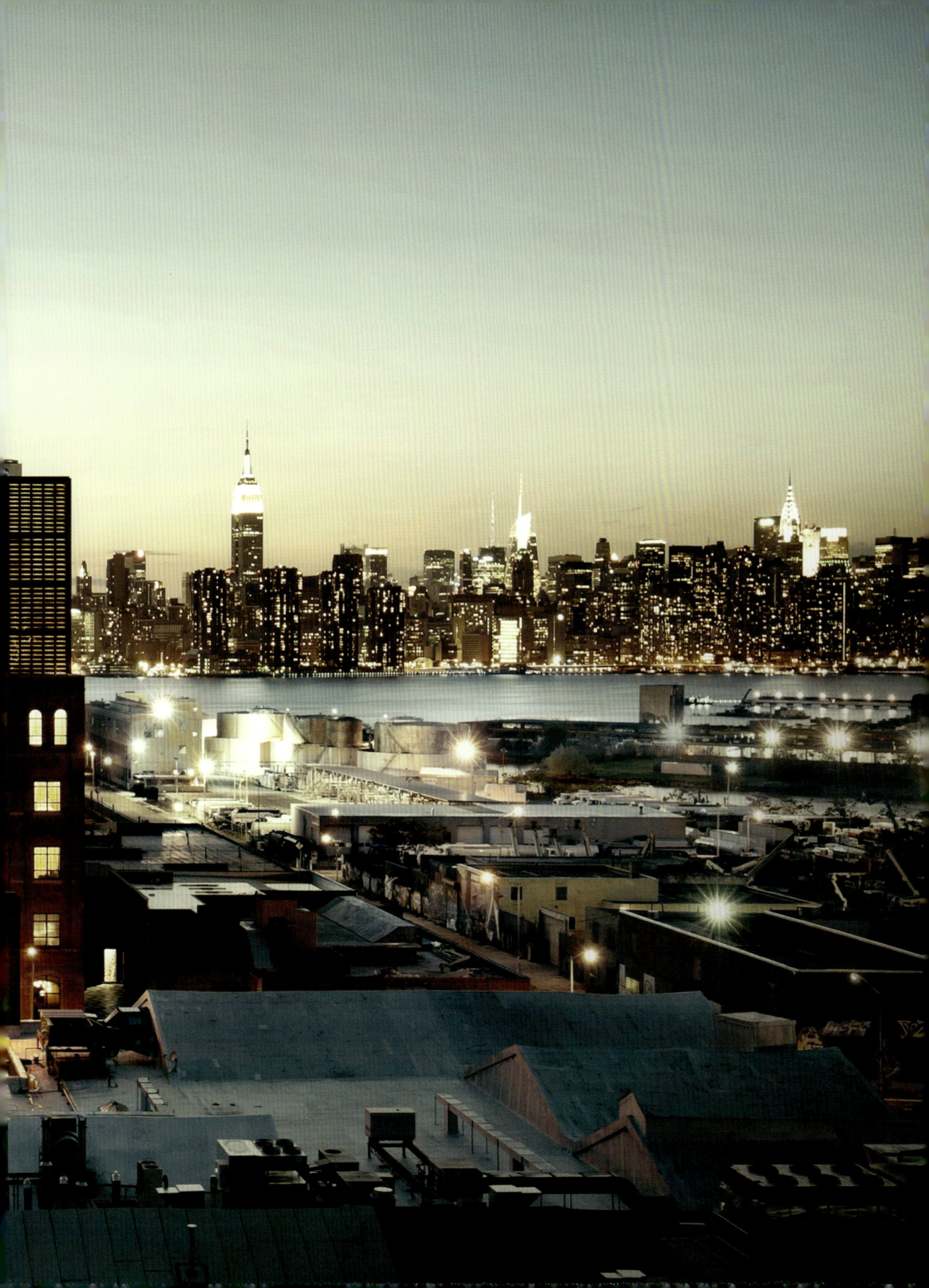

Palihouse Santa Monica, California

ADDRESS | 1001 Third Street, Santa Monica, California, USA
ROOMS | 37
OPENED | June 2013
ARCHITECT | Arthur E. Harvey (1927)
INTERIOR DESIGN | Avi Brosh and Paligroup Management
GRAPHIC DESIGN | Paligroup Management

Palihouse in Santa Monica contains only thirty-seven boutique rooms in a Spanish Colonial Revival-style building. The hotel, featuring lush courtyards and a gracious lobby, invites guests to experience residential comfort without compromising on location, style, amenities or service.

In operation since 1927, the building boasts classic examples of Moorish-influenced Mediterranean Revival Architecture which has been meticulously maintained over the course of several decades. So much so, that in 2001 the property was deemed a historic landmark by the City of Santa Monica.

The Palihouse brand has been designed so that guests can explore the people and places they visit 'authentically' — with space, style, sophistication and individuality. From fully furnished studio suites to two-bedroom residences, Palihouse accommodates a wide variety of travellers.

The identity itself has been applied across collateral in a mixture of traditional and modern interpretations but all predominantly feature the simplified 'P' icon. The logo reflects the hotel's historical influences, whereas its applications allow the identity to be applied with a more contemporary approach.

'The Palihouse brand has been designed so that guests can explore the people and places they visit 'authentically' — with space, style, sophistication and individuality.'

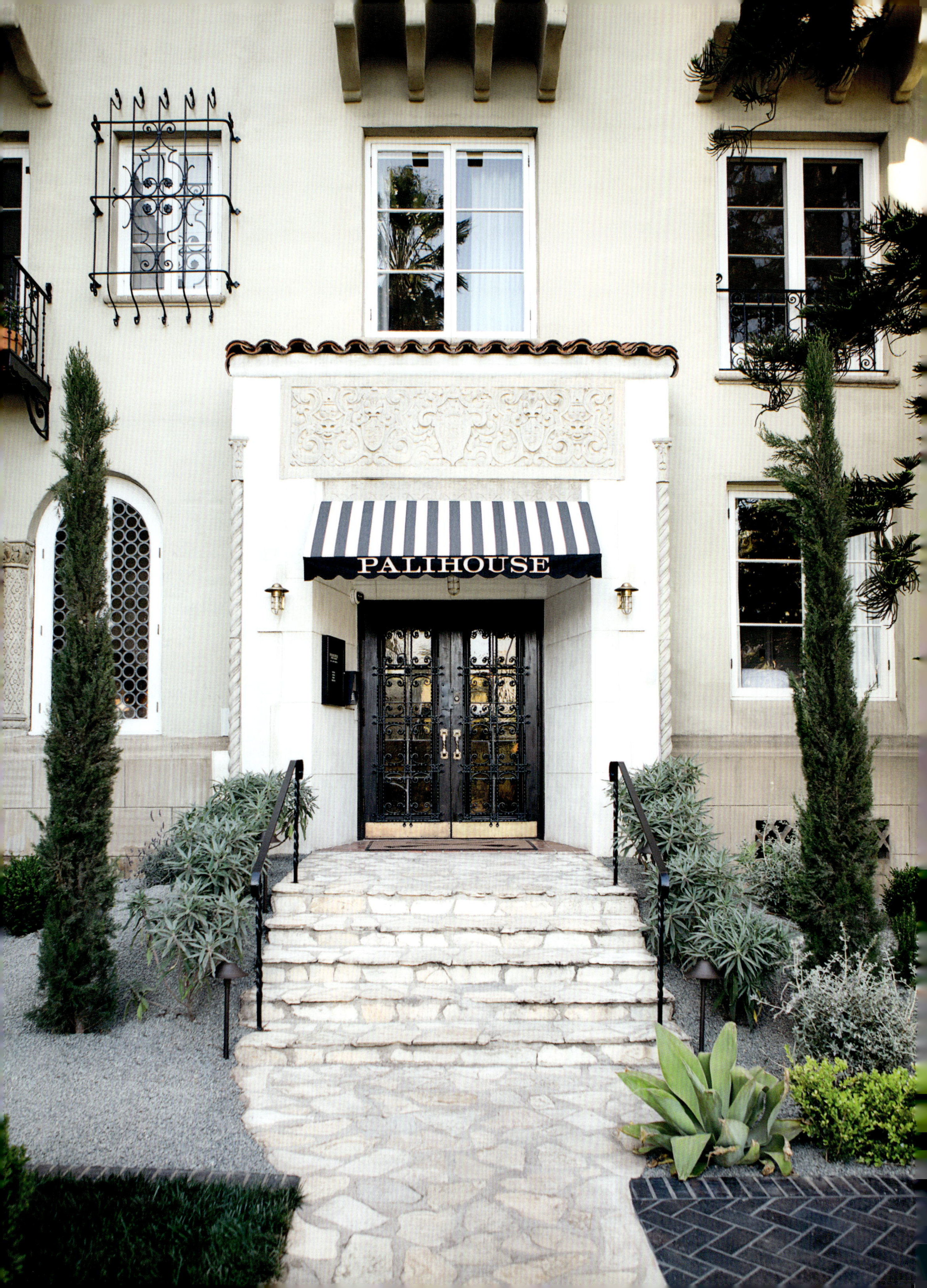
PALIHOUSE

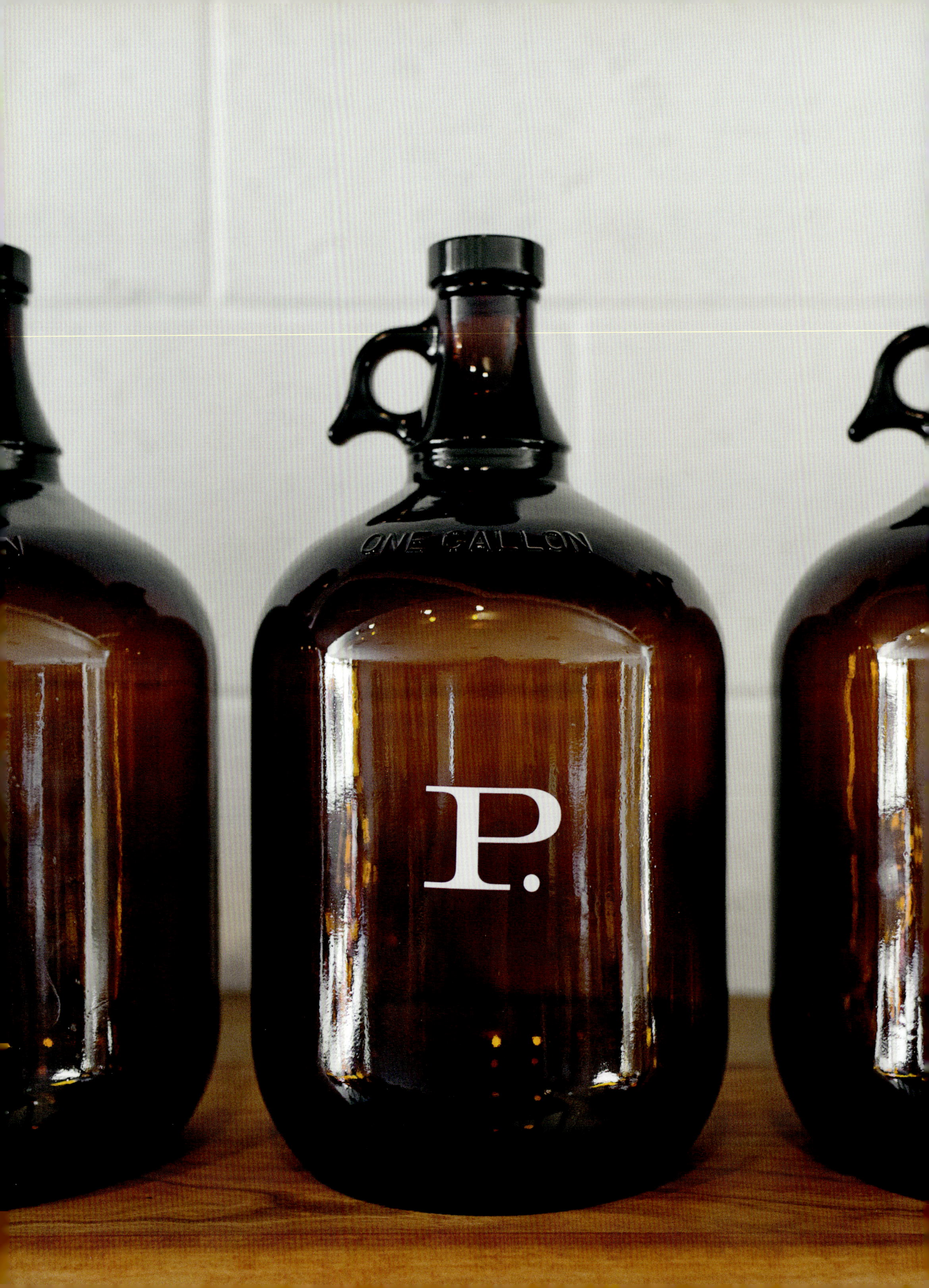
ONE GALLON
P.

PALIHOUSE

PALIHOUSE
LIVING·ROOMS

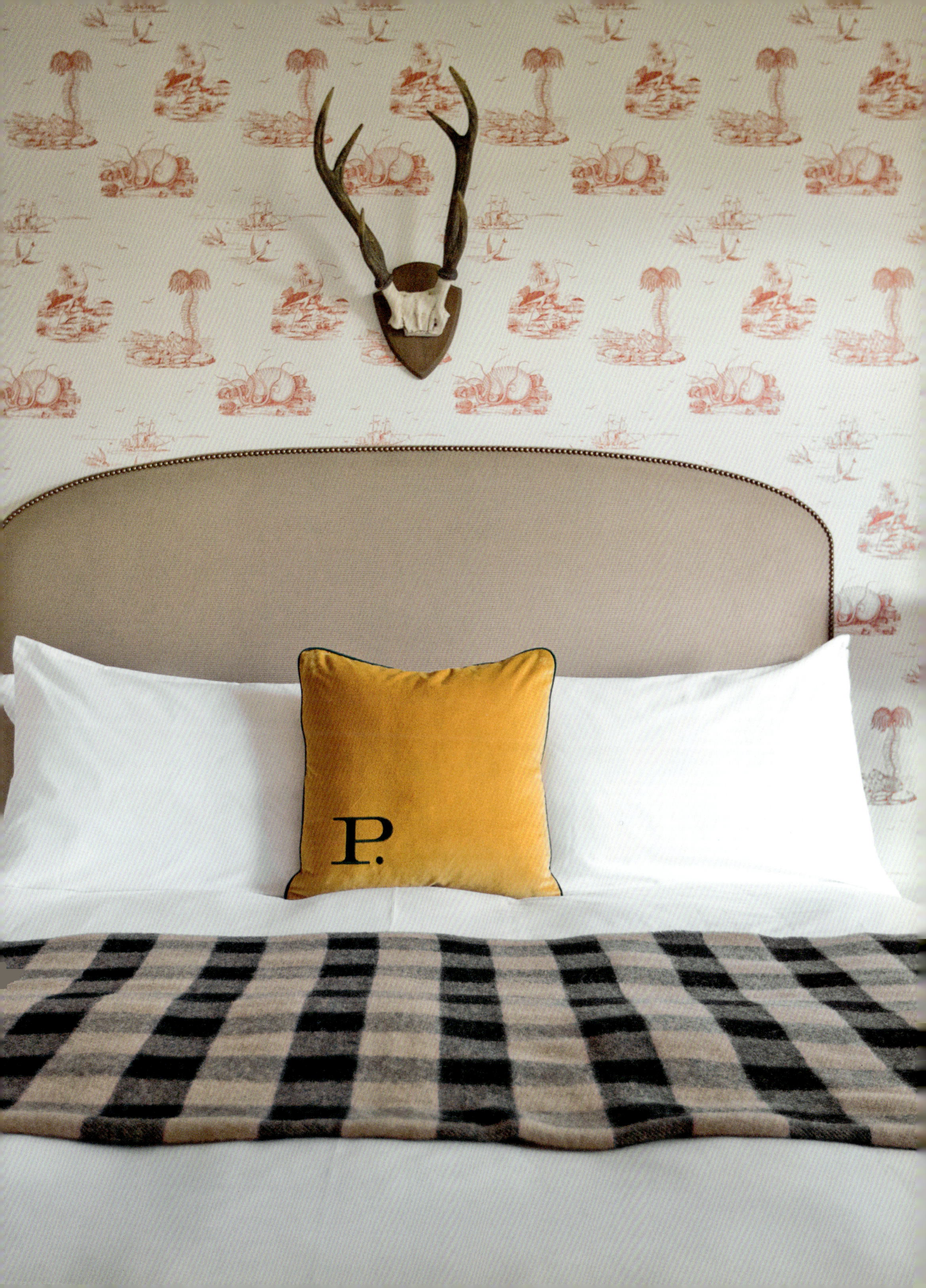
P.

AMERICA | SANTA MONICA

PALIHOUSE

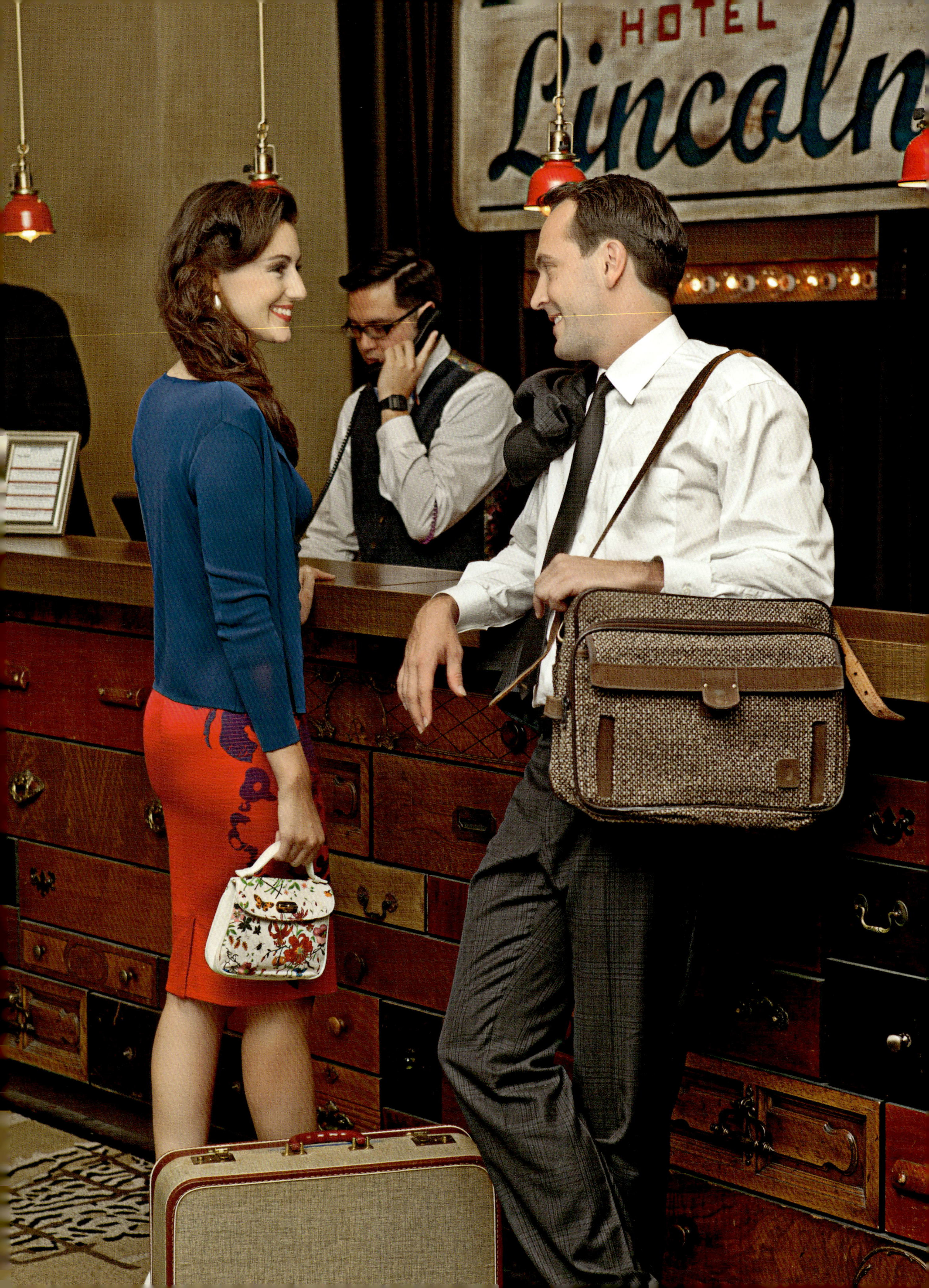
HOTEL
Lincoln

AMERICA | CHICAGO | HOTEL LINCOLN

Hotel Lincoln Chicago, Illinois

ADDRESS | 1816 North Clark Street, Chicago, Illinois, USA
ROOMS | 184
OPENED | March 2012
ARCHITECT | Loewenberg & Loewenberg (original building)
INTERIOR DESIGN | Andrew Alford of Dirty Lines Design and Lisa McClung of INT Inc.
GRAPHIC DESIGN | Joie de Vivre Hotels

Hotel Lincoln is an eclectic mix of retro, vintage, old and new. Originally built in 1928, the building has been transformed into a twelve story hotel with an all-season rooftop bar, restaurant and coffee shop.

Inspired by the notion of staying in a friend's home (who happens to be a design enthusiast), the hotel's public spaces are quirky, colourful and unique. The hotel features a 'wall of bad art' — the name given to the wall of 168 pieces of art, stacked gallery style, that appear from floor to ceiling.

In addition, the front desk is built from more than thirty vintage dresser drawers (some that open and some that don't) sourced from antique shops across the Midwest. The experience at this hotel steps you back in time — from 60s style employee uniforms to embroidered cushions and an eccentric mismatch of furniture.

The brand identity itself is very traditional, with just a hint of old newsprint to complement the hotel's eclectic nature. With its sweeping views of Lake Michigan and the Lincoln Park neighbourhood, this hotel returns to an era of old fashioned service, nostalgia and enduring charm.

'With its sweeping views of Lake Michigan and the Lincoln Park neighbourhood, Hotel Lincoln returns to an era of old fashioned service, nostalgia and enduring charm.'

HOTEL LINCOLN

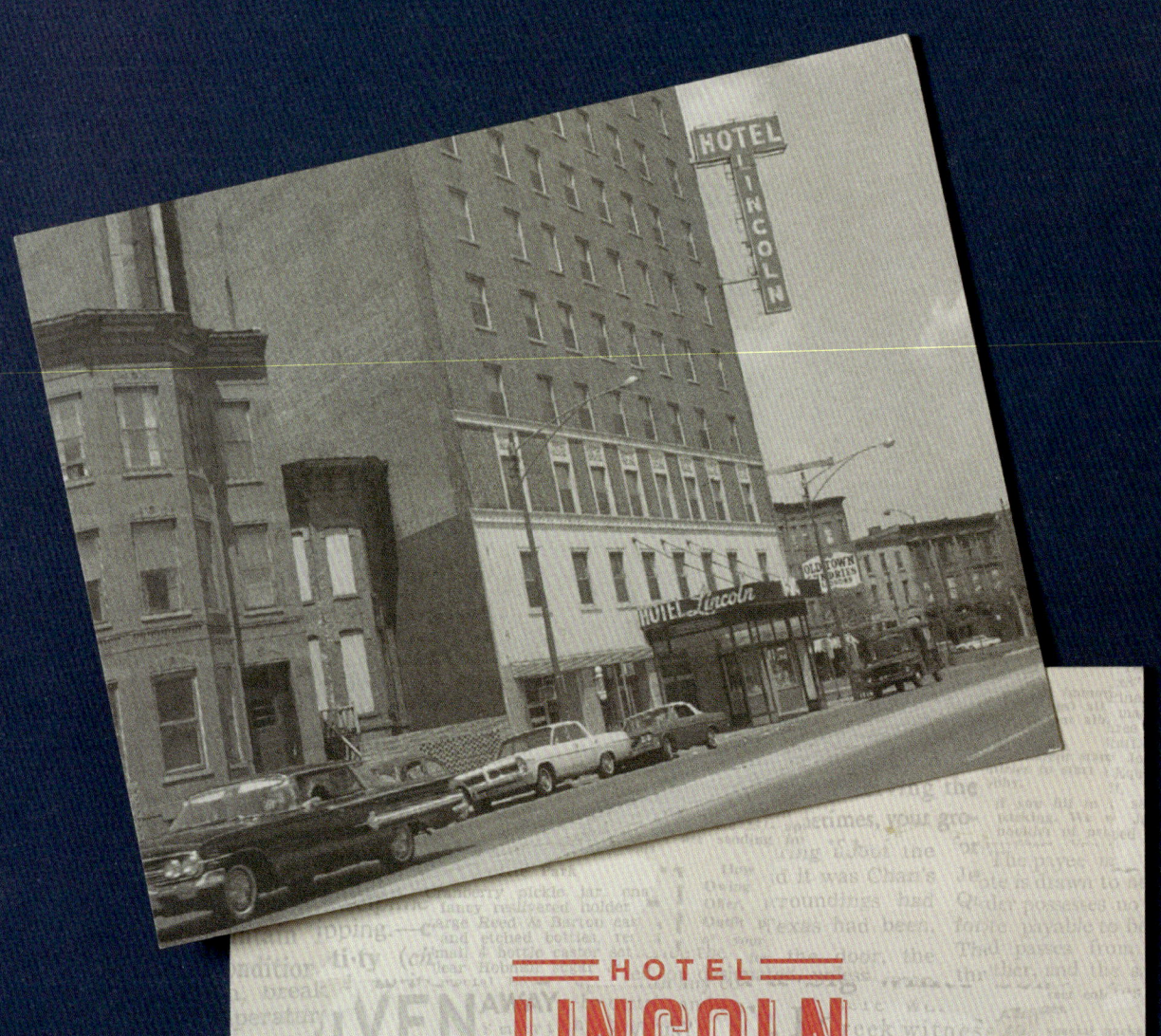

HOTEL LINCOLN

1816 North Clark Street
Chicago, Illinois 60614
hotellincolnchicago.com
T 312.254.4700 F 312.254.4701

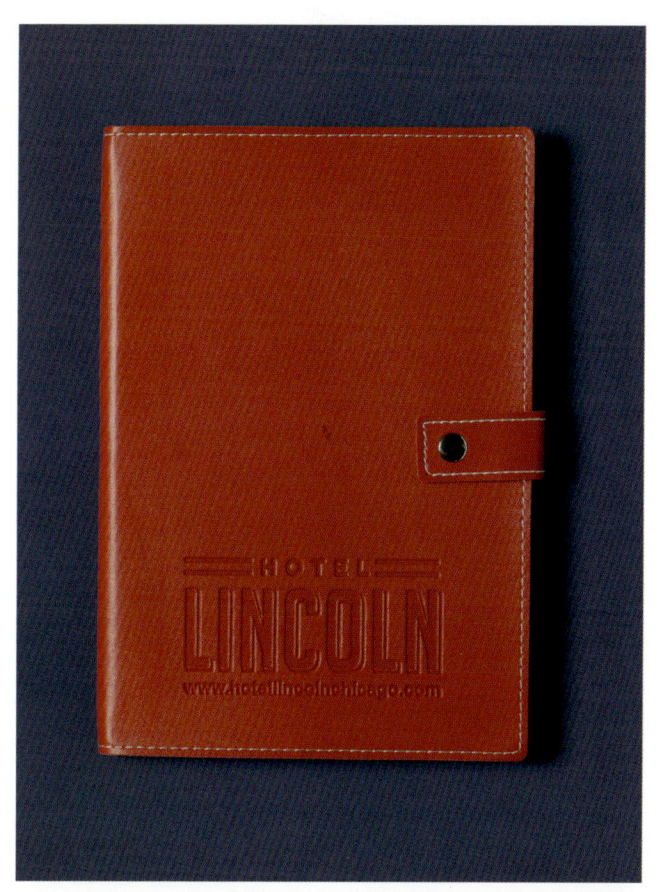

HOTEL LINCOLN

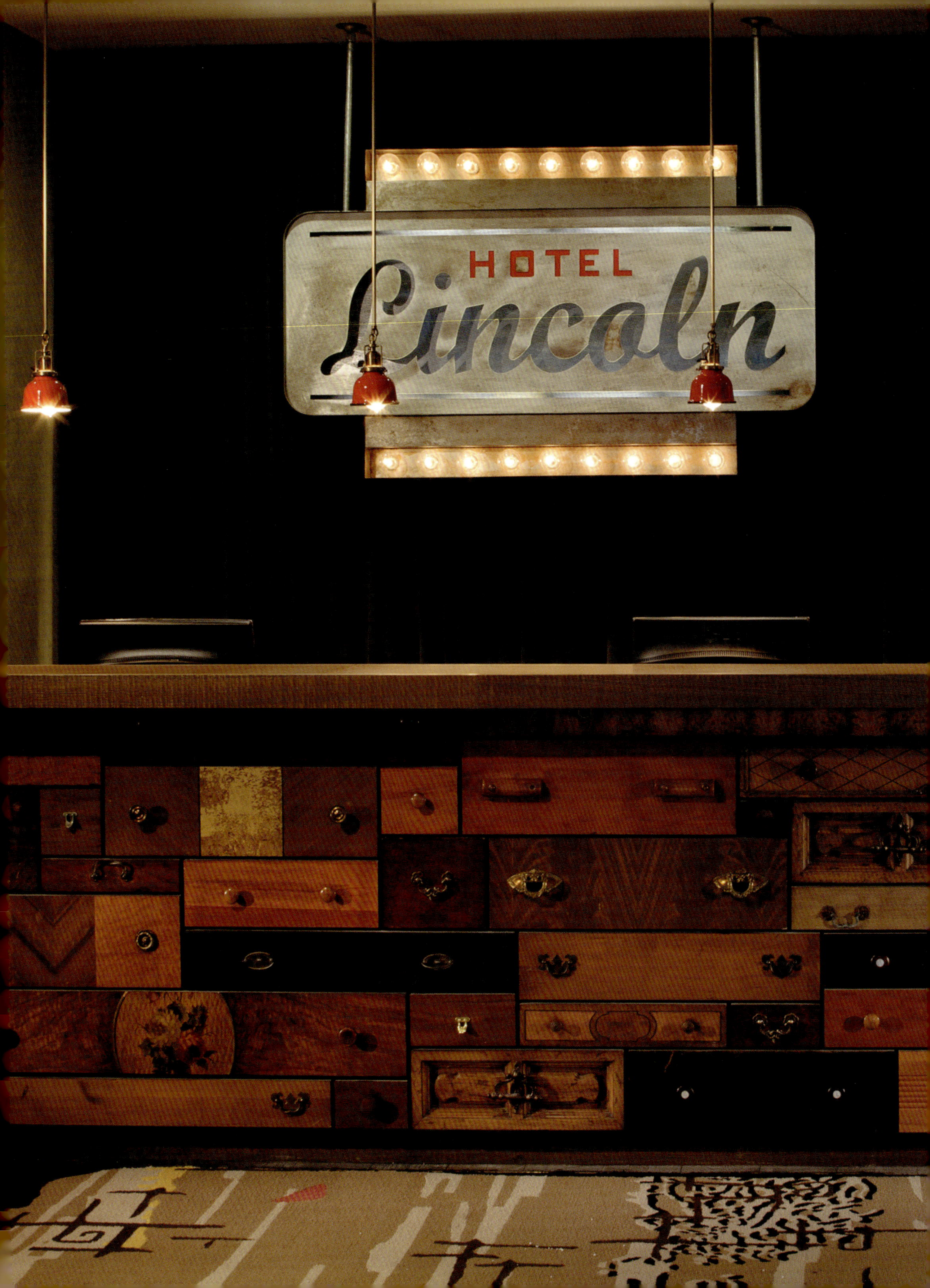
HOTEL
Lincoln

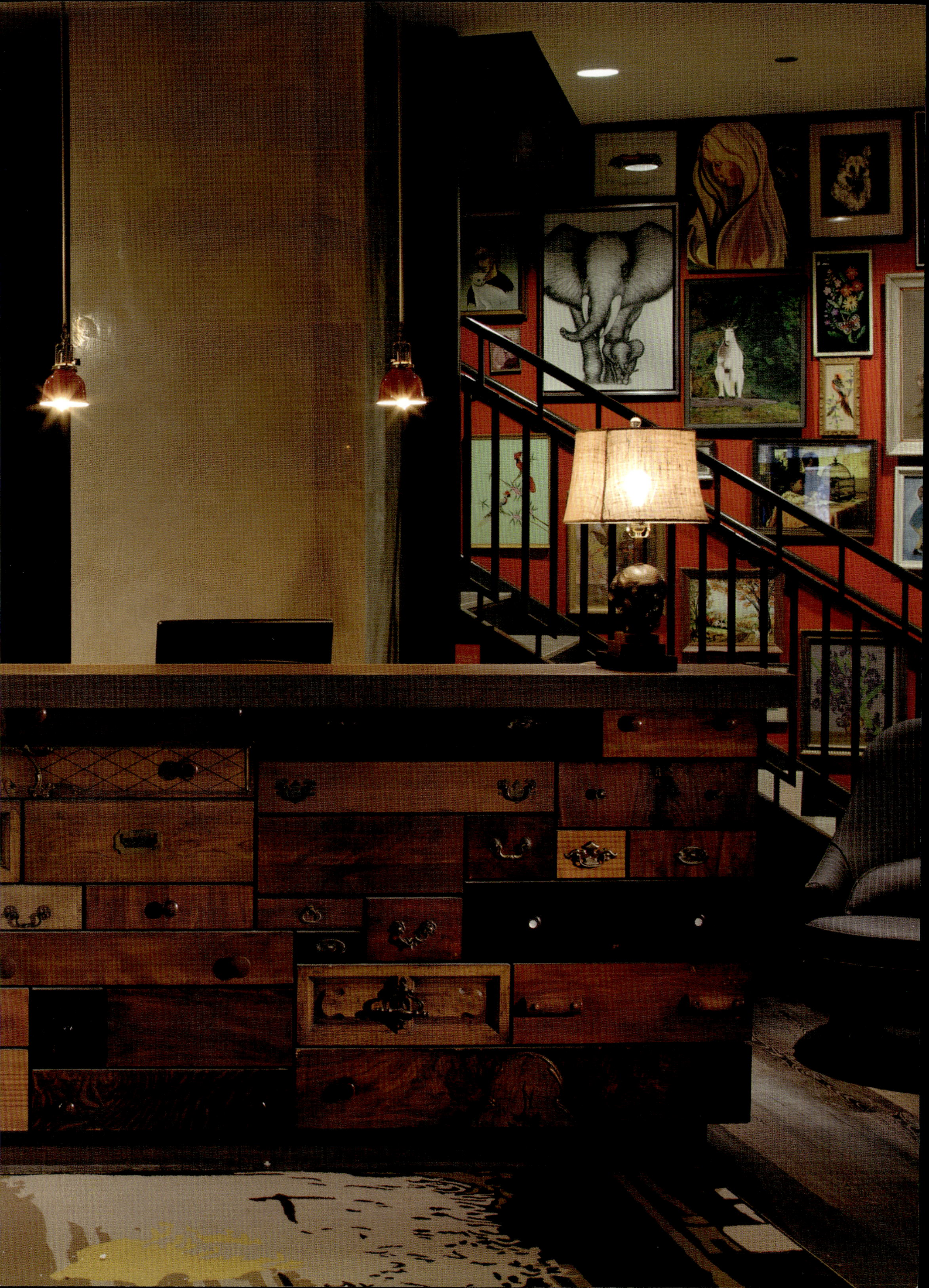

AMERICA | CHICAGO

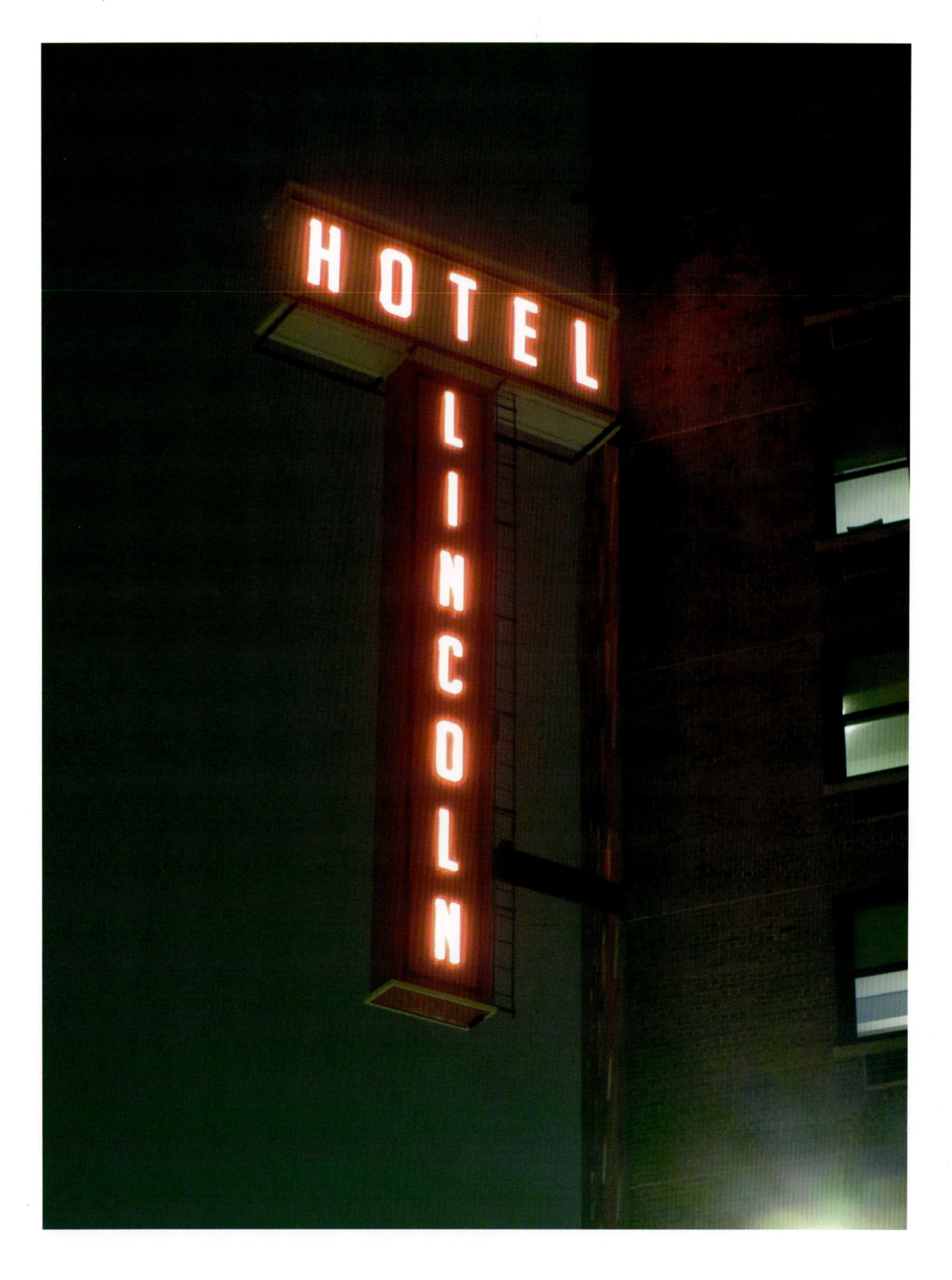

HOTEL LINCOLN

1816 CLARK

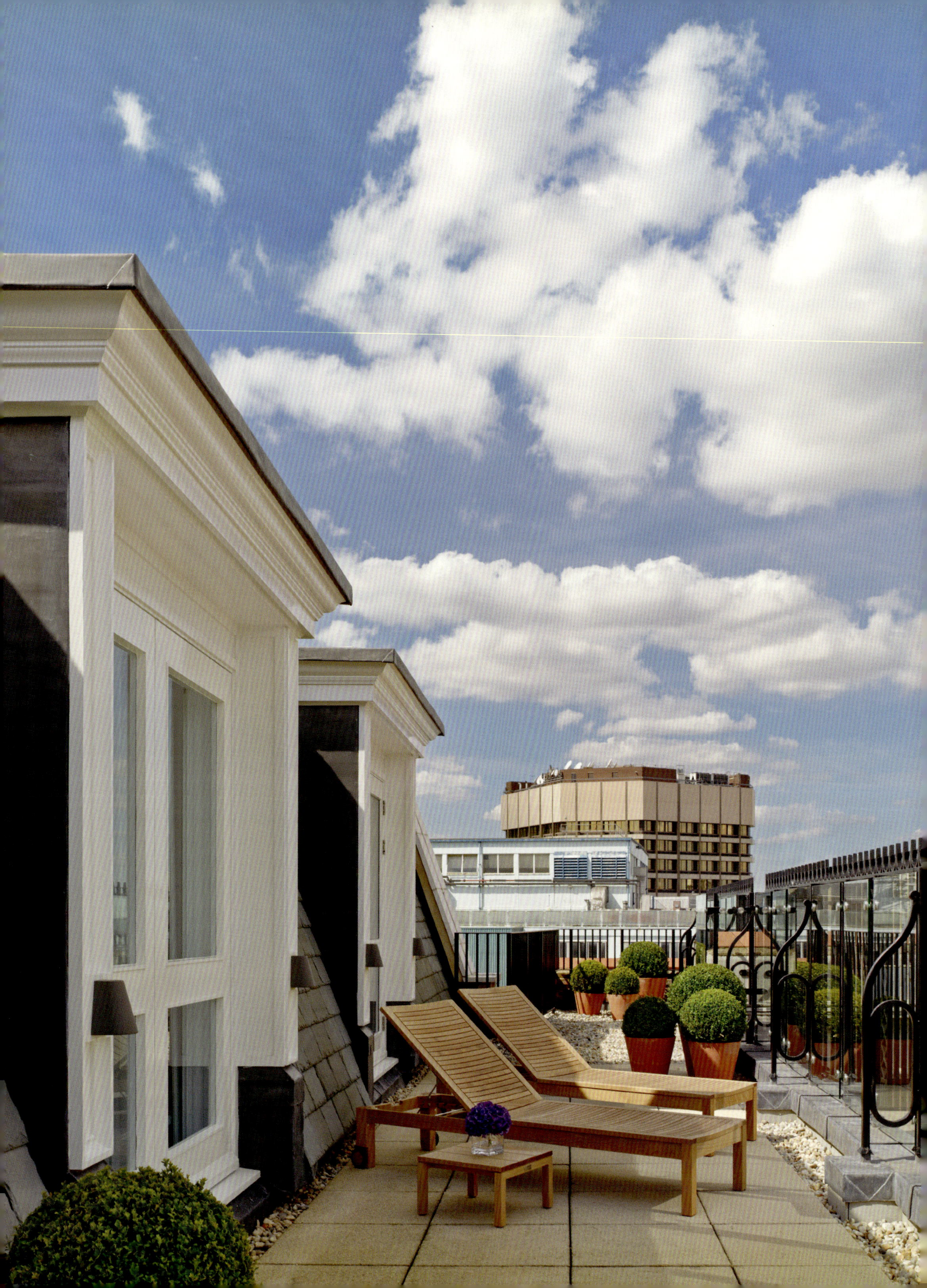

Europe

'Hotels are about dream-making,
about creating a story you want to tell.'

— Petter A. Stordalen

citizenM says:
London, you look like you need a new place to sleep
citizen
hotel
citizenM.com
citizen
friends who

EUROPE | LONDON | CITIZENM

citizenM London, England

ADDRESS | 20 Lavington Street, London, England, United Kingdom
ROOMS | 192 rooms
OPENED | July 2012
ARCHITECT | Concrete
INTERIOR DESIGN | Concrete
GRAPHIC DESIGN | KesselsKramer

The citizenM hotel in London caters to a new traveller called 'mobile citizens' who share a common desire of 'affordable luxury for the people.' According to the hotel, 'these modern individuals are explorers, cultural seekers, professionals and shoppers,' and citizenM reflects this philosophy not only in their interiors but also in conjunction with their branding.

This hotel features stylish design, great value, quality products, technology and a social atmosphere — all within the one central location of Bankside. Upon arrival, there is no lengthy check in; instead, touch screen kiosks ensure this process is seamless and efficient. In the event that you do require assistance, there is always an employee (known as a brand ambassador) willing to help.

In order to be democratic, all rooms within the hotel are exactly the same size, albeit on the smaller side (inevitably to maximise the space within this central London location). Within each room, however, you can control temperature, lighting and music to the mood of your choice. Whether you want to work, relax, meet friends, browse design books or wake up in the morning 'gently' or 'wildly' to an alarm, you can do it all at citizenM.

'citizenM hotels cater to a new traveller called 'mobile citizens' who share a common desire of 'affordable luxury for the people.' These modern individuals are explorers, cultural seekers, professionals and shoppers.'

**societyM
meeting rooms**

**elevator
luggage storage**

toilets

canteenM

no smoking

citizenM hotels

To all travellers long and short haul. To the weary, the wise and the bleary-eyed. To the suits, weekenders, fashion baggers and **affair-havers. To the explorers, adventurers and dreamers.** To all locals of the world from Amsterdam, Boston and Cairo to Zagreb. To all **who travel the world with wide eyes and big hearts.** To all who are independent yet united in a desire for positive travelling. To those **who are smarter than a dolphin with a university degree** and realize you can have luxury for not too much cash. To those who need **a good bed, a cold drink and big fluffy towels.** To all who are mobile citizens of the world. citizenM **welcomes you all.**

EUROPE | LONDON

citizenM says:

hello

citizenM hotels

CITIZENM

EUROPE | LONDON

All branding, created by KesselsKramer, communicates the hotel's personality in a conversational tone with a sense of humour that elevates the brand to a new level. citizenM appeals to their clientele and offers insight into their playful philosophy through multiple applications, from check-in procedures to the wide range of accessories for guests' use.

68

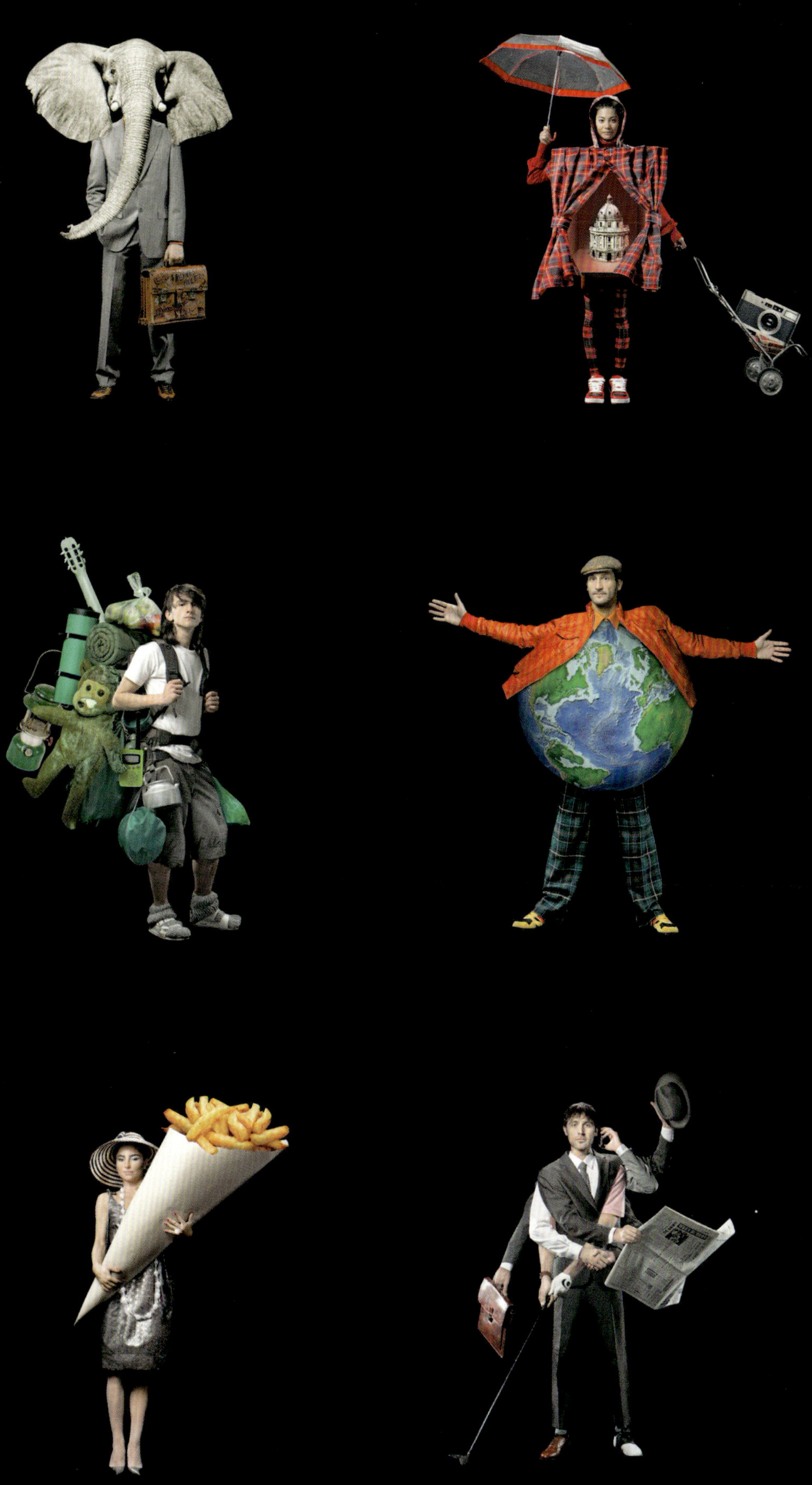

EUROPE | LONDON | CLARIDGE'S

Claridge's London, England

ADDRESS | Brook Street, London, England, UK
ROOMS | 197 rooms, including 67 suites
OPENED | 1856
ARCHITECT | CW Stephens (original building 1898)
INTERIOR DESIGN | Basil Ionides and Oswald Milne (1929); Diane von Furstenberg (2000); David Linley (2012)
GRAPHIC DESIGN | Construct London

Claridge's is an art deco masterpiece that has been favoured by the most distinguished figures of every generation. With a reputation that is unsurpassed by any other, this historic luxury hotel is regularly frequented by royalty, celebrities, socialites and the business elite. Guests have included Winston Churchill, Queen Elizabeth, Cary Grant, Audrey Hepburn, Anna Wintour and Kate Moss to name but a few.

In order to sustain this level of clientele, Claridge's provides extraordinary attentiveness and absolute discretion to their guests. The immaculately presented employees provide a traditional English service that is intuitive and personal to every guest, regardless of their status or position in society.

The combination of this hotel's elegance and timeless glamour creates an experience that guests return to time and time again. In addition, their branding reflects this grandness through a bold and opulent palette inspired by the hotel's architecture and features.

This sophisticated colour palette of jade and gold, mixed with white and black chevron patterns, provides elements of surprise and delight, and appears not only on hotel stationery but other branded keepsakes as well.

'With a reputation that is unsurpassed by any other, this historic luxury hotel is regularly frequented by royalty, celebrities, socialites and the business elite.'

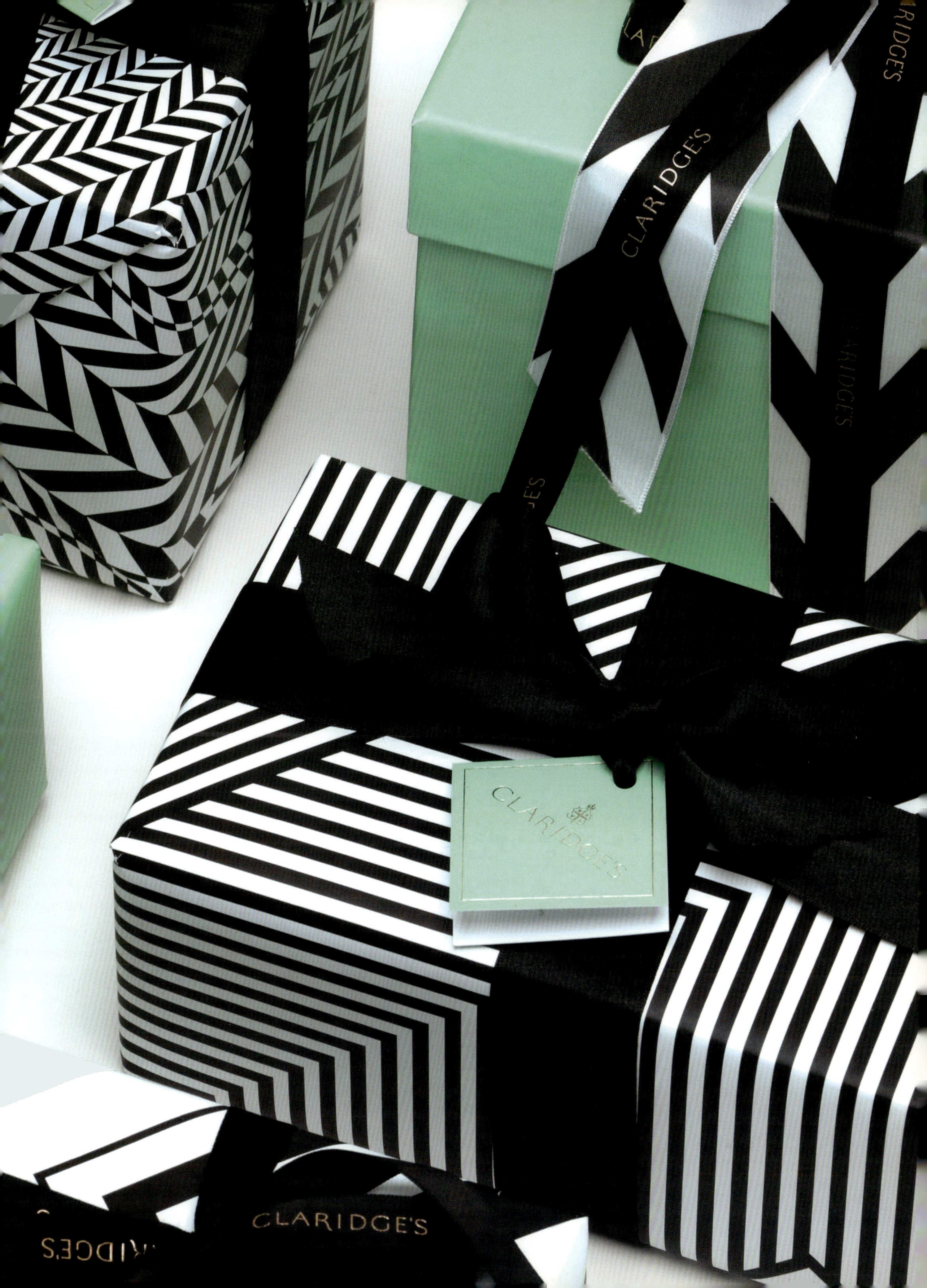
CLARIDGE'S
CLARIDGE'S
CLARIDGE'S
CLARIDGE'S
CLARIDGE'S

EUROPE | LONDON

CLARIDGE'S

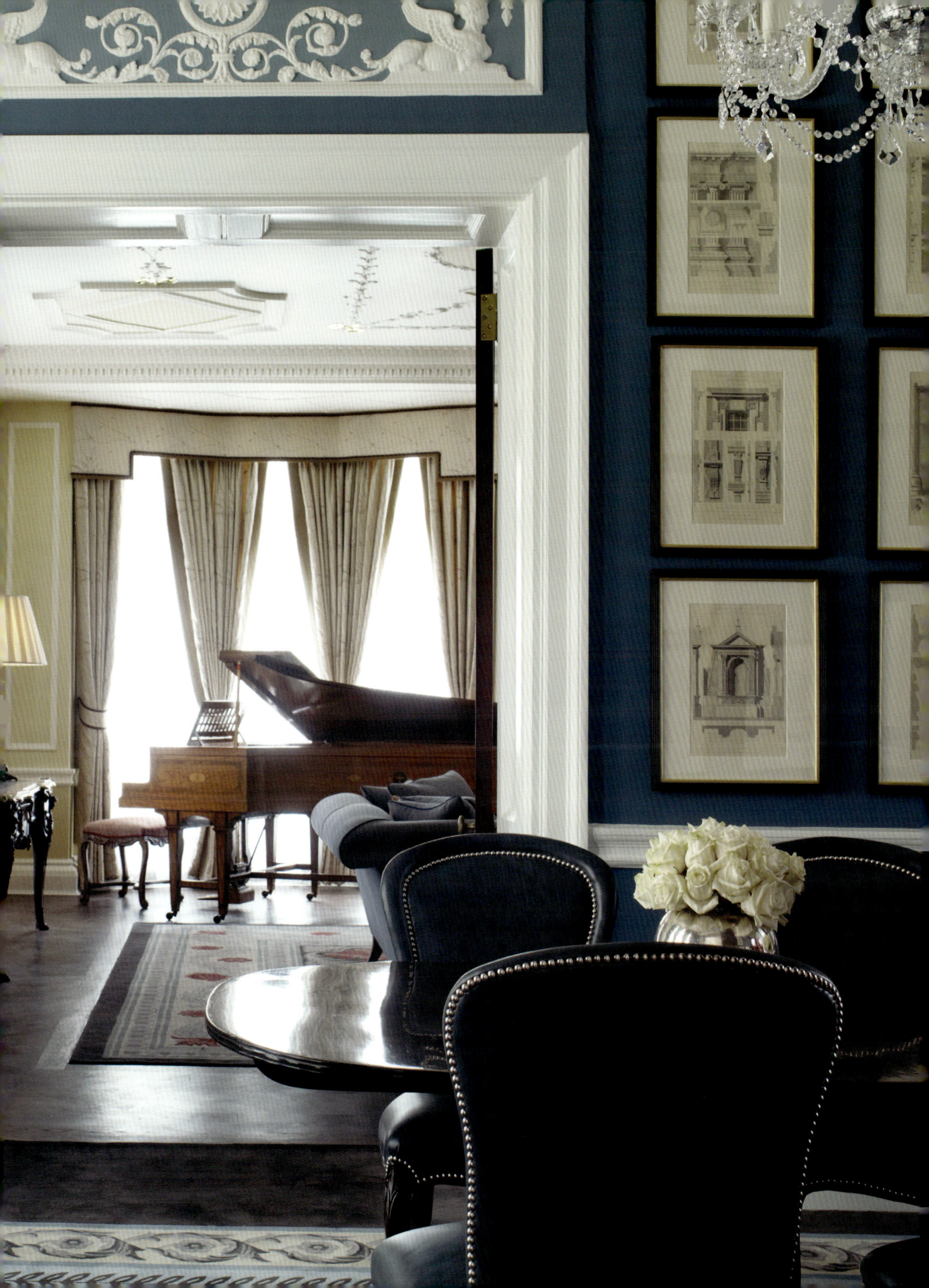

EUROPE | LONDON

'We put aside design dogma that prescribes the corporate and repetitive approach of a consistent logo on every item possible in the belief that if you see it often enough it will be remembered.'

— Georgia Fendley, Construct London

CLARIDGE'S

Claridge's is the insider's choice when in London

Our guest list is a "Who's Who" of world power and glamour. Our guests choose us because of the steps we take to ensure their comfort, security and privacy in today's constantly changing world.

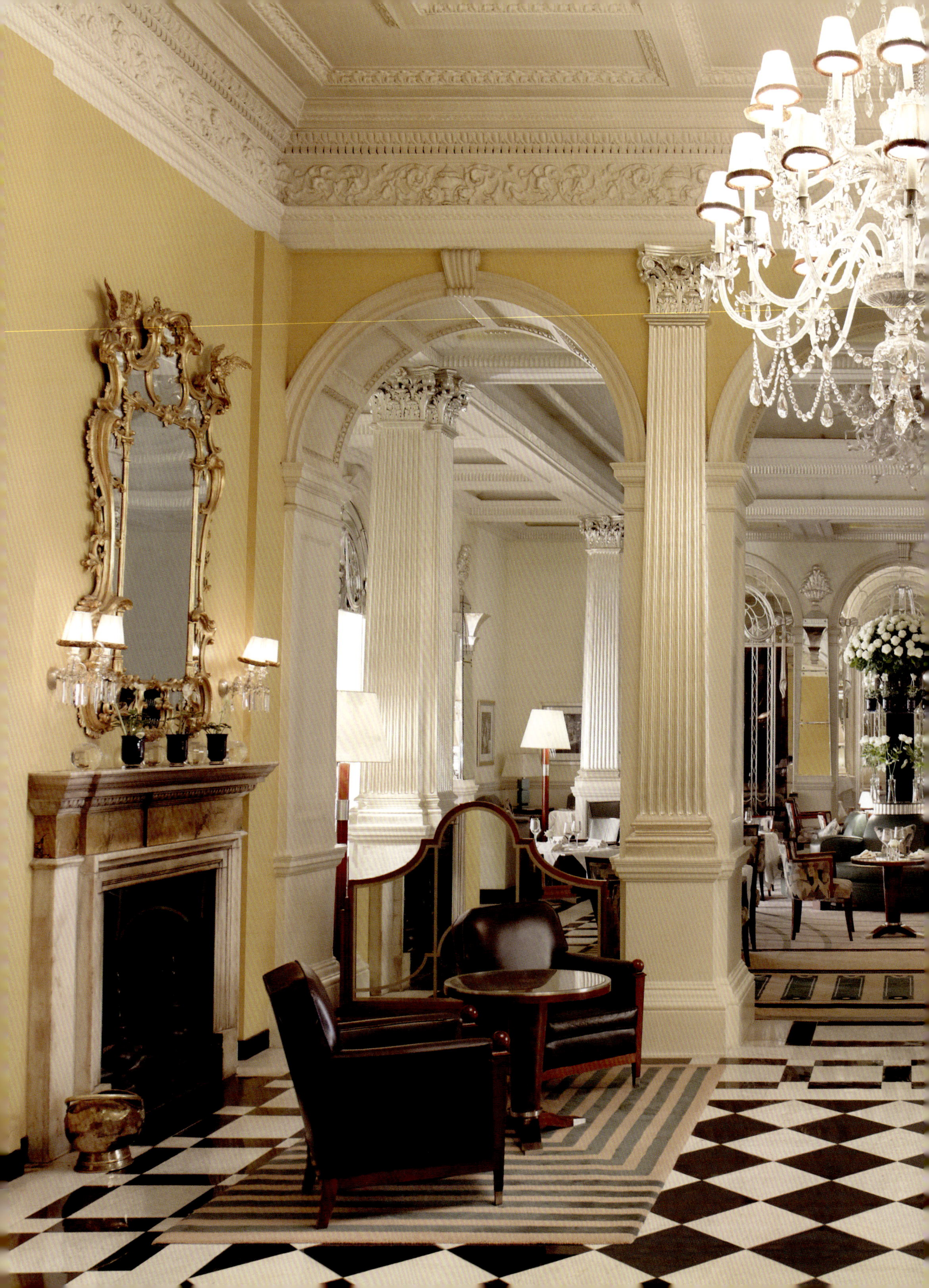

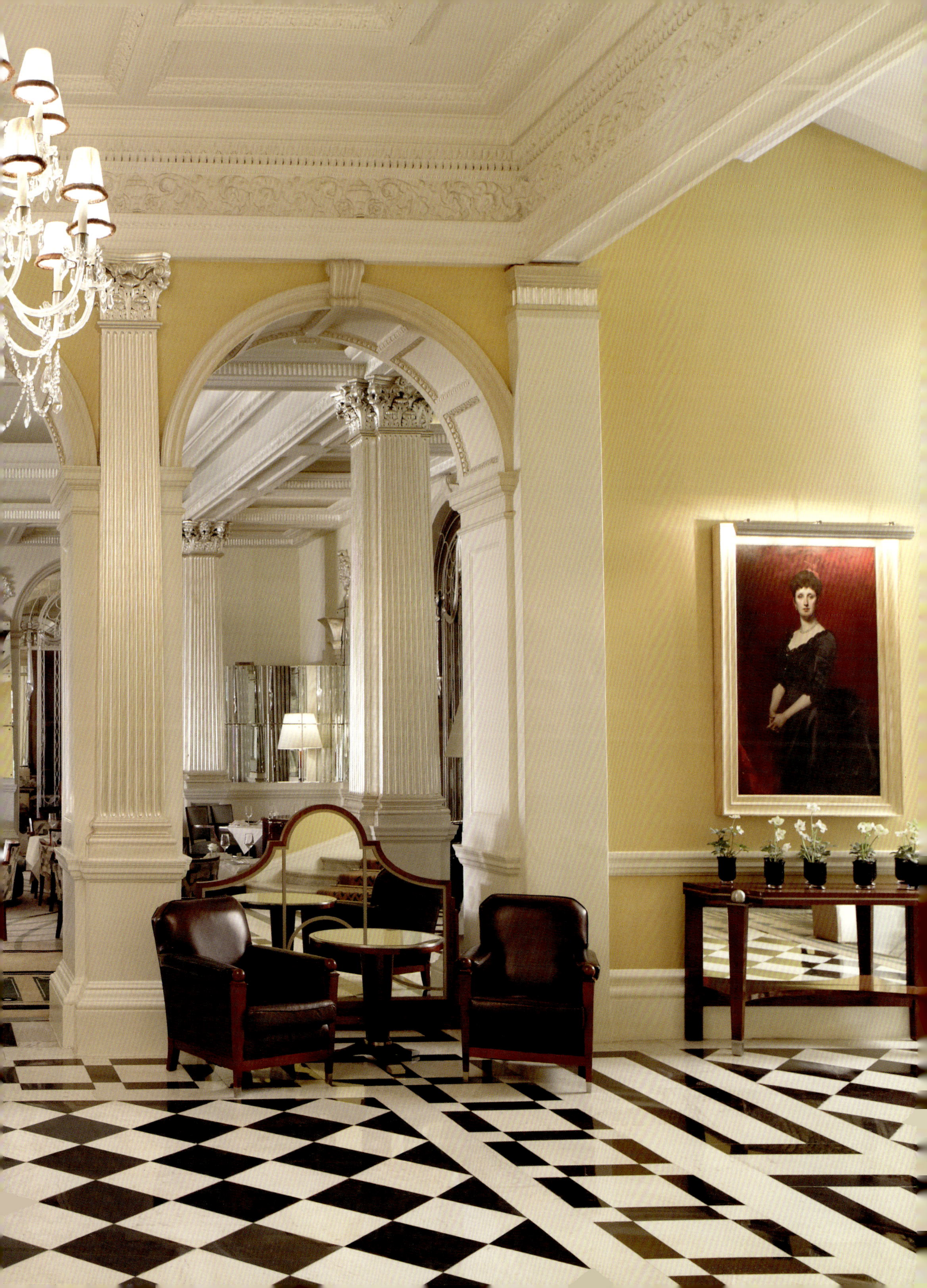

EUROPE | LONDON | THE AMPERSAND HOTEL

The Ampersand London, England

ADDRESS | 10 Harrington Road, London, England, UK
ROOMS | 111 suites
OPENED | Summer 2012
ARCHITECT | Dextor Moren Associates
INTERIOR DESIGN | Dextor Moren Associates
GRAPHIC DESIGN | Goosebumps Brand Consultancy

The Ampersand Hotel is a privately owned hotel with a Victorian façade that dates back to 1888. Located in South Kensington, it is conveniently situated nearby Knightsbridge, Hyde Park, the Victoria and Albert Museum, the Natural History Museum, the Science Museum as well as the Royal Albert Hall.

The interior design for the hotel works to connect it with its vibrant location in the midst of a diverse arts and culture neighborhood. On each floor, for example, the wallpaper and artwork is based on the five themes of Botany, Music, Geometry, Ornithology and Astronomy.

Not confined to only the interiors, the location has also inspired the identity for the hotel. The name and use of the ampersand represents the connection between guests and the best of South Kensington. The identity utilizes a number of playful applications — the entrance mat states 'Hello & Welcome,' the umbrella was designed on the expression 'It's raining cats & dogs' and bathroom amenities also utilize the ampersand. These applications demonstrate that the hotel not only understands guests but utilizes language that is friendly and sophisticated.

Furthermore, the colour palette (primarily charcoal and dove accentuated with salmon, teal and lemon) is not only harmonious, but stylish and inviting, much like the hotel experience itself.

'The location for this South Kensington hotel has inspired the identity — the name and use of the ampersand not only brings the hotel closer to the guest but connects them to the local area.'

THE
AMPERSAND
HOTEL

EUROPE | LONDON

THE
—
AMPERSAND
—
HOTEL

WARM
—|—
&
—|—
DRY

EUROPE | LONDON

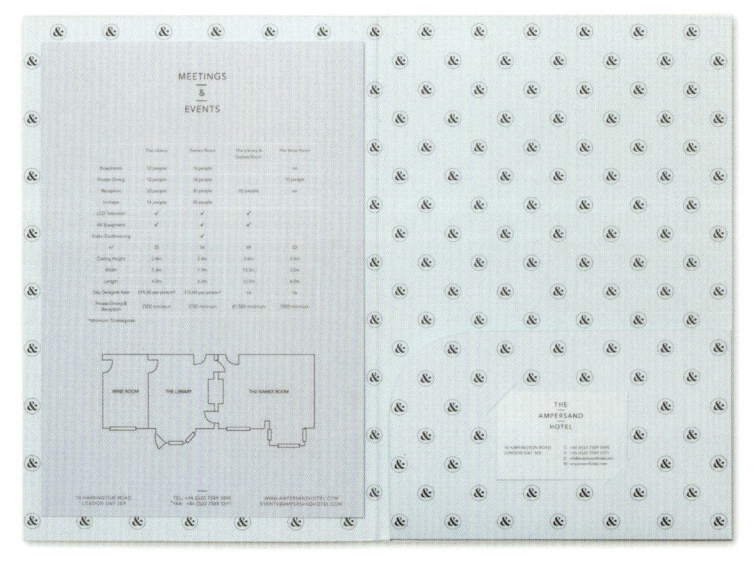

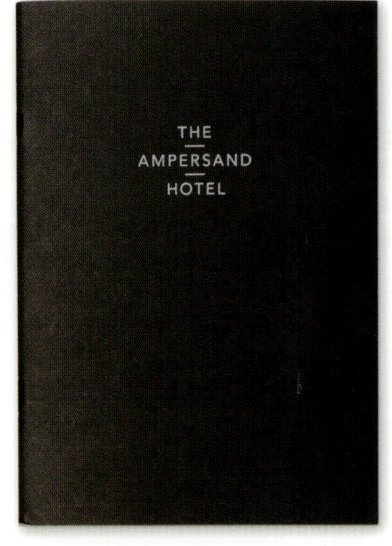

The hotel's name, modeled after the universal symbol of connection, has been applied in a thoughtful and stylish manner across the hotel collateral.

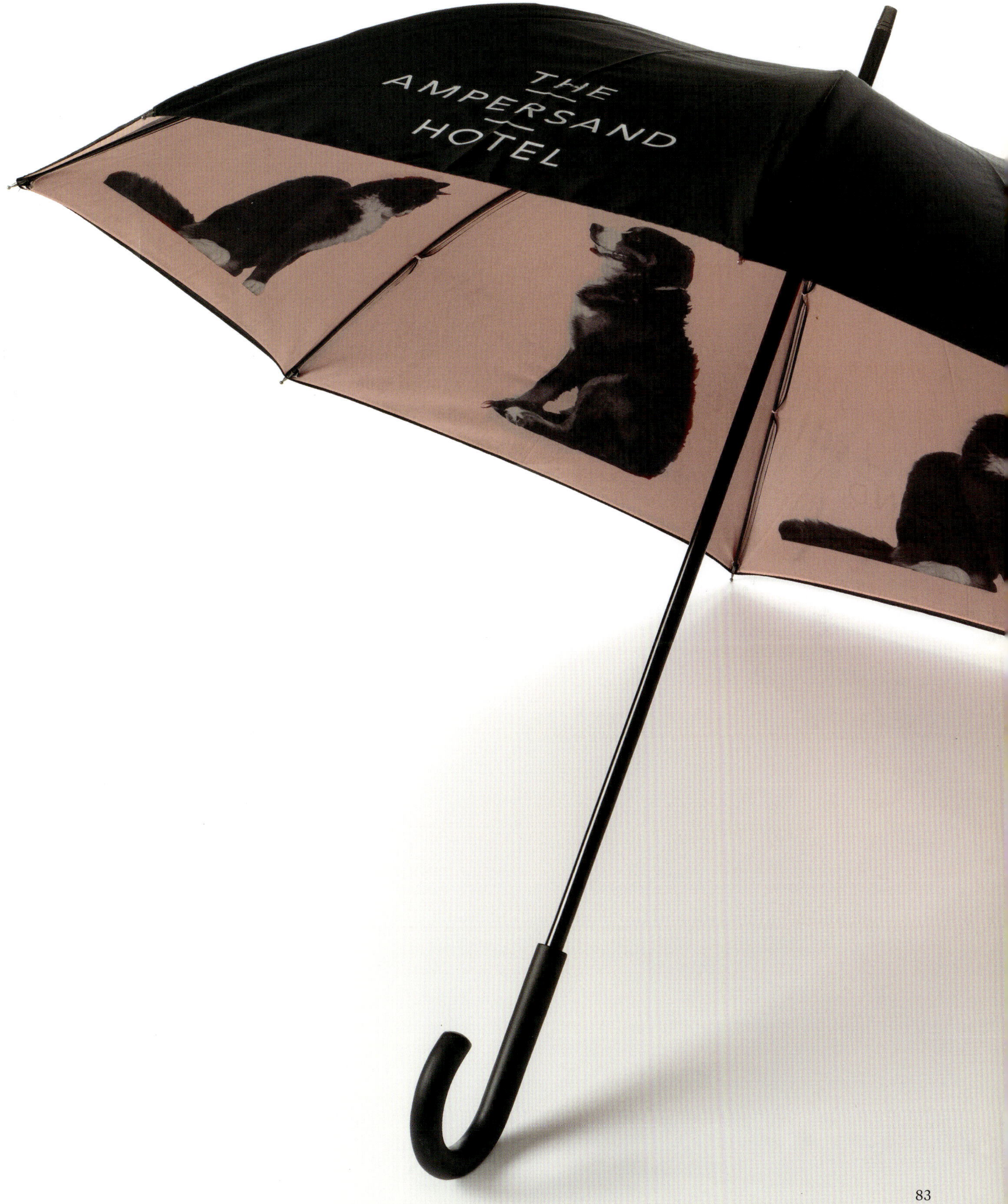
THE
AMPERSAND
HOTEL

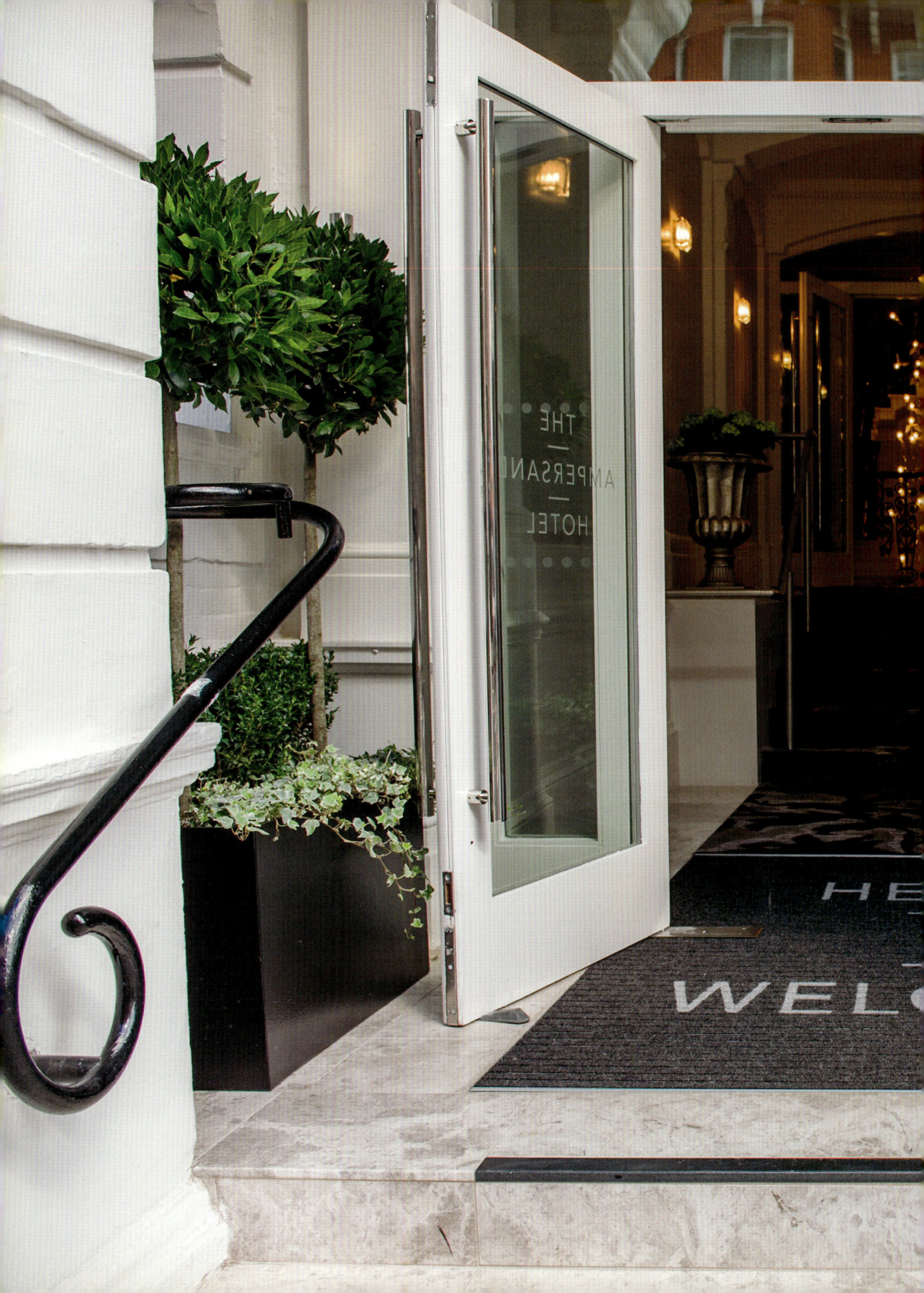
THE
HOTEL

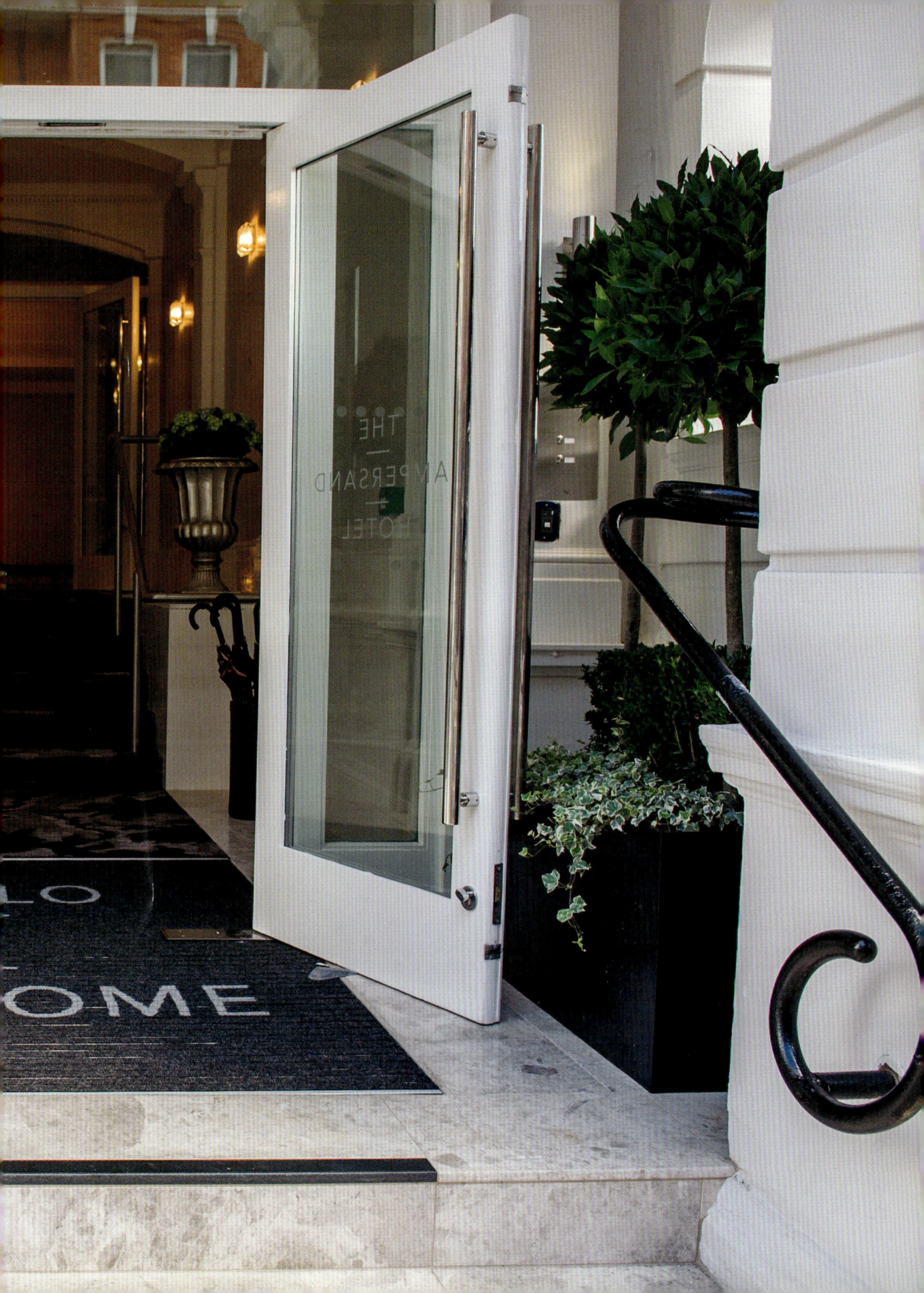
THE
AMPERSAND
HOTEL

The London EDITION London, England

ADDRESS | 10 Berners Street, London, England, United Kingdom
ROOMS | 173 rooms
OPENED | September 2013
ARCHITECT | Shepherd Construction
INTERIOR DESIGN | Yabu Pushelberg with Ian Schrager Company
GRAPHIC DESIGN | Baron & Baron

The London EDITION is housed in a row of Georgian terraces that have been renovated and sealed with the approval of none other than Ian Schrager. Schrager's influence has ensured that the integrity and charm of the original historic building has been retained and a sophisticated and contemporary design sensibility added to the hotel.

The lobby and bar exist in a state of organized chaos, furnished with an eclectic mix of unique pieces that include British and European designs interpreted with unexpected twists. These spaces include Donald Judd inspired sofas in pale green velvet; leather-upholstered modern wingback chairs; an oversized, deep tufted leather khaki sofa; Christian Liaigre black metal furniture and lighting; twenty-four karat gold Salvador Dali inspired floor lamps; an antique billiard table; mustard velvet slipper chairs; and Ingo Mauer's spaceship-like polished silver sphere light that presides over the entrance.

The branding is elegant and simple, with only black and white versions of the identity. However, the addition of black foil on black backgrounds elevates the branding to a level of style and class. No doubt this was Ian Schrager's intention for the hotel itself.

'Located in Fitzrovia, on the edge of London's Soho neighborhood, The London EDITION preserves the finest aspects of an iconic landmark building, while reinventing the spaces within to create a dynamic fusion of old and new, past and present.'

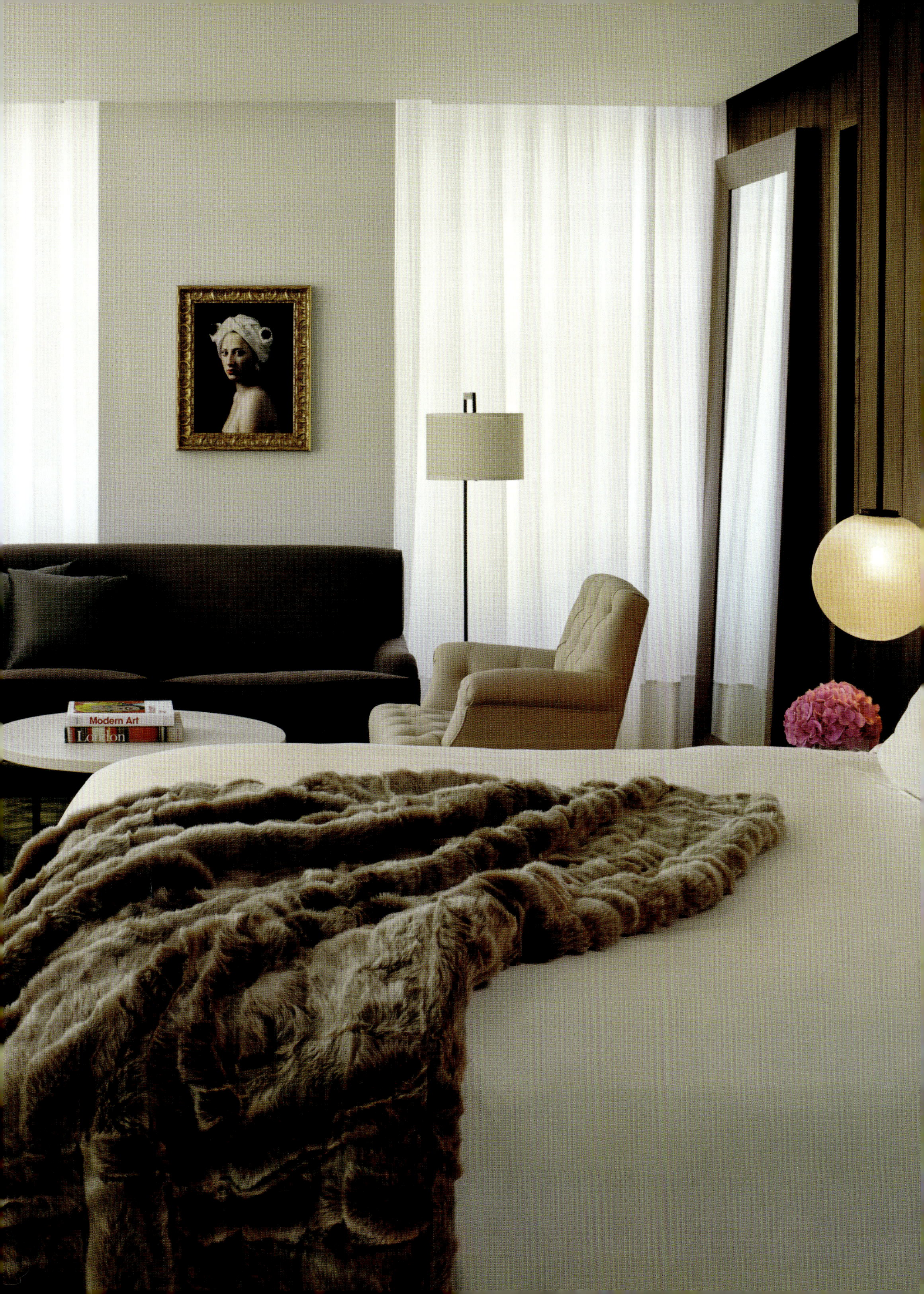
Modern Art
London

EUROPE | LONDON

10 BERNERS STREET
LONDON, W1T 3NP, UNITED KINGDOM
PHONE 020 7781 0000 FAX 020 7781 0100
WWW.EDITIONHOTELS.COM

THE LONDON EDITION

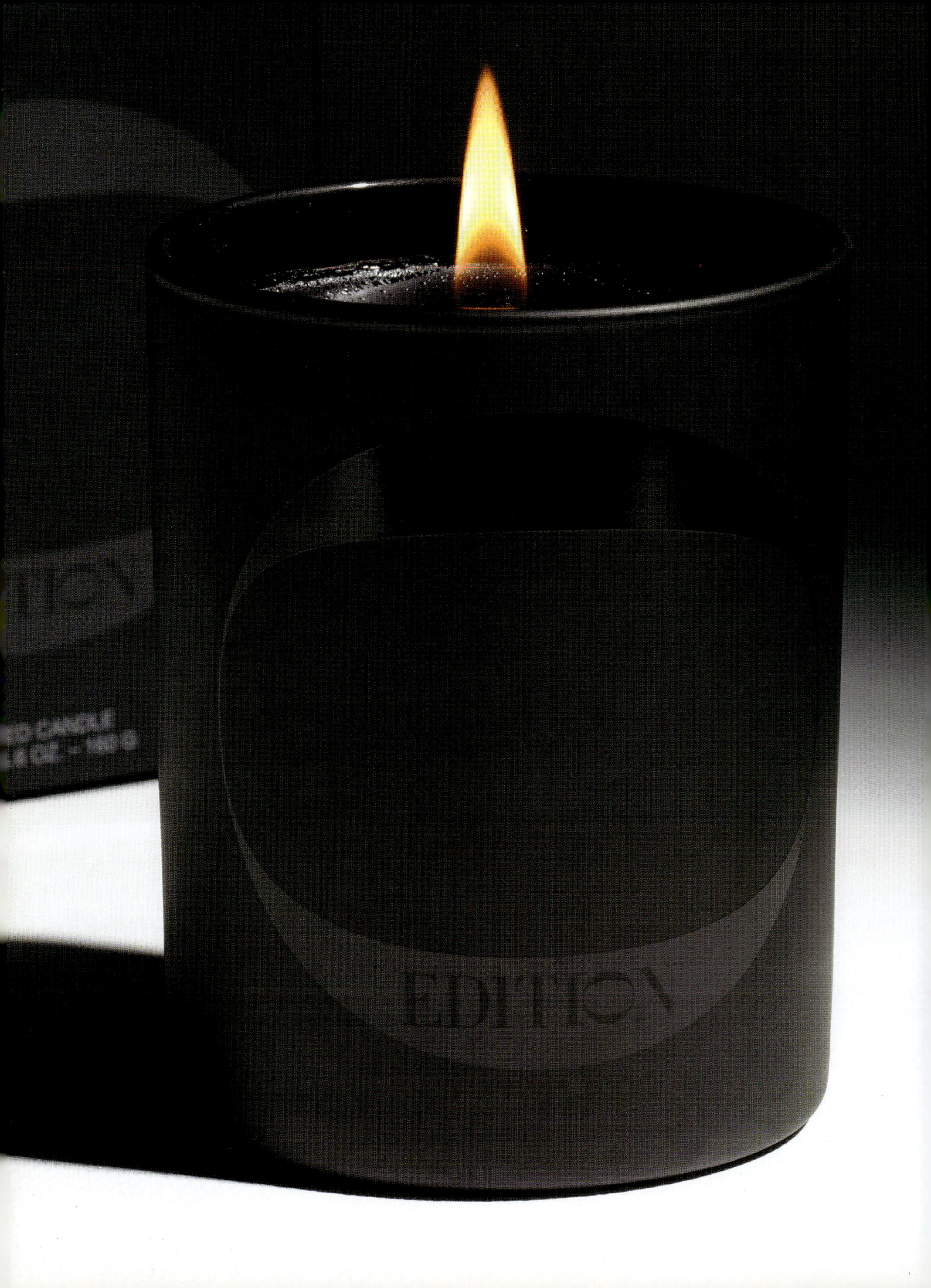
EDITION

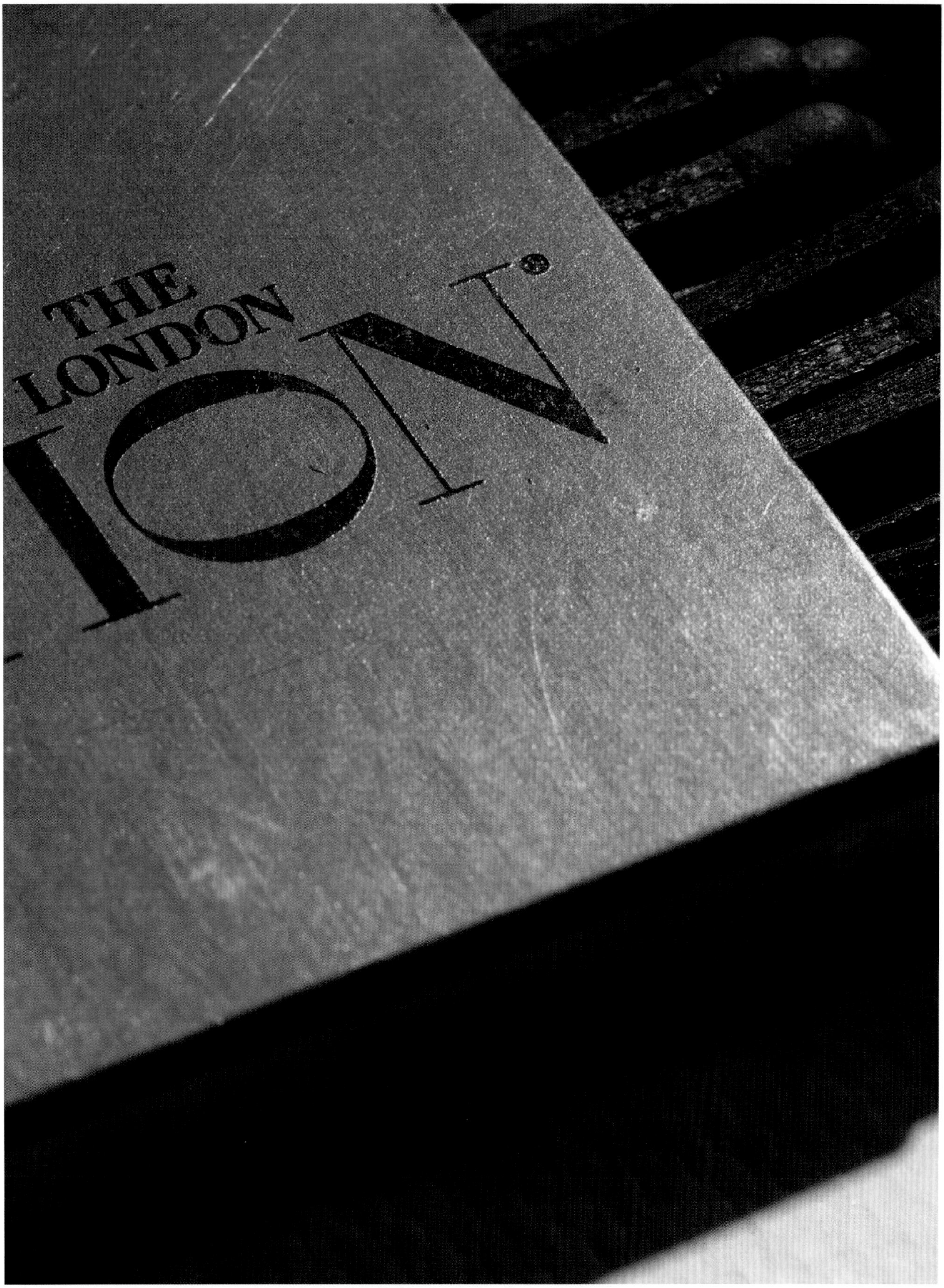
THE
LONDON

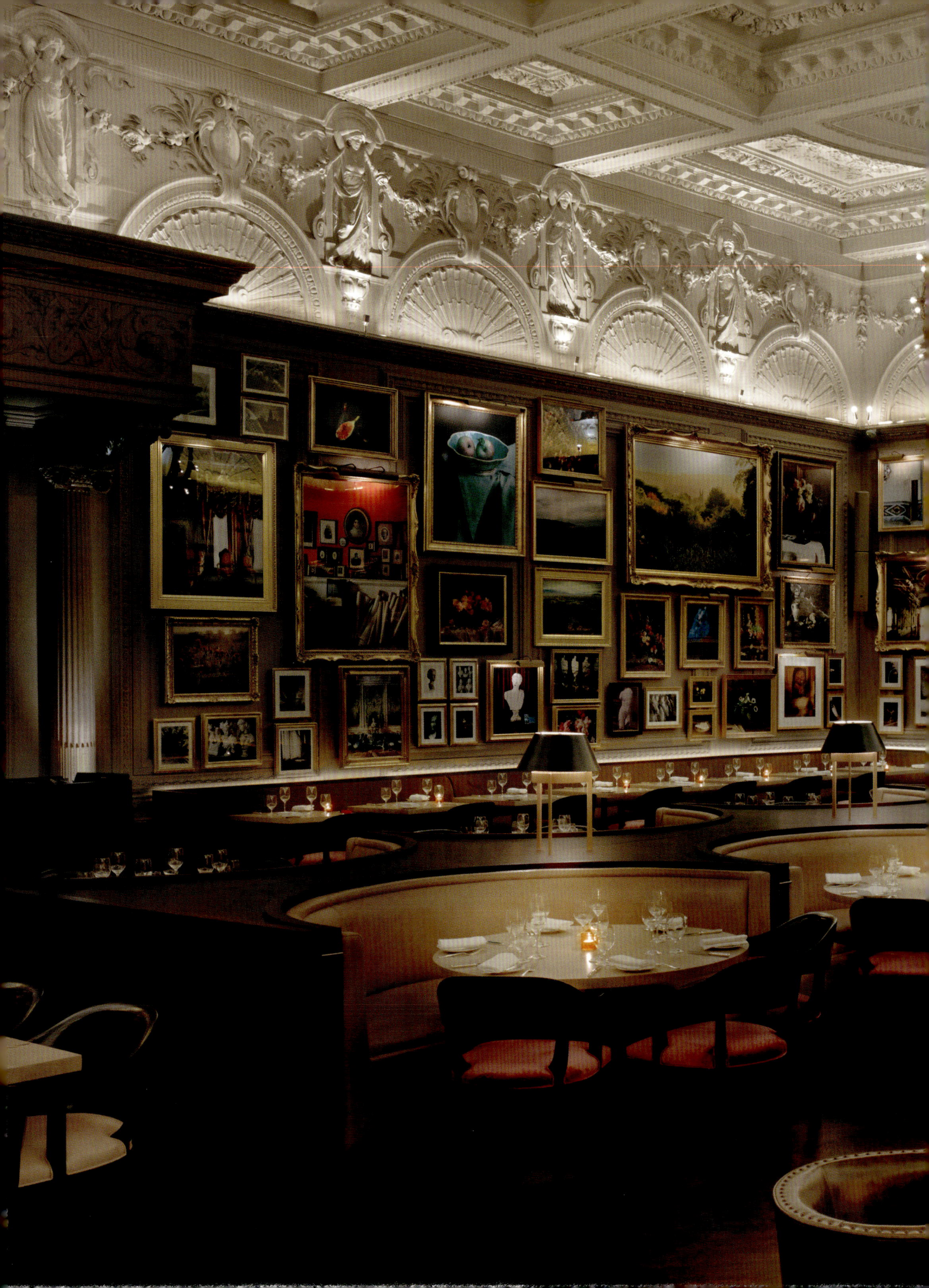

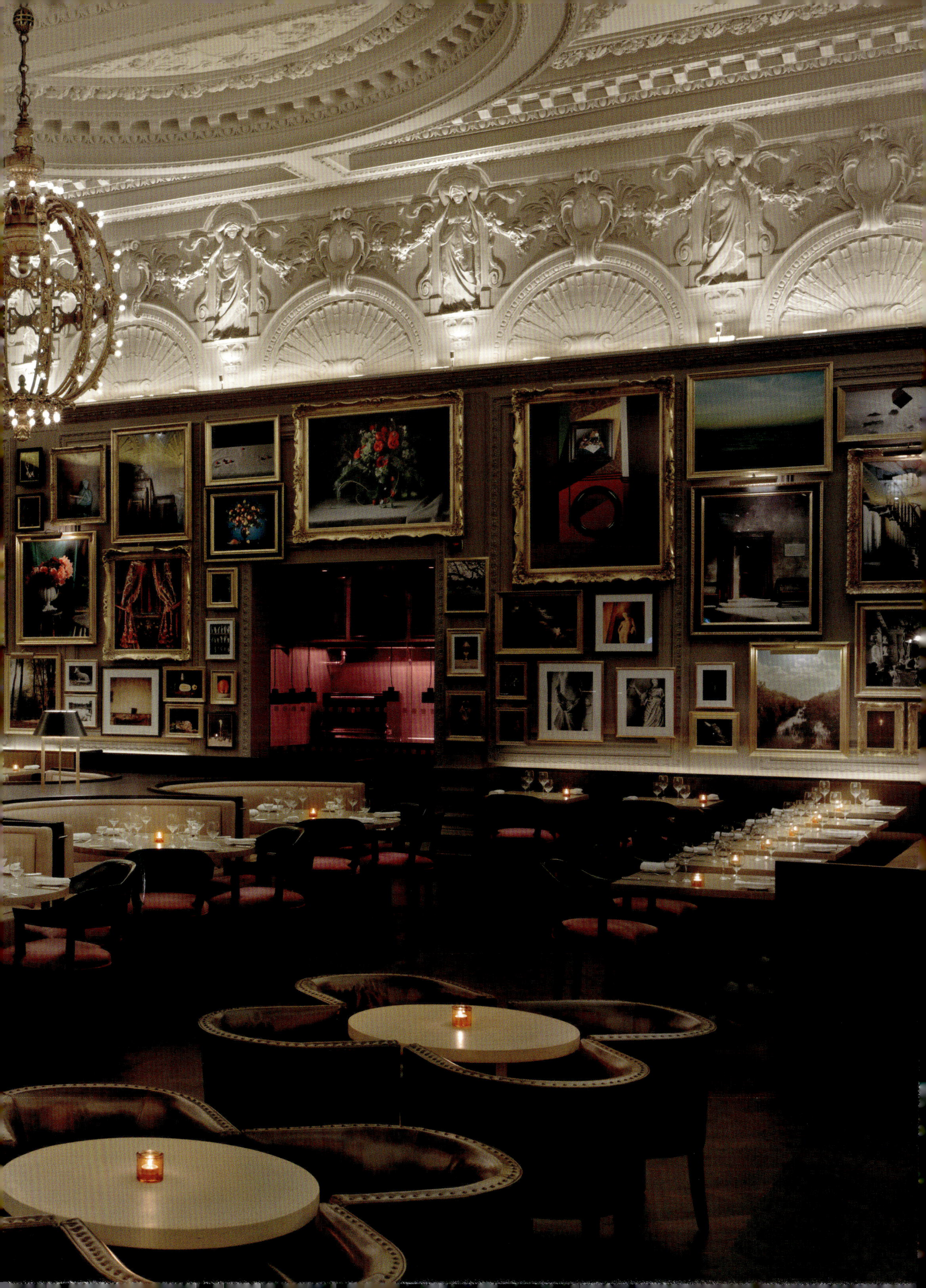

SHARE YOUR WIESLER MOMENTS

WITH THE ONES YOU LOVE

EUROPE | GRAZ | HOTEL WIESLER

Hotel Wiesler Graz, Austria

ADDRESS | Grieskai 4—8, Graz, Austria
ROOMS | 98, 41 refurbished rooms
OPENED | 2011
ARCHITECT | Marcel Kammerer
GRAPHIC DESIGN | Moodley Brand Identity

Hotel Wiesler has a long and proud history that has been 'inspiring since 1909.' The interior design features mismatched chairs, an old record player, typewriters and a treasure chest; these are just some of the items that can be found nestled throughout the art nouveau/modern design masterpiece.

In fact, owner Florian Weitzer's main aim was to create instantly recognisable details and give items with soul and history a place. The entrance hall is home to custom made furniture (sourced from recycled materials), breakfast is served under the Art Nouveau mosaic 'Spring' by Leopold Forstner and their own 'Speisesaal' restaurant is decorated with street art by artist Josef Wurm. Together they combine to create a source of inspiration for their guests.

The integration of the branding into the hotel is the creative work of Moodley Brand Identity. It respects the tradition of the hotel through its neutral tones combined with whimsical, conversational language. Through the use of a variety of finishes and textures, the identity pays homage to the vintage era while adding a new layer of modernity that matches the new romantic feel of the hotel.

'The polaroid corner, where you can 'Share your Wiesler moments with the ones you love,' demonstrates the branding extending itself beyond the walls of the hotel.'

Für Stadtgespräche.
Und weiter.

Für Gespräche mit Ihren Freunden, Kollegen, dem Pizzadienst oder Tante Ulla in Berlin wählen Sie bitte die Null vor. Innerhalb des Wieslers telefonieren Sie kostenfrei und müssen sich dafür praktischerweise nur eine einzige Nummer merken: 75. That's it. Damit erreichen Sie die Rezeption, die immer alles weiss.

FOR LOCAL CALLS AND BEYOND.

For calling your friends, colleagues, the pizza service or Auntie Anne in Berlin please dial '0' before the actual number. All phone calls within the Wiesler are free and you only need to know one number: 75. That's it. This is the number of the reception desk where you'll get help, answers to all your questions.

HOTEL WIESLER

The owner's main aim was to create instantly recognisable details and give items with soul and history a place as a source of inspiration and comfort for guests from all over the world.

WIESLER

since 1909

THE WIESLER
HOTEL.

IN THE CENTRE
OF GRAZ.

1 Der
2 Trib
3 Kuns
4 Kwrl
5 Murin
6 Stadtn
7 Schloßb
8 Old city
9 Townh

HOTEL WIESLER

EUROPE | GRAZ

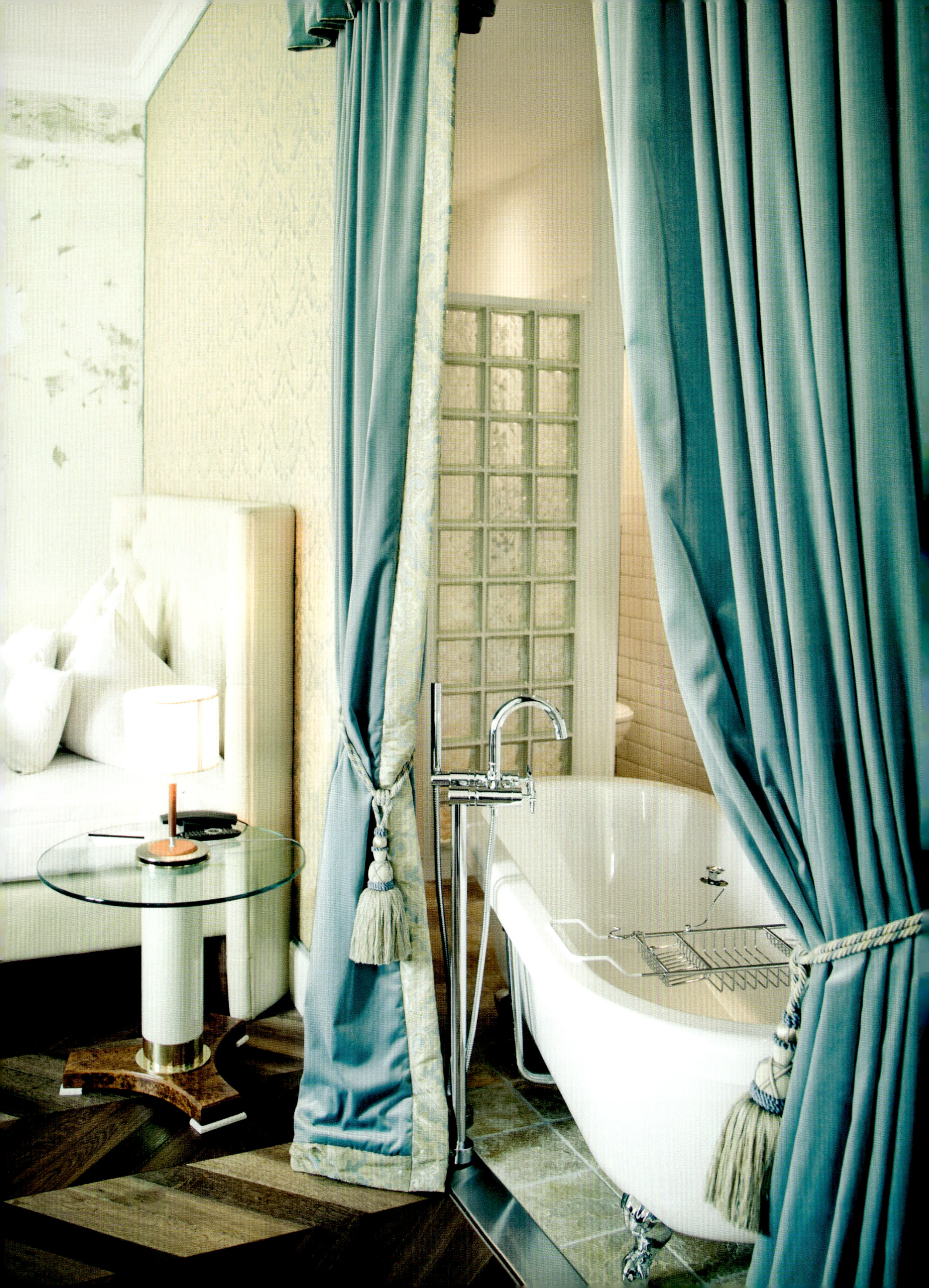

Hotel Daniel Vienna, Austria

ADDRESS | Landstraßer Gürtel 5, Vienna, Austria
ROOMS | 116
OPENED | 2012
ARCHITECT | Georg Lippert and Roland Rohn (original building 1962); Atelier Heiss Architects (restoration 2011)
GRAPHIC DESIGN | Moodley Brand Identity

Originally founded by Alois Daniel in 1886, it wasn't until 1962 that Hotel Daniel was transformed into the existing structure by architects Georg Lipper and Roland Rohn. The original building was unfortunately destroyed after the Second World War; later, the office block, known as the Hoffman—La Roche building, was restored to the building that exists today.

As it now stands, Hotel Daniel is based around the concept of reinterpreted luxury, known as 'Smart Luxury.' The hotel's owner, Florian Wietzer (who is also responsible for Hotel Wiesler in Graz), created the hotel specifically for attracting what he calls the 'modern traveller' — one whose needs are as little as possible. Therefore, you won't find anything superfluous or any complicated frills — Hotel Daniel is built on minimalism, function and style.

Hotel Daniel's identity is not based on merely one logo. Instead, there are several alternatives (all with a similar look and feel) that can work individually or collectively. Similar to the notion of the 'modern traveller,' all versions are simple, monochrome but with a strong personal touch (some versions even include the owner himself).

In addition, the hotel's store offers guests the opportunity to purchase their own branded products, including honey from their own rooftop beehive.

'The identity varies across a range of collateral according to each application's purpose. Using a variety of materials (including leather and metal) and different methods of applications (such as spray painting), the identity demonstrates how interestingly branding can be applied.'

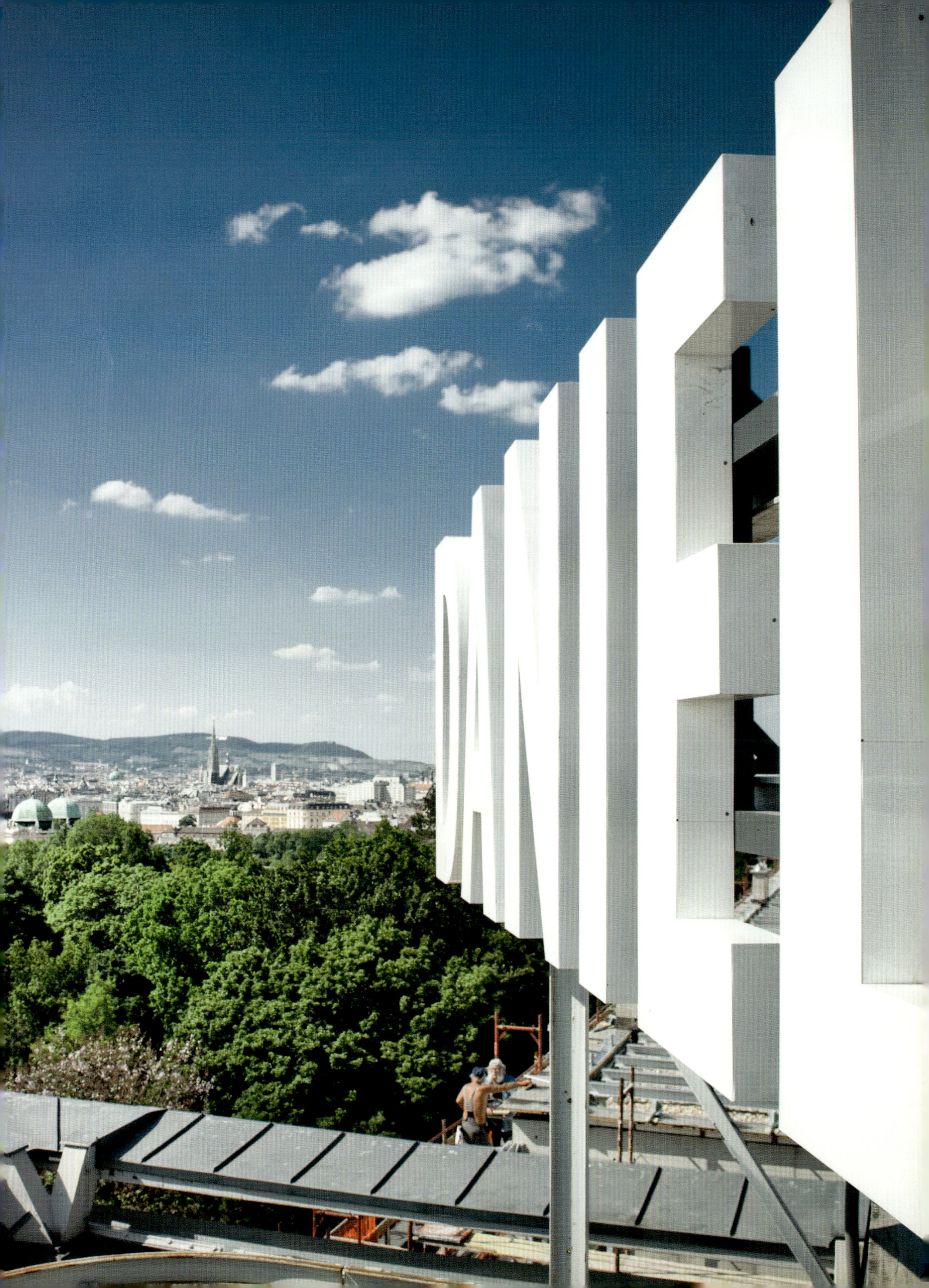

EUROPE | VIENNA

The hotel's motto is 'Urban Stay — Smart Traveller.' Urban Stay offers modern travellers a vibrant blend of innovative ideas which are far removed from cumbersome hospitality and the conventional charm of hotel chains. The idea has also gone down well with local city dwellers, making Hotel Daniel an urban meeting place which adds up to a lot more than simply 'a good place to stay overnight.'

— Hotel Daniel

HOTEL DANIEL

105

SORRY, WE'RE CLOSED.
EINLADUNG
OPENING HOTEL DANIEL VIENNA
Übrigens: Erwin Wurm enthüllt sein neues Werk
DATE:
31. Mai 2012
TIME:
18.30 Uhr
PLACE:
Landstraßer Gürtel 5, 1030 Vienna
URBAN STAY
DANIEL
SMART LUXURY
ALOIS DANIEL
DANIEL
HOTEL EST 1886
WELCOME
GREAT TO HAVE YOU HERE
FLORIAN WEITZER
URBAN STAY
DANIEL
SMART LUXURY
1886
ALOIS DANIEL
DANIEL
BODY & HAIR WASH
URBAN STAY
DANIEL
SMART LUXURY
HOTEL DANIEL VIENNA
WORLDHOTELS

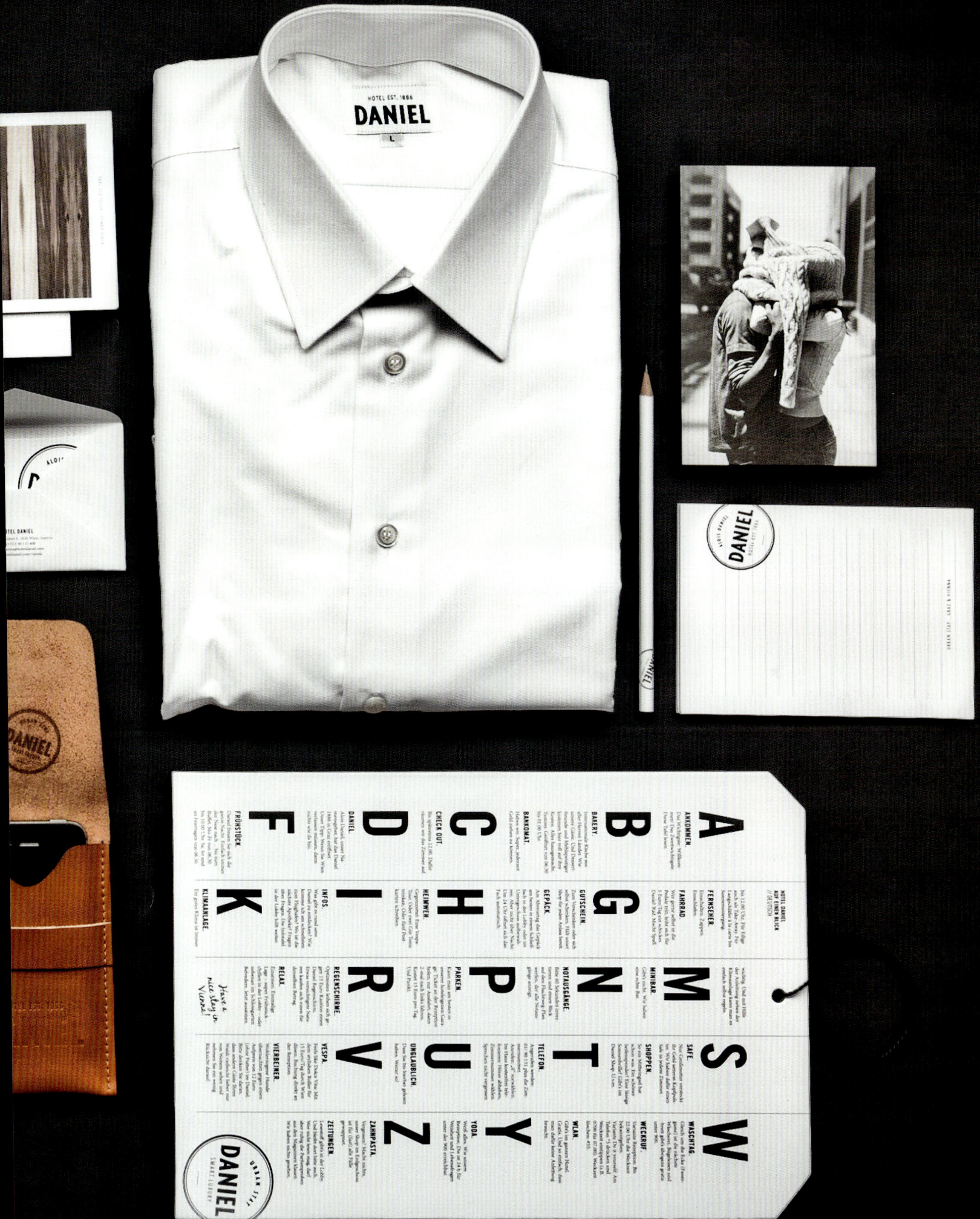
HOTEL EST. 1886
DANIEL
L

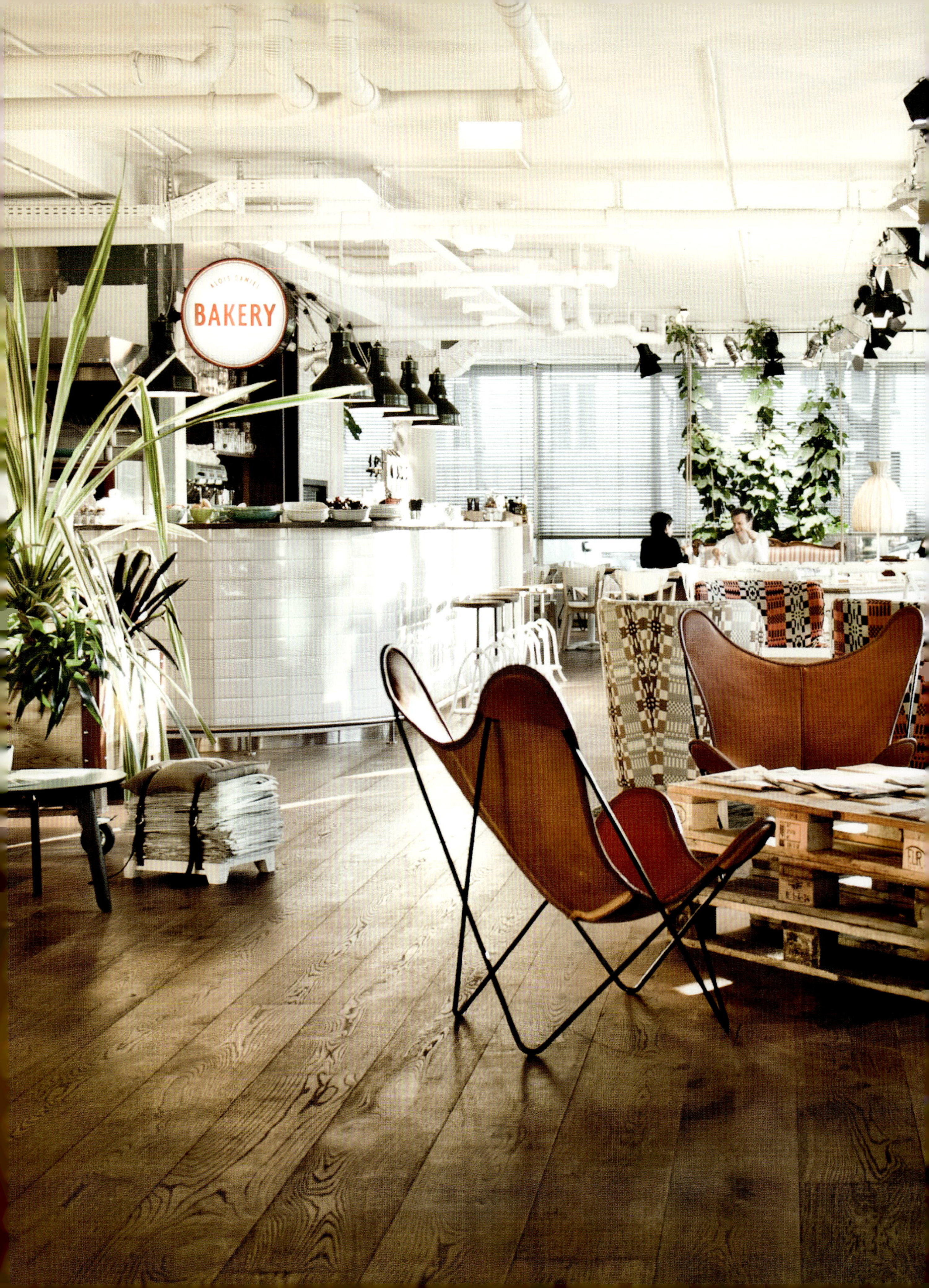
BAKERY

The hotel's bakery, which also acts as lobby, breakfast room and restaurant, uses the same design elements as the main identity but is distinguished by the color red.

surface et symbole.
Ceux qui vont voir sous
la surface le font à leurs
risques et périls.
même que ceux qui cherchent à déchiffrer le symbole.
ON A OUBLIÉ CE POTEAU

EUROPE | PARIS | MAMA SHELTER

Mama Shelter Paris, France

ADDRESS | 109 Rue de Bagnolet, Paris, France
ROOMS | 172
OPENED | September 2008
ARCHITECT | Roland Castro
INTERIOR DESIGN | Philippe Starck
GRAPHIC DESIGN | GBH

Formerly a multistory car park, Mama Shelter is located in the Saint Blaise quartier in the east side of Paris. With Philippe Starck as interior designer, you can expect nothing less than whimsical, ultra modern, yet quirky interiors that entertain and delight.

Chalkboard ceilings are covered in graffiti — with phrases such as, 'Let's trash the place!' and 'Can we hire a room by the hour?' adding to the visual interest and intrigue. This signature white script also appears as a collection of odd facts and anecdotes dispersed throughout the hotel, with guests provided markers to make their own contribution.

The Mama Shelter brand is its own universe. The name 'Mama' denotes a mother that takes care of you, while 'Shelter' refers to a place where everyone is welcome. This hotel has no pretences and accepts all socioeconomic backgrounds with open arms, merely inviting guests to enjoy the spaces that surround them.

The hotel's branding, along with all associated marketing material, complements the modern interiors with sexy, fun and playful creations. Bold, unconventional and unique, the identity plays on the name — for example in the word 'Mama' a chicken sits over the name while the negative space makes the shape of an egg. These additional layers of clever branding, combined with unique interiors, create the Mama Shelter experience.

'The design collateral for Mama Shelter varies every six to twelve months to ensure that the hotel experience remains new and exciting — guests can always expect an element of surprise.'

EUROPE | PARIS

'Come to Mama and experience an intriguing mix of warmth, friendliness and community, wrapped in chic style, eclecticism and a drop of surreal humour — qualities that are very much reflected in Mama's brand identity.'

— GBH

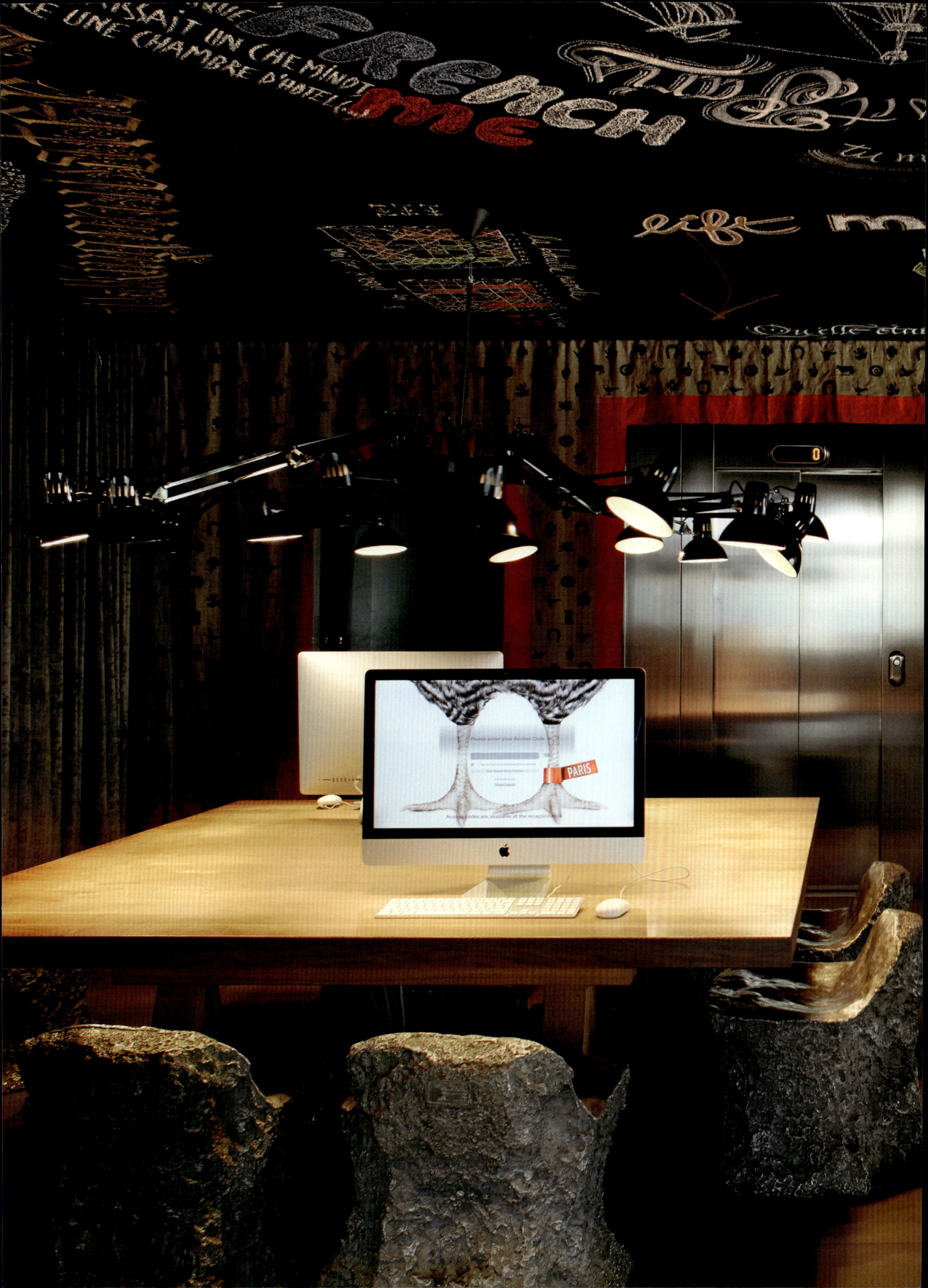
FRENCH
me
Please enter your Access Code
PARIS

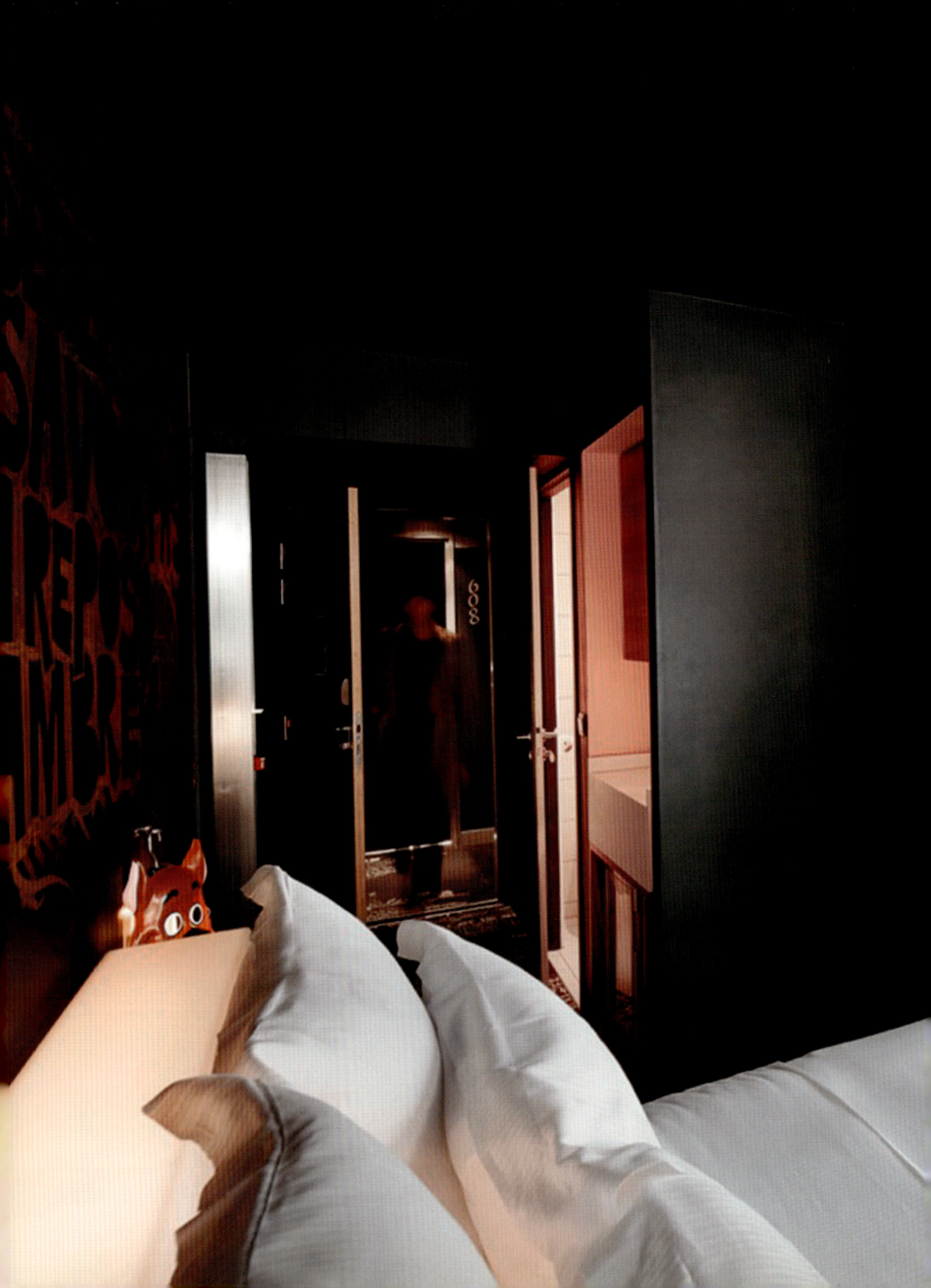
608

MAMA SHELTER

Mama, don't disturb me!

Mama, please clean my room!

Flying Like
into Time
eyes
The shrinkage
in the
These
RICARD
MICROPUZZLES

MAMA SHELTER

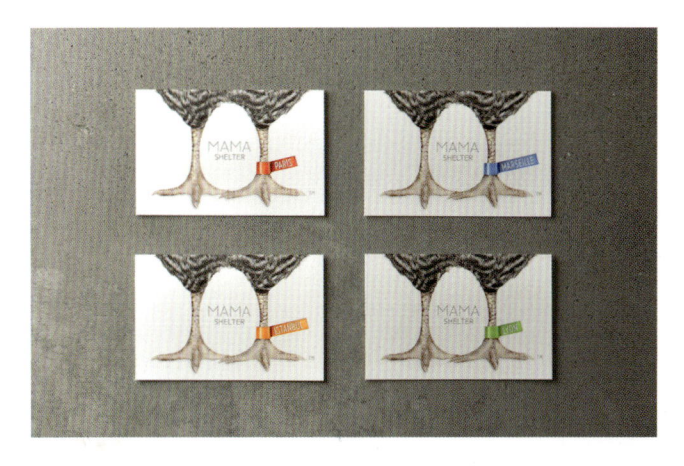

Mama Shelter now has a hotel in six locations, Paris, Marseille, Lyon, Bordeaux, Istanbul and Los Angeles, with many more opening in the coming years. Each location varies the brand through not only their interiors but also designed elements, such as key card holders, 'do not disturb' signs and restaurant menus, to create a unique and distinct Mama Shelter universe.

117

EUROPE | BERLIN | CASA CAMPER

Casa Camper Berlin, Germany

ADDRESS | Weinmeisterstrasse 1, Berlin, Germany
ROOMS | 51 rooms and suites
OPENED | September 2009
ARCHITECT | Jordi Tió
INTERIOR DESIGN | Fernando Amat
GRAPHIC DESIGN | America Sanchez

The Camper brand is known all over the world for their shoes — they have over four hundred stores in more than sixty countries. In 2005 they extended their brand to include hotels, and now have a hotel each in Barcelona and Berlin.

The Camper company's philosophy is based on 'the luxury of simplicity' which has now been adopted across both of their hotels. Casa Camper Berlin, located in the Mitte district, practices environmentally friendly methods such as solar energy and water recycling, in addition to providing bicycles for all of their guests. Each room is simple, clean and practical with the only embellishments being stylish necessities from the likes of Muji, Artemide and Vitra.

In addition to room numbers on each door, you can also identify your room from the outside by the numbers printed on the hotel curtains. This feature demonstrates that Camper is not afraid to reinterpret the standard format of a hotel room, a philosophy also reflected in the rooms' layout — all bathrooms have views of Berlin while the bed remains centrally located within the room.

The branding throughout the hotel is clear, playful and distinctly minimal in keeping with the interior design of the hotel. This is what Camper cares most about — functional design that provides nothing more (or less) than is required.

'The Camper company's philosophy is based on 'the luxury of simplicity,' an extension which has now been adopted across their hotels.'

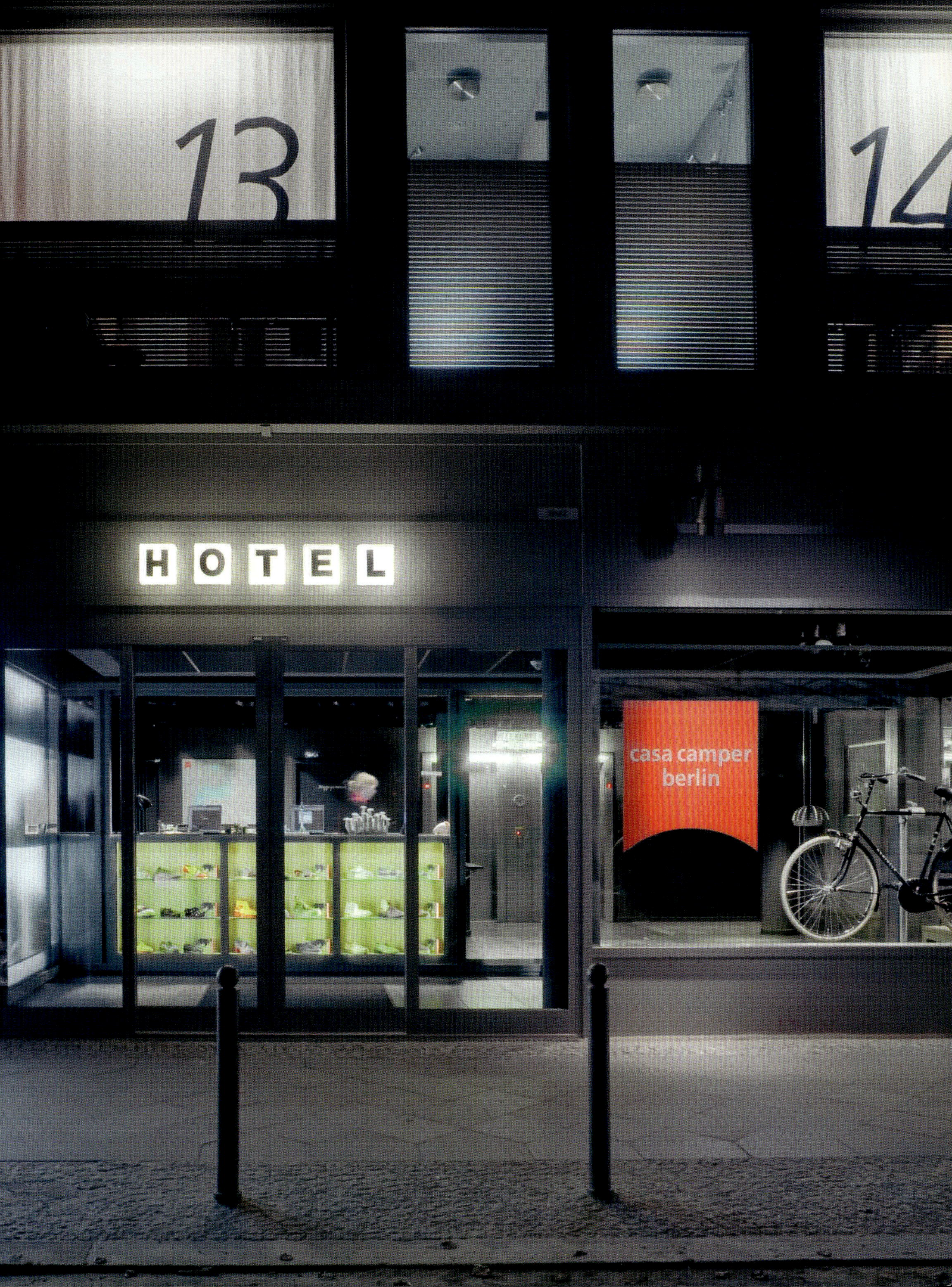
13
14
HOTEL
casa camper
berlin

EUROPE | BERLIN

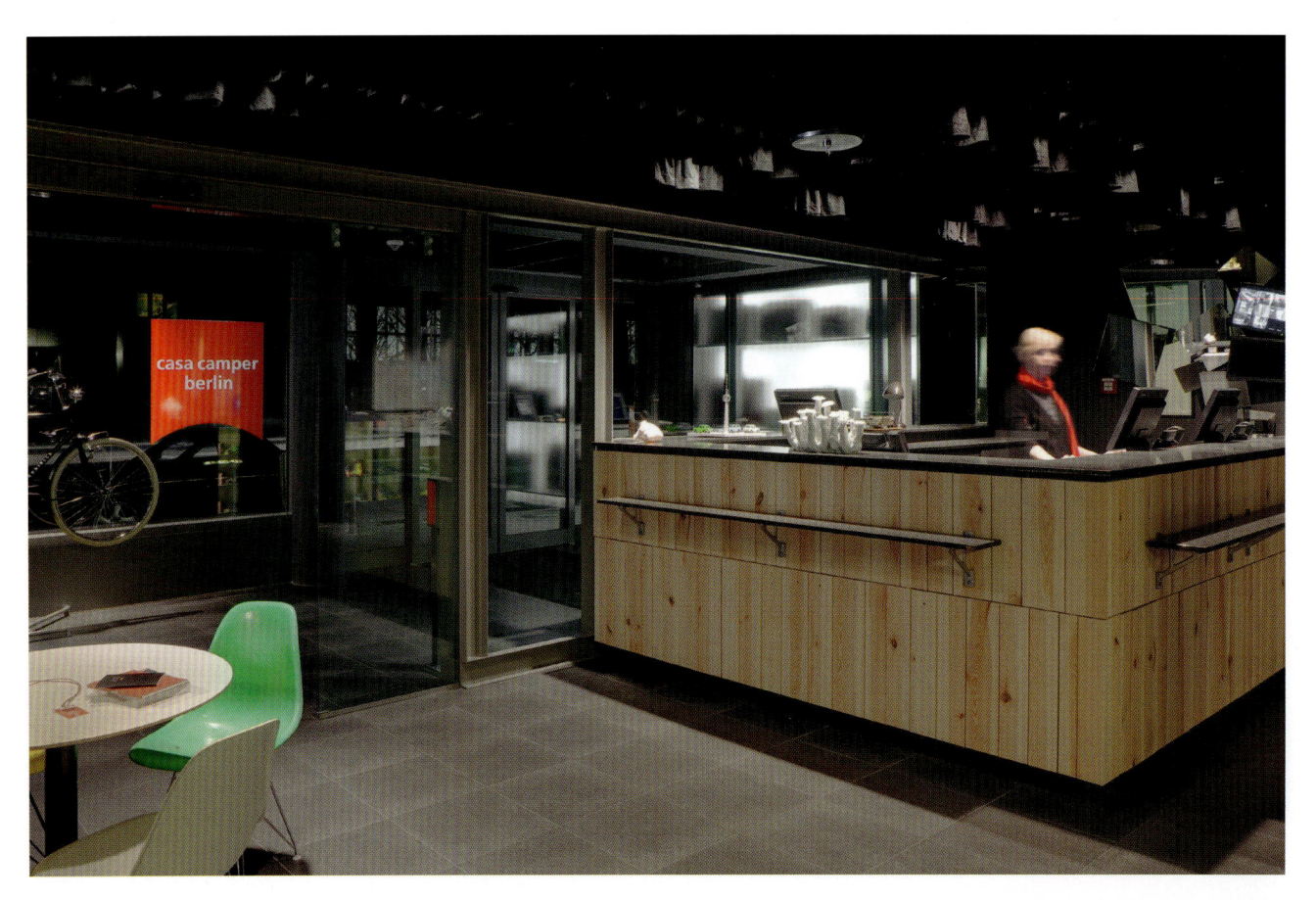

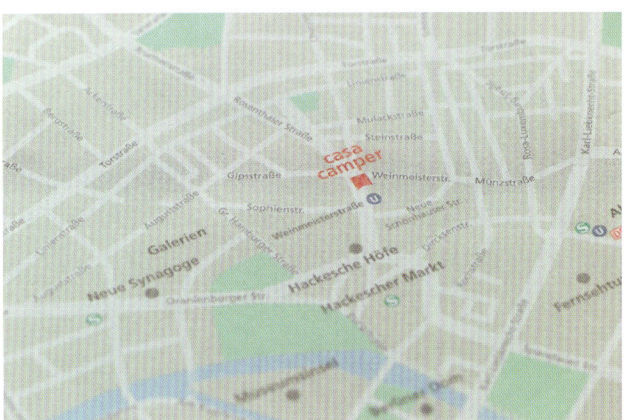

CASA CAMPER

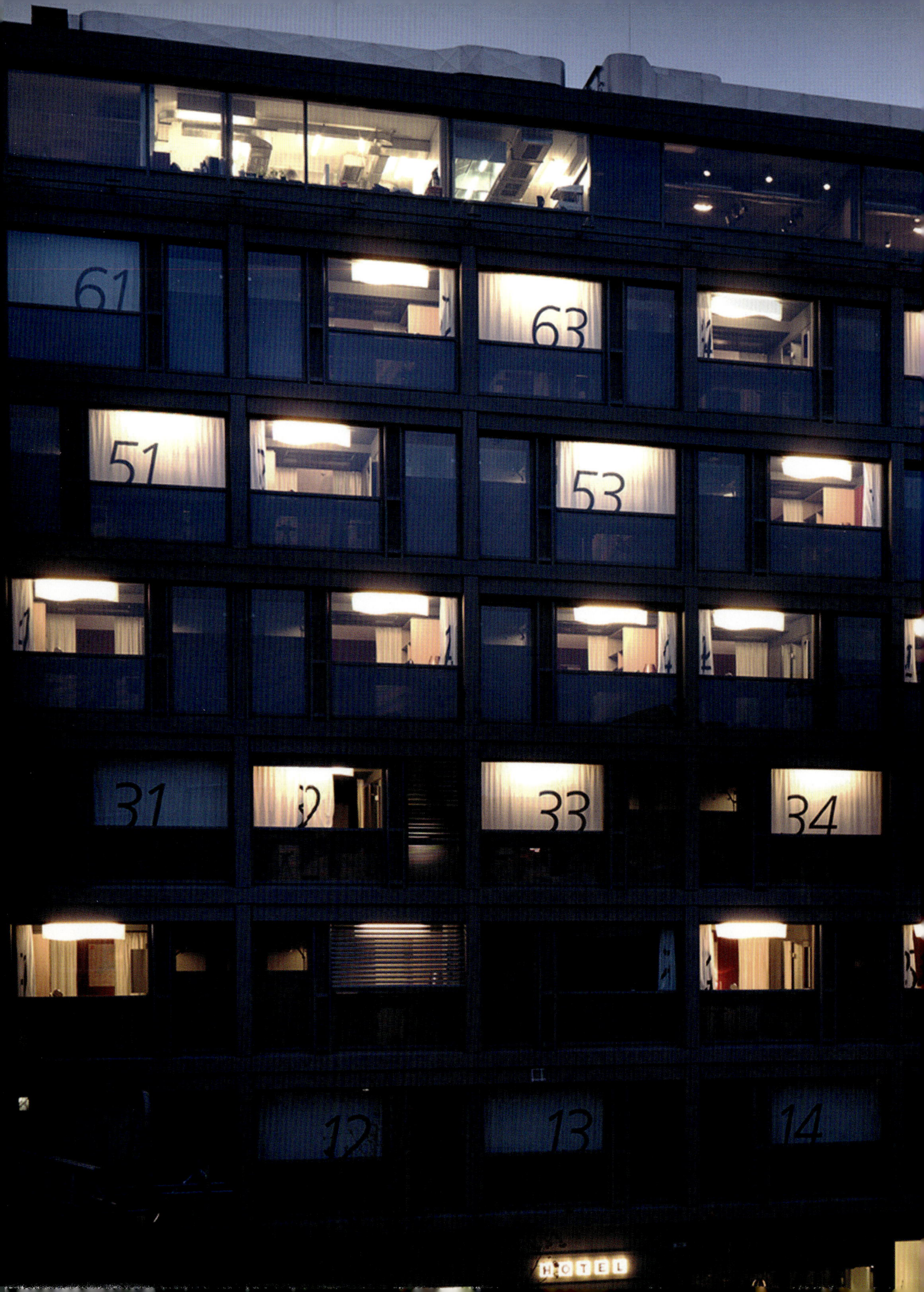
61
63
51
53
31
33
34
12
13
14
HOTEL

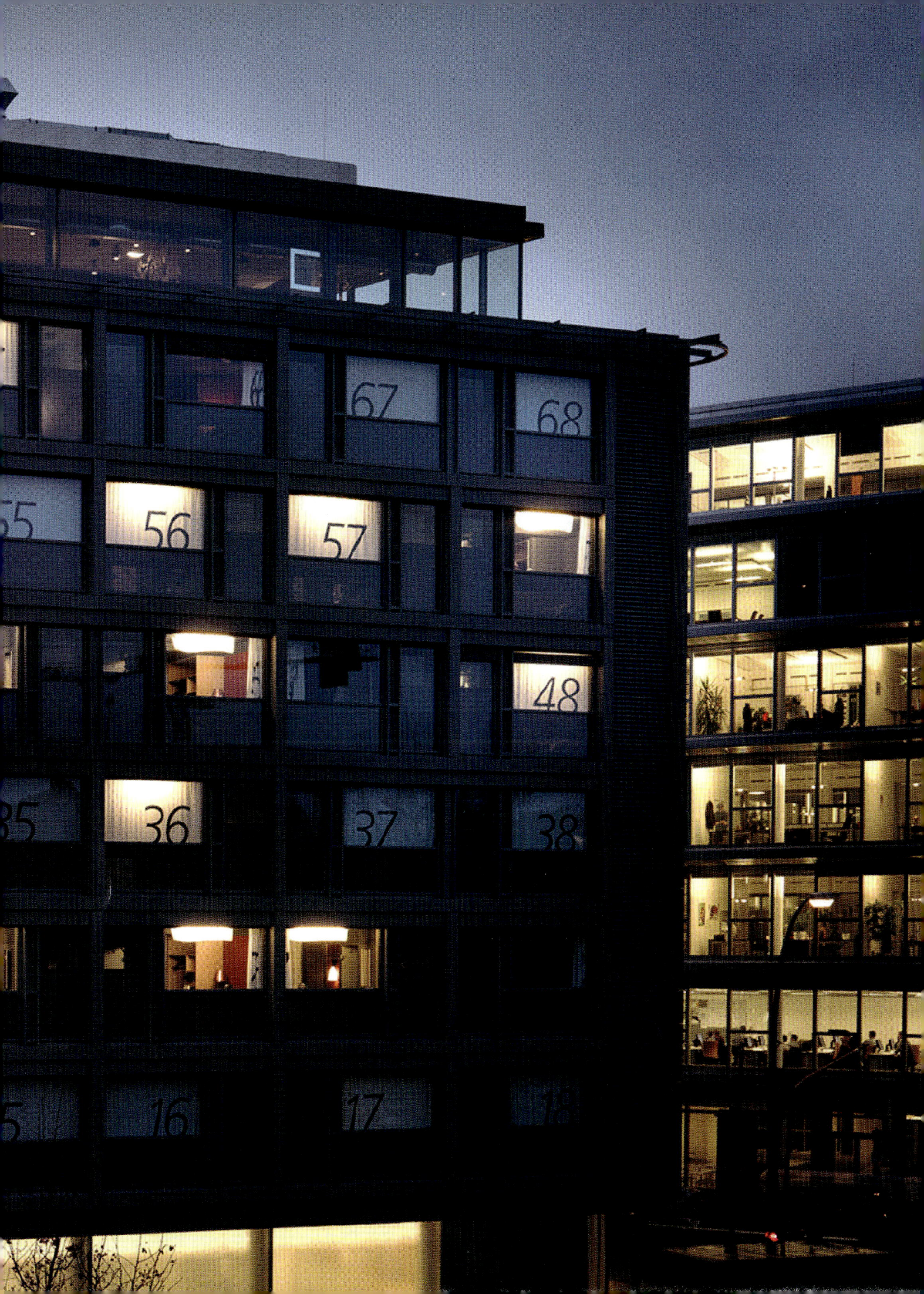
67
68
56
57
48
36
37
38
16
17

EUROPE | BERLIN

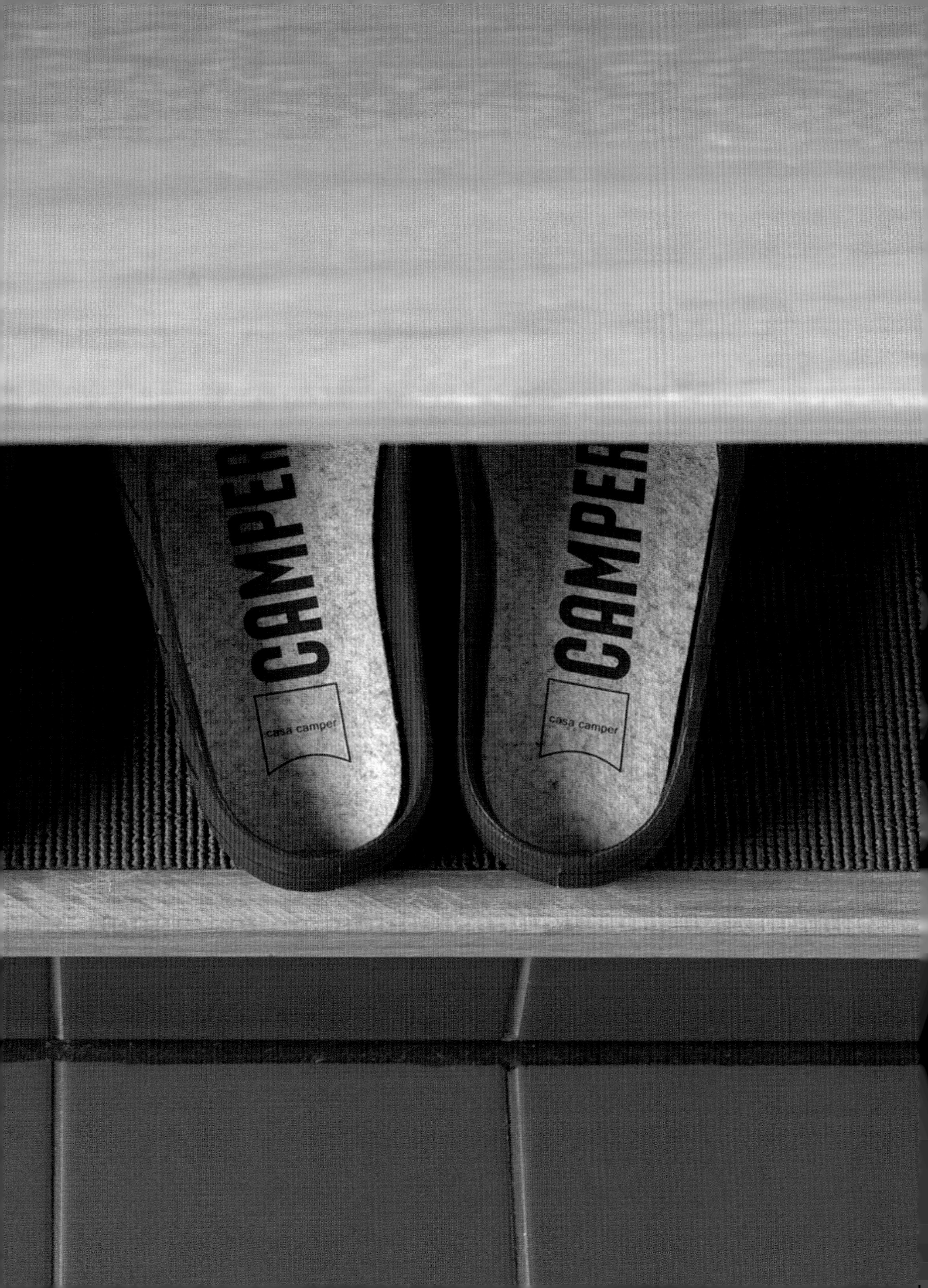
CAMPER
casa camper
CAMPER
casa camper

BERLIN

Michelberger Hotel Berlin, Germany

ADDRESS | Warschauer Straße 39/40, Berlin, Germany
ROOMS | 119
OPENED | September 2009
ARCHITECT | Werner Fricker and Ingenieure
INTERIOR DESIGN | Studio Aisslinger
GRAPHIC DESIGN | Azar Kazimir

The Michelberger Hotel caters to guests with an adventurous spirit, creating a sense of family unlike that of a traditional hotel. The interiors, created by internationally renowned designer Werner Aisslinger, provide a playful design aesthetic to a relaxed, laid back atmosphere that remains open to all walks of life.

Within the hotel there is an eclectic mix of design elements, mostly comprised of unique hand-made items, from light shades to signage. In conjunction with the diverse interior, the hotel replaces traditional printed type with handwritten script on everything from menus and signage to various iterations of the identity itself.

Led by the creative direction of Azar Kazimir, the Michelberger Hotel evolves organically with designs that are frequently updated to remain interesting and engaging. There are no rules within the creative team, and this sense of freedom transcends to the materials they create.

Although the hotel combines many elements under the same roof, the one consistency is that all creations reflect the spirit of the hotel — loads of creativity and an abundance of delight.

> 'The Michelberger Hotel is comprised of an eclectic mix of design elements. There is no one distinguishable typeface to recognise the hotel's identity, instead the designs grow and evolve organically.'

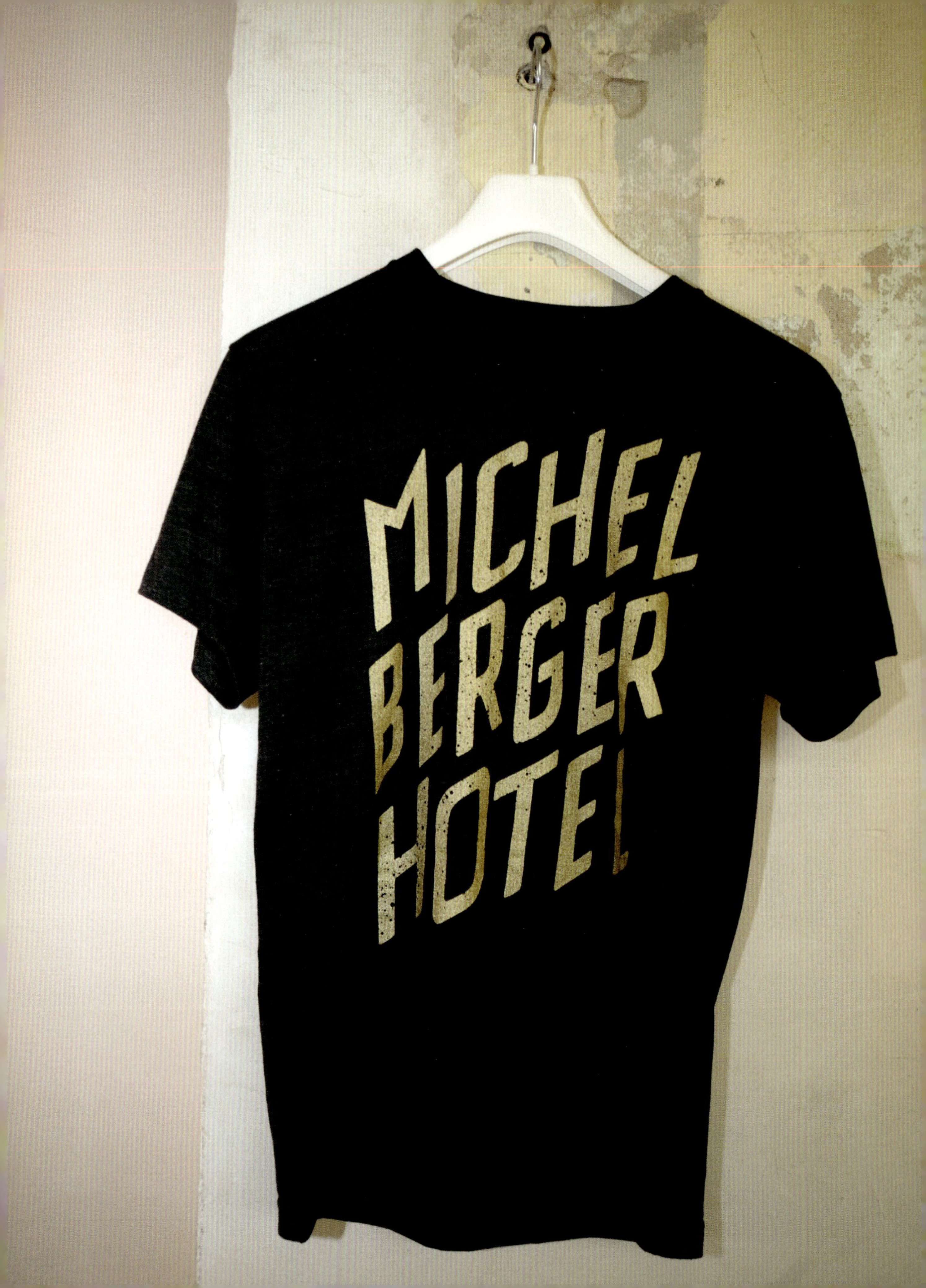
MICHEL
BERGER
HOTEL

MICHELBERGER HOTEL

EUROPE | BERLIN

130

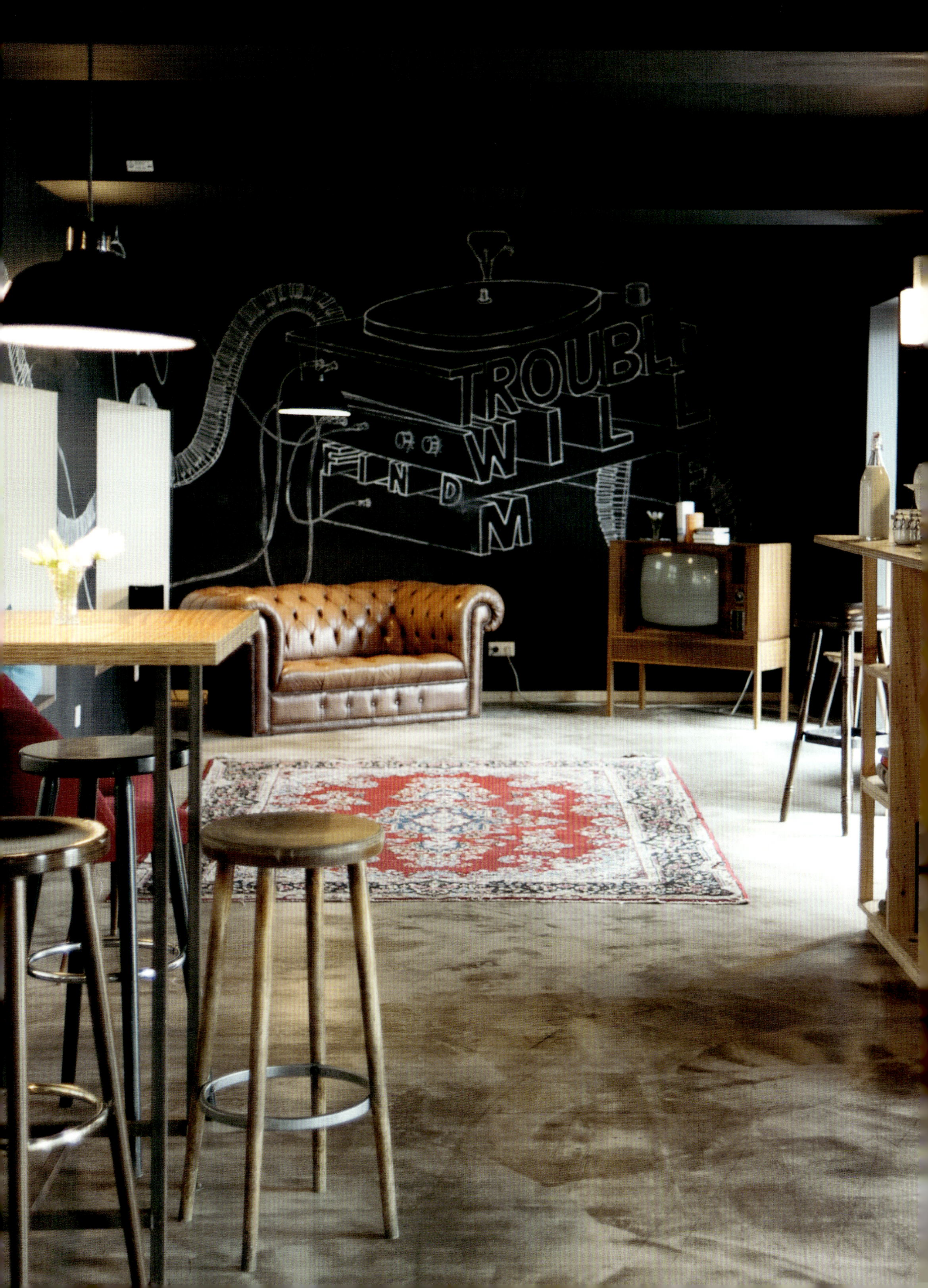

STILL -OR- SPARKLING
FOR YOU IT'S FREE DUDE!
REHYDRATE WITH
MICHEL BERGER WATER
MAKE YOUR
no more expensive beauty products needed ever!!
1.5L maybe
BE COOL.

MICHELBERGER HOTEL

The creative spirit of the Michelberger Hotel has extended to their own range of 'Fountain of Youth' coconut water and Michelberger Booze Schnapps available to purchase during your stay.

133

Hotel The Exchange Amsterdam, Netherlands

ADDRESS | Damrak 50, Amsterdam, Netherlands
ROOMS | 61 unique rooms
OPENED | 2011
ARCHITECT | Onswerk
INTERIOR DESIGN | Amsterdam Fashion Institute
GRAPHIC DESIGN | Studio INA MATT

Hotel The Exchange is located on the Damrak, Amsterdam's oldest street, opposite the former stock exchange. The location has influenced the naming, not only for the hotel itself, but also for its associated webstore (Options!) and eatery (Stock Café).

This street is considered the 'red carpet' of Amsterdam as it welcomes the main thoroughfare to the city from the Central Station. However, the concept for the hotel, by Suzanne Oxenaar and Otto Nan, is based around this area looking more like a catwalk. Based on this, they approached the AMFI (Amsterdam Fashion Institute) and through collaboration with eight fashion designers, created sixty-one unique rooms around the theme of 'rooms dressed as models.'

This unique approach has created a design hotel that playfully weaves together fashion and architecture, including public spaces whereby the reception represents a handbag. The approach was to dress the hotel as a 'naked body' with materials that connect deeply with fashion.

Perhaps even more interesting for a hotel is that it accommodates a range of guests and budgets. Rooms on each level range from one star to five stars to create a truly different approach to hotel accommodation.

'Hotel The Exchange collaborated with eight fashion designers from the AMFI (Amsterdam Fashion Institute) to create sixty-one unique rooms around the theme of 'rooms dressed as models.' The identity also leverages off the 'x' shaped crosses in the red and black shield from Amsterdam's coat of arms.'

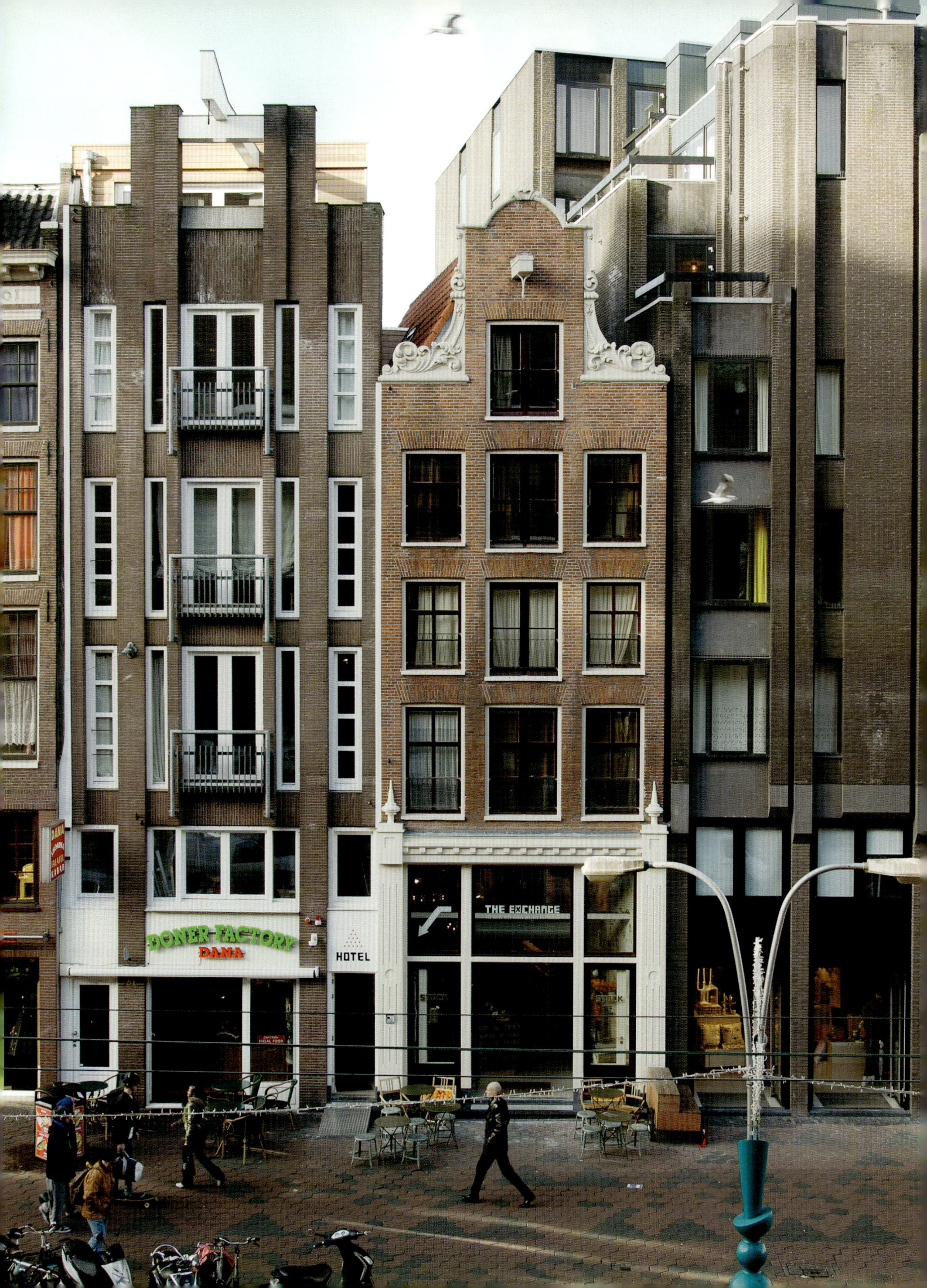
DONER FACTORY
DANA
HOTEL
THE EXCHANGE

EUROPE | AMSTERDAM

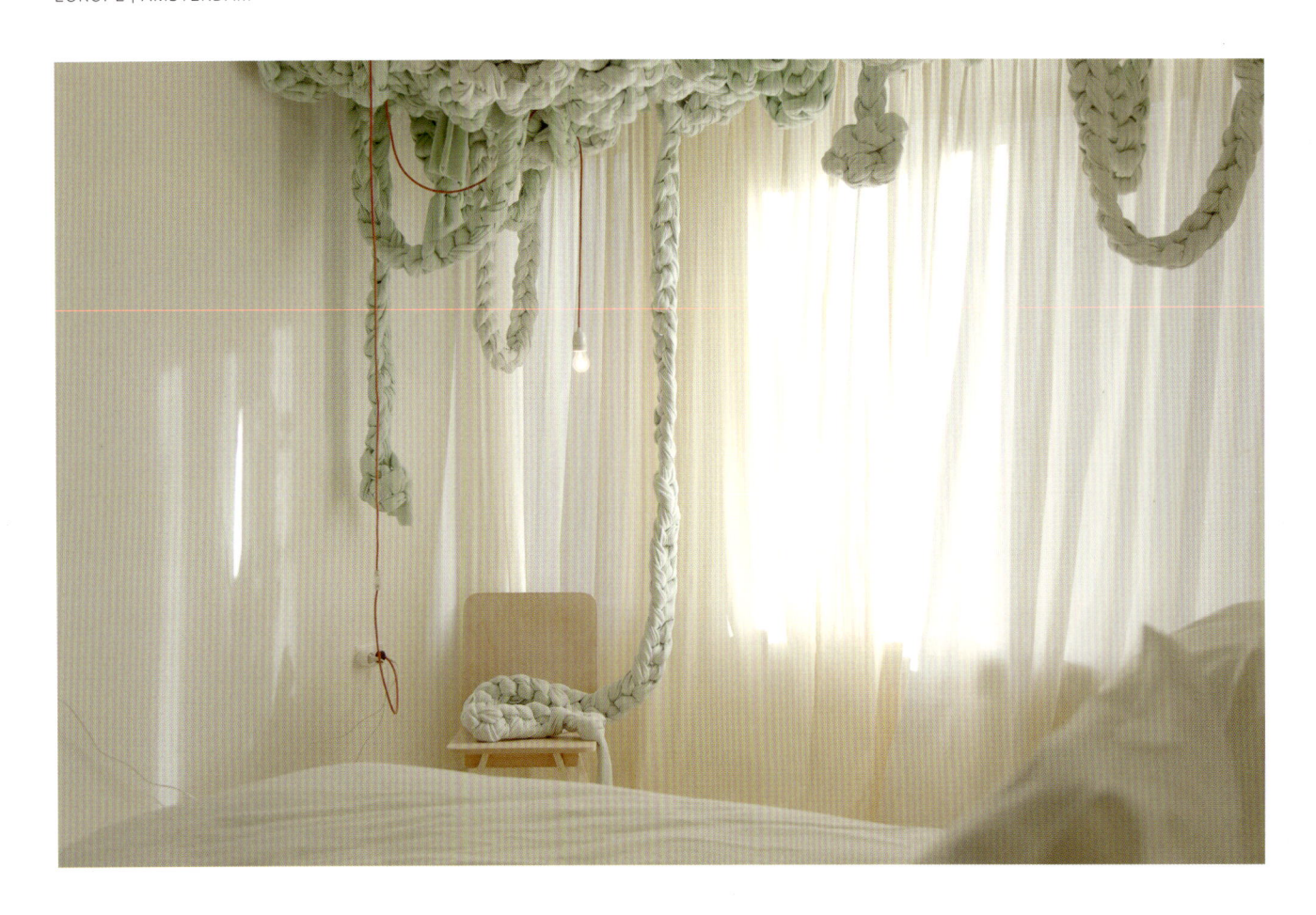

SO!X

STOCK   OPTIONS!   THE EXCHANGE

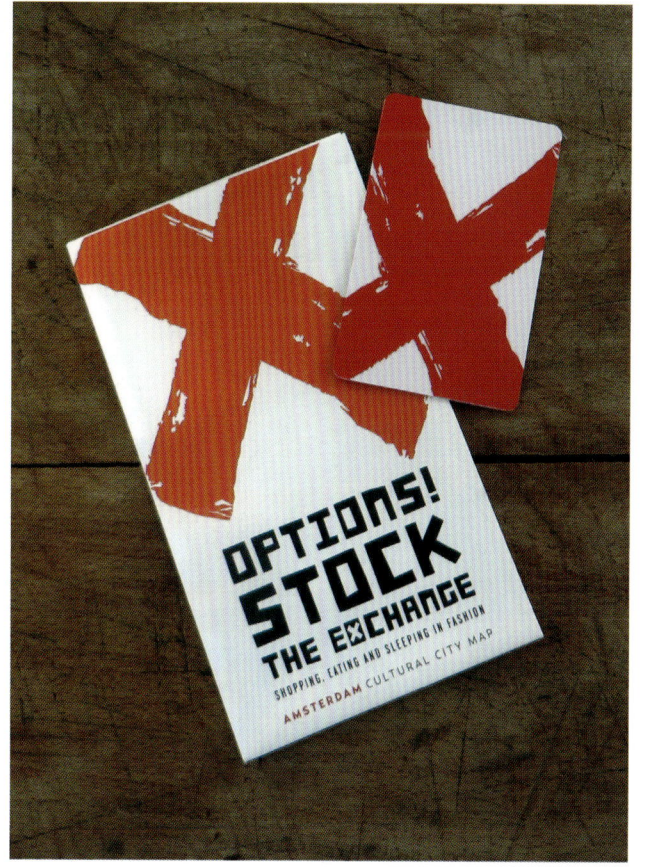

HOTEL THE EXCHANGE

EUROPE | AMSTERDAM

The hotel's notion of collaboration also extends to their branding. Within the café, for example, the walls are filled with hand-drawn illustrations from each contributor to the hotel — aiming to represent the different visitors the hotel would house in the future. Referencing the stock exchange building opposite, the café itself has been created using faux bars of gold.

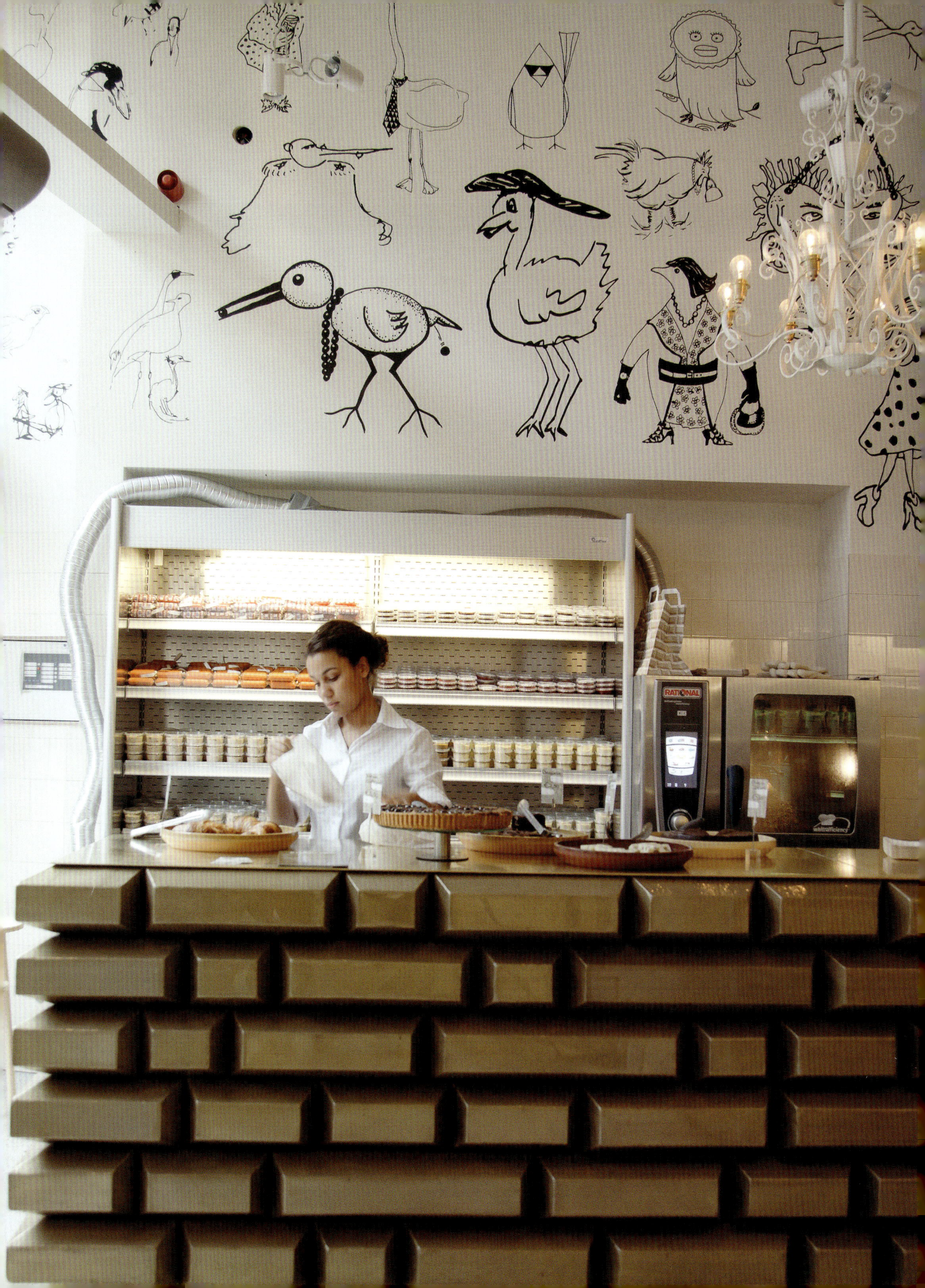
RATIONAL

The Options! webshop features fashion, interior and student design collections.

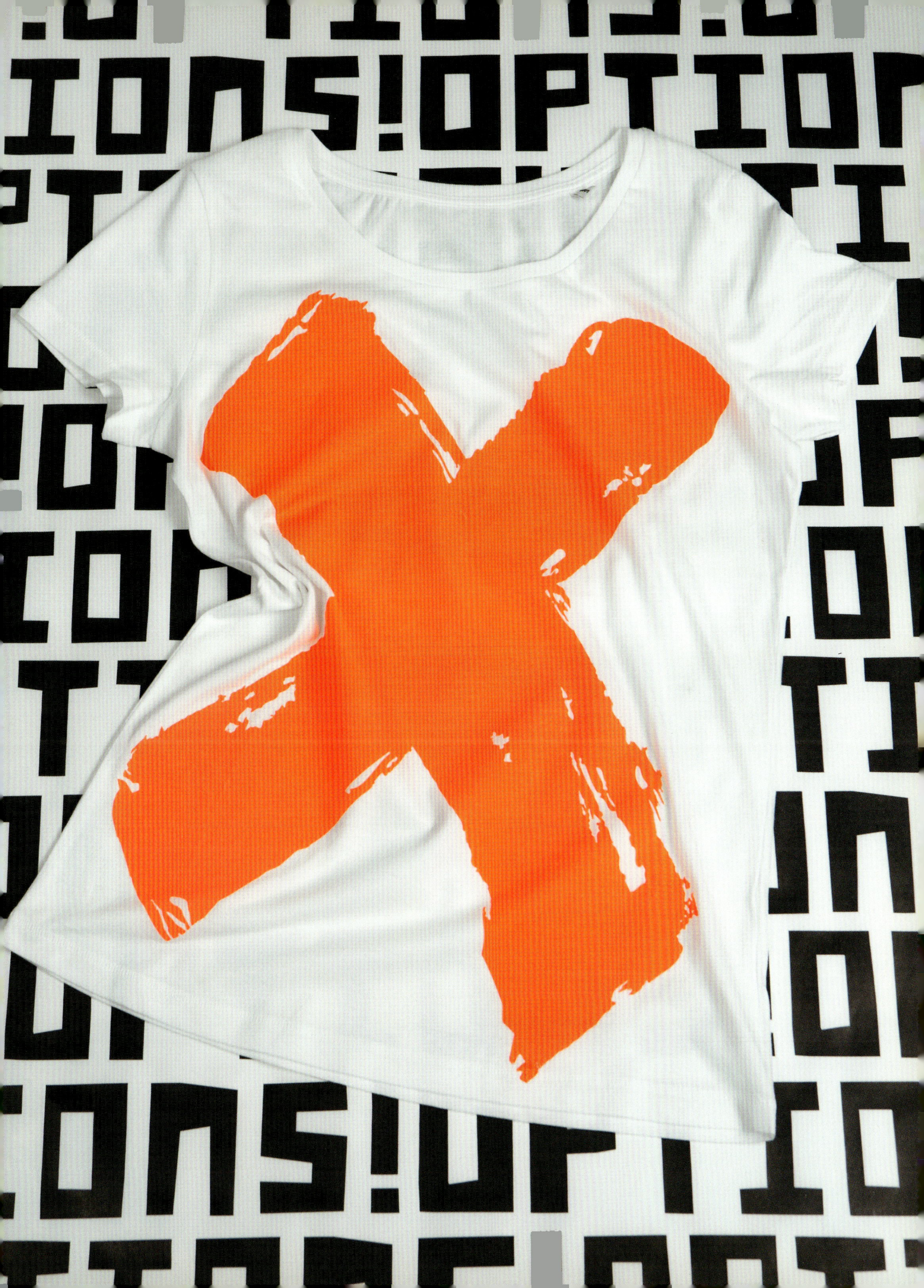
IONS!OPTIO
ONS!OPTIO

EUROPE | AMSTERDAM | THE STUDENT HOTEL

The Student Hotel Amsterdam, Netherlands

ADDRESS | Jan van Galenstraat 335, Amsterdam, Netherlands
ROOMS | 707 rooms
OPENED | September 2013
ARCHITECT | A&E Architects
INTERIOR DESIGN | ...,staat creative agency
GRAPHIC DESIGN | ...,staat creative agency

The Student Hotel in Amsterdam is an evolution of the traditional student housing idea — combining designer interiors and shared spaces to create a fun, exciting and affordable place for students (or the young-at-heart) to stay for either a short or long time.

Designed and branded by Amsterdam's creative agency ...,staat, the hotel spreads over three multi-story buildings and embraces exposed concrete walls and ceilings to create an industrial, yet modern, look for this unique offering that merges student with hotel.

The hotel not only has all the modern facilities expected from a traditional hotel (minus the room service), but also a range of shared facilities to encourage social interaction between students. Everything a student would need is here, including a games room with ping pong and foosball, a gym, free bicycle rentals for stays longer than a month, a basketball court, lounge area, and a canteen/restaurant. Of course, all the practical requirements, such as free wifi, quiet study areas, a DIY laundry and a library are also included.

The branding, featuring a bespoke typeface combined with a daring colour palette of black and yellow, is confident and striking — perhaps a reflection of the guests the hotel caters towards.

'The Student Hotel spreads over three multi-story buildings and embraces exposed concrete walls and ceilings to create an industrial, yet modern, look to this unique offering.'

THE STUDENT HOTEL

EUROPE | AMSTERDAM

THE STUDENT HOTEL

The branding reflects the hotel's audience with playful patterns interspersed with large quotes that feature on the walls. These messages, such as 'You can't be spoiled if you do your own ironing,' 'Too much ego will kill your talent' and 'The beach is boring' add another level of engagement and understanding of the hotel's primary audience.

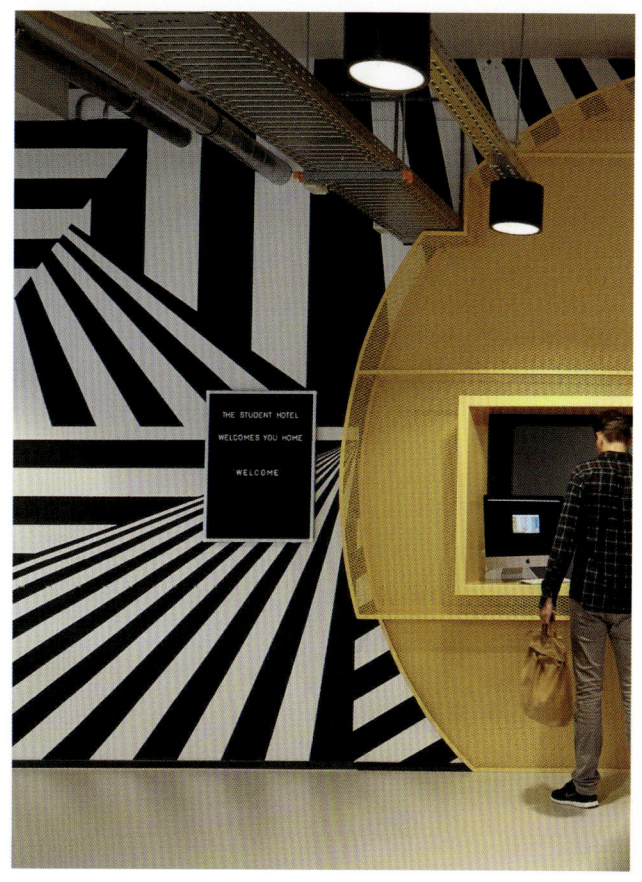

145

EUROPE | AMSTERDAM

IT'S A HOTEL *AND* A HOME.
SOMEWHERE YOU CAN SLEEP, EAT, DRINK AND STUDY.
WHERE YOU LEARN ABOUT LIFE.
WHERE YOU CAN MEET NEW PEOPLE
AND MAKE NEW FRIENDS
SOME WHO'LL BE FRIENDS FOR LIFE
OR EVEN LIFELONG PARTNERS.
A PLACE YOU CAN PARTY OR PLAY PING PONG.
WORKOUT OR CHILLOUT.
WHERE YOU CAN WAKE-UP WITH FRESHLY BREWED COFFEE
OR SIMPLY REST YOUR HEAD AFTER
A GREAT NIGHT OUT.

THE STUDENT HOTEL

A HOME FROM HOME

OPENING THIS SEPTEMBER. BOOK NOW!

Fully furnished rooms & studios, including private gym, café, study rooms, bikes and more.
Book now online at **www.thestudenthotel.com** or call **010-760 2000**

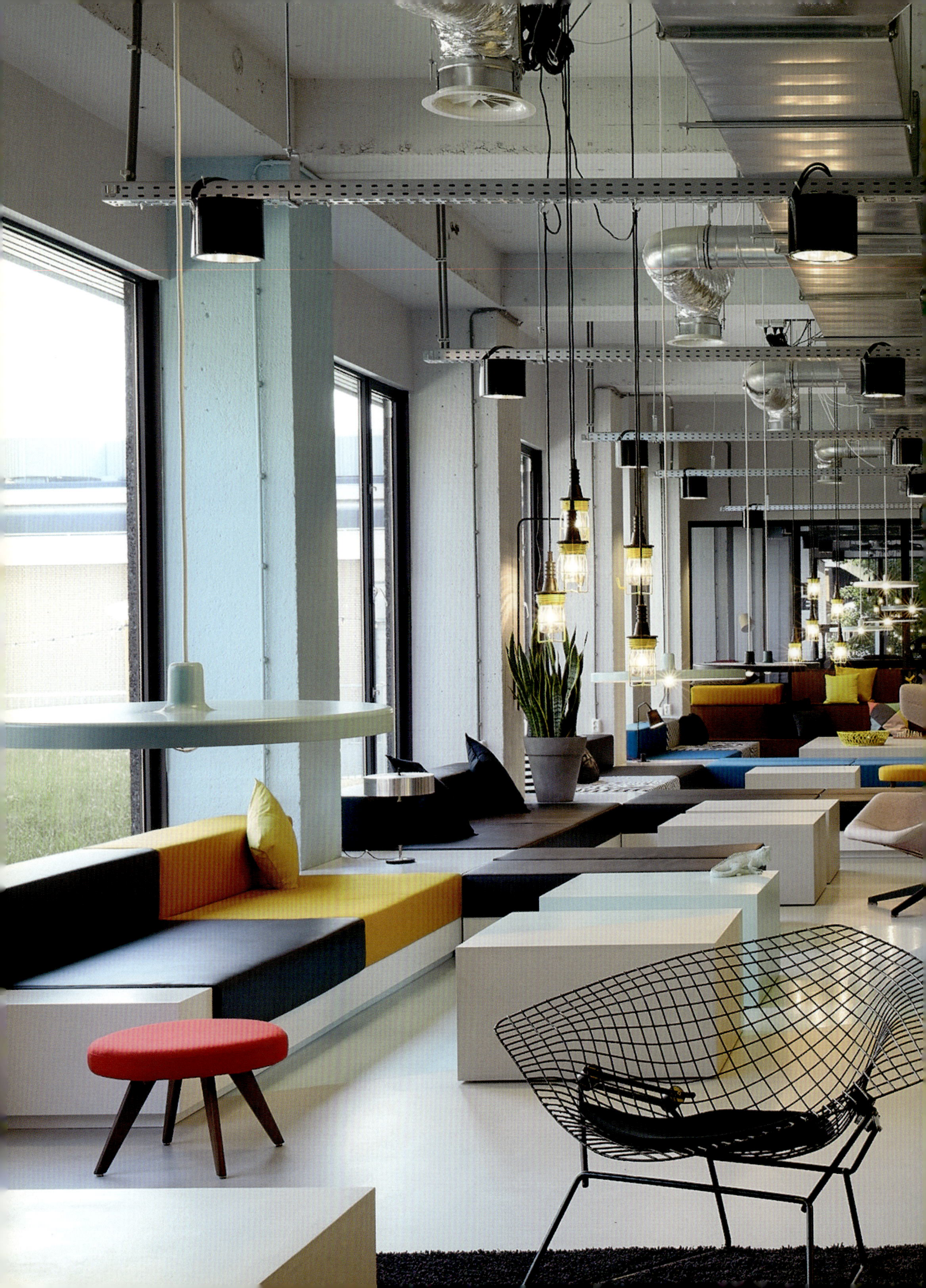

The Student Hotel provides an alternative to living on a university campus while still creating a strong sense of community. They are currently active in Rotterdam, The Hague and Liege, and plan to spread the concept internationally soon.

THE
THIEF

The Thief Oslo, Norway

ADDRESS | Landgangen 1, Oslo, Norway
ROOMS | 118 rooms
OPENED | January 2013
ARCHITECT | Mellbye Architects
INTERIOR DESIGN | Anemone Wille Våge
GRAPHIC DESIGN | Fete Typer

The Thief hotel, privately owned by billionaire Petter A. Stordalen, has a mission 'to steal you away from everyday life.' Located on Tjuvholmen (Thief Islet), which was once said to be overrun by robbers and prostitutes in the 18th century, the hotel boasts an impressive art collection (through their relationship with the nearby Astrup Fearnley Museum of Modern Art).

Sune Nordgren (former director of the National Museum of Art, Architecture and Design in Oslo) curated the hotel's permanent art collection, valued at over three million pounds. Works from Andy Warhol, Sir Peter Blake, Richard Prince and British contemporary artist Julian Opie are strategically placed throughout the hotel. But it is not only the art collection that makes this hotel impressive. The interior design (filled throughout with Tom Dixon lights), impeccable service, attention to detail and the use of technology throughout the hotel (the building's lighting operates on motion sensors) combine to create an experience for guests that is hard to forget.

This is a hotel that also understands the importance of branding. From their main identity, where the 'I' and 'F' have cleverly been 'stolen' to create 'The,' to the extension of the brand across a range of collateral, the identity is well considered and cleverly executed. Indeed, just like the hotel itself.

'The Thief has a mission 'to steal you away from everyday life.' With its impressive art collection and impeccable service, the hotel achieves this and more.'

THE
THIEF

THE THIEF

The Thief identity has been applied across a variety of quality materials, including wood, silk and leather.

153

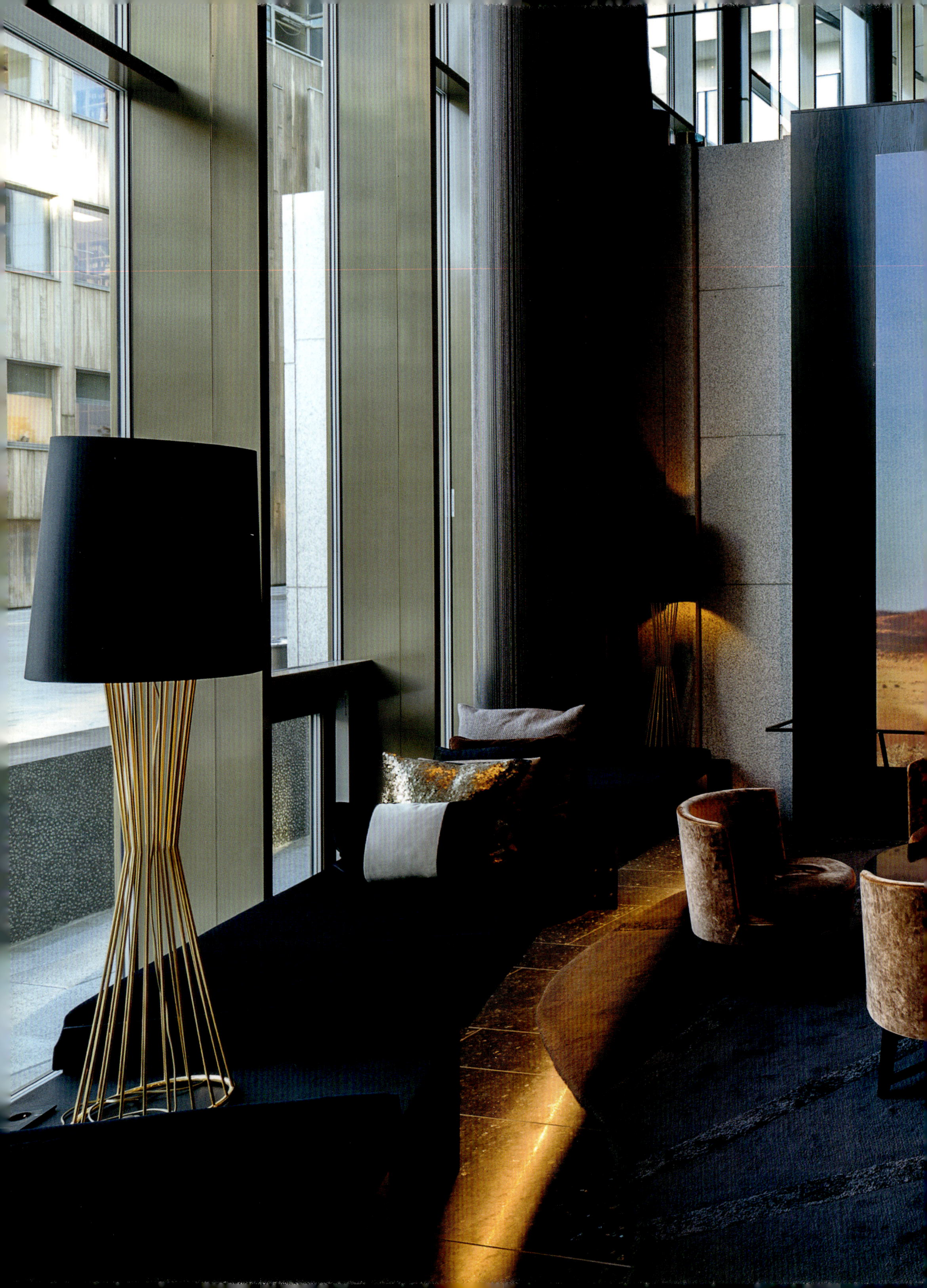

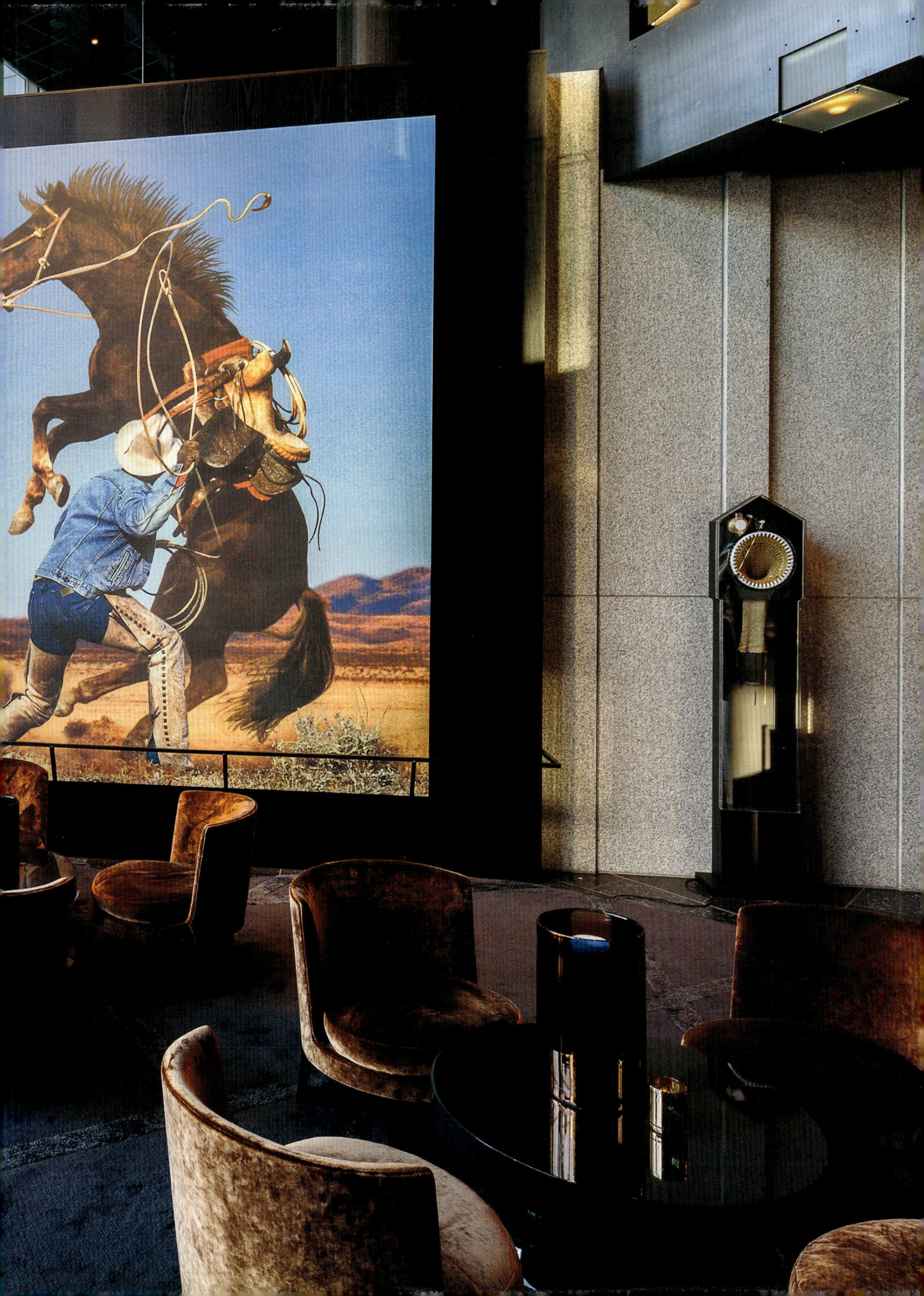

THE THIEF

THE
THIEF

AWAY FROM EVERYDAY LIFE
WWW.THETHIEF.COM

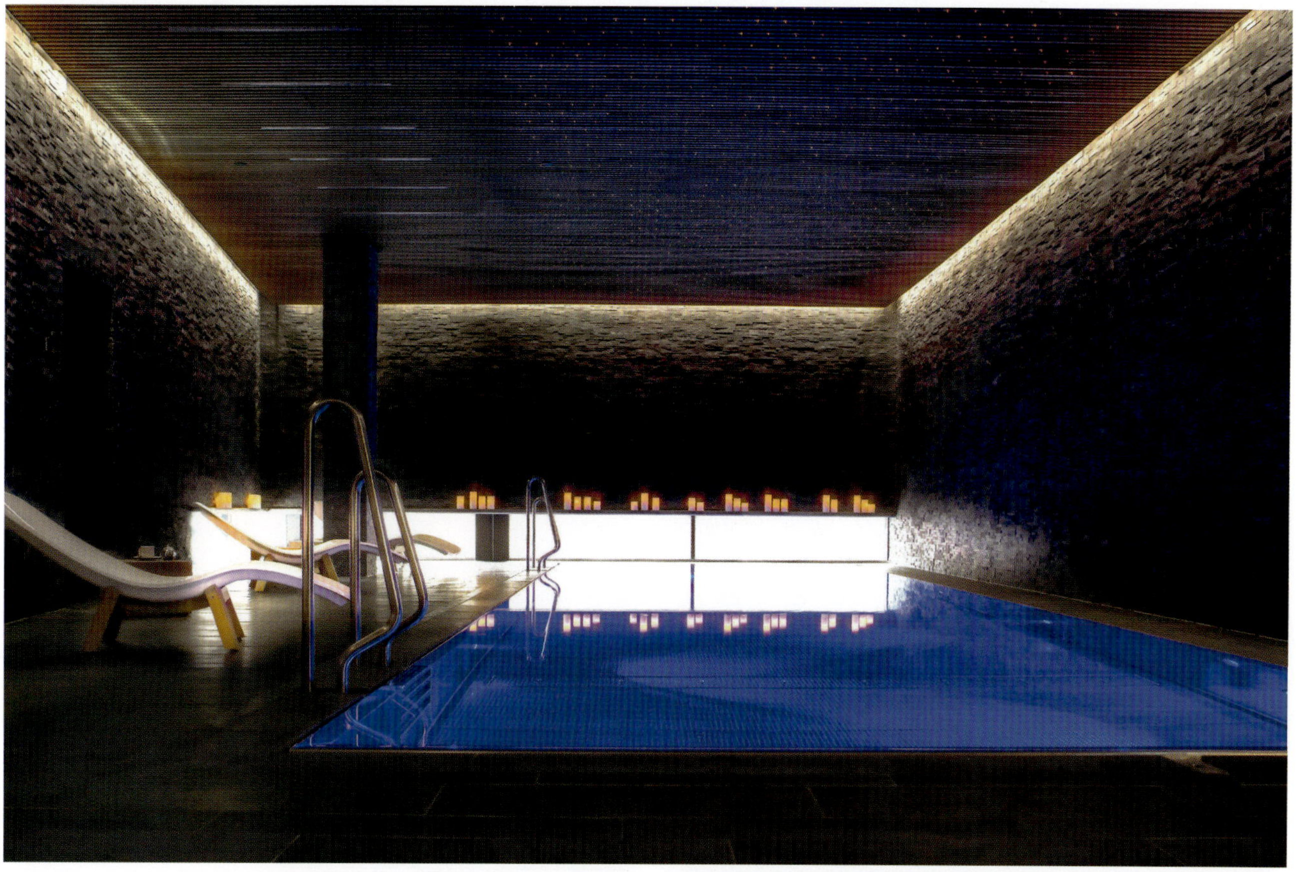

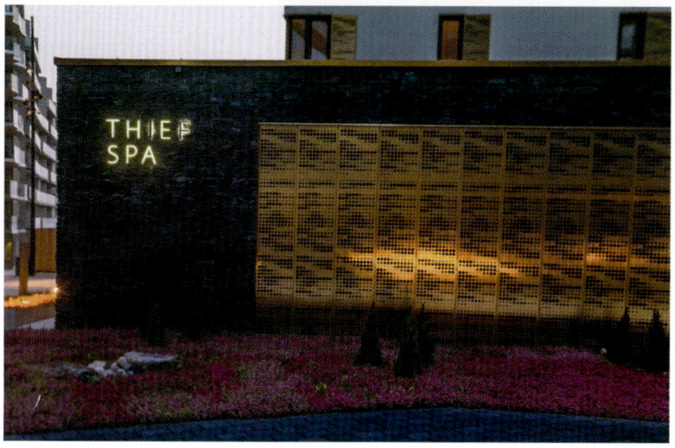
THIEF
SPA

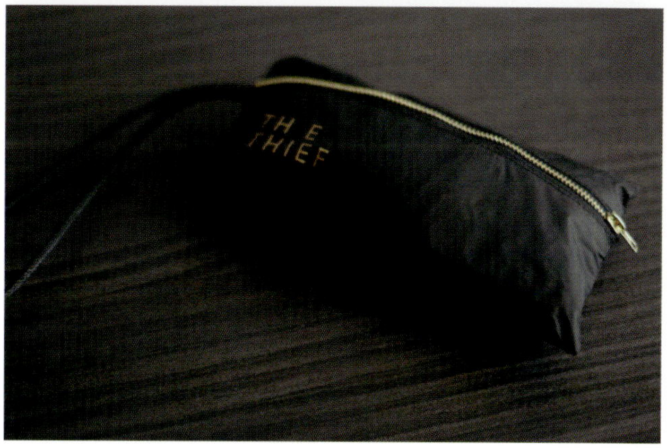
THE
THIEF

SPACIOMM
SPACIOMM
SPACIOMM
SPACIOMM
SPACIOMM
SPACIOMM
SPACIOMM

EUROPE | BARCELONA | HOTEL OMM

Hotel OMM Barcelona, Spain

ADDRESS | Rosselló 265, Barcelona, Spain
ROOMS | 91
OPENED | 2003
ARCHITECT | Juli Capella, Capella Arquitectura and Design
INTERIOR DESIGN | Sandra Tarruella and Isabel López
GRAPHIC DESIGN | Mario Eskenazi

Hotel OMM is a meeting point for visitors and locals in Barcelona. The desire to experience the city and integrate with the locals inspired its structure and design, which creates an environment where the pace of Barcelona feels more leisurely and relaxed.

The hotel was built using traditional materials and shapes, such as stone façades, balconies that open onto the street and an inside courtyard. Each area within the hotel is multifunctional and aesthetically pleasing.

The lobby lounge comprises the Roca Moo, a one-star Michelin restaurant and the Roca Bar which offers an innovative selection of street food and dishes to share any at time. In addition, the roof of the building offers a unique terrace, covered with ipe wood, a deck with a pergola and a swimming pool to take in the views of Casa Milá, Sagrada Familia and the lights of Montjuïc.

In addition, the hotel's spa, Spaciomm, features natural materials (such as wood, stone, iron and coconut matting) with soft lighting, aromas and low music to create a peaceful ambiance.

The branding for Hotel Omm is simple and sophisticated, applied predominantly in black, white and grey. The hotel itself is an example of all the characteristics that have made Barcelona a city renowned for its style, architecture and design.

'The desire to experience the city and integrate with the locals has inspired Hotel OMM's structure and design, which creates an environment where the pace of Barcelona feels more leisurely and relaxed.'

Hotel Omm
Barcelona

OMM

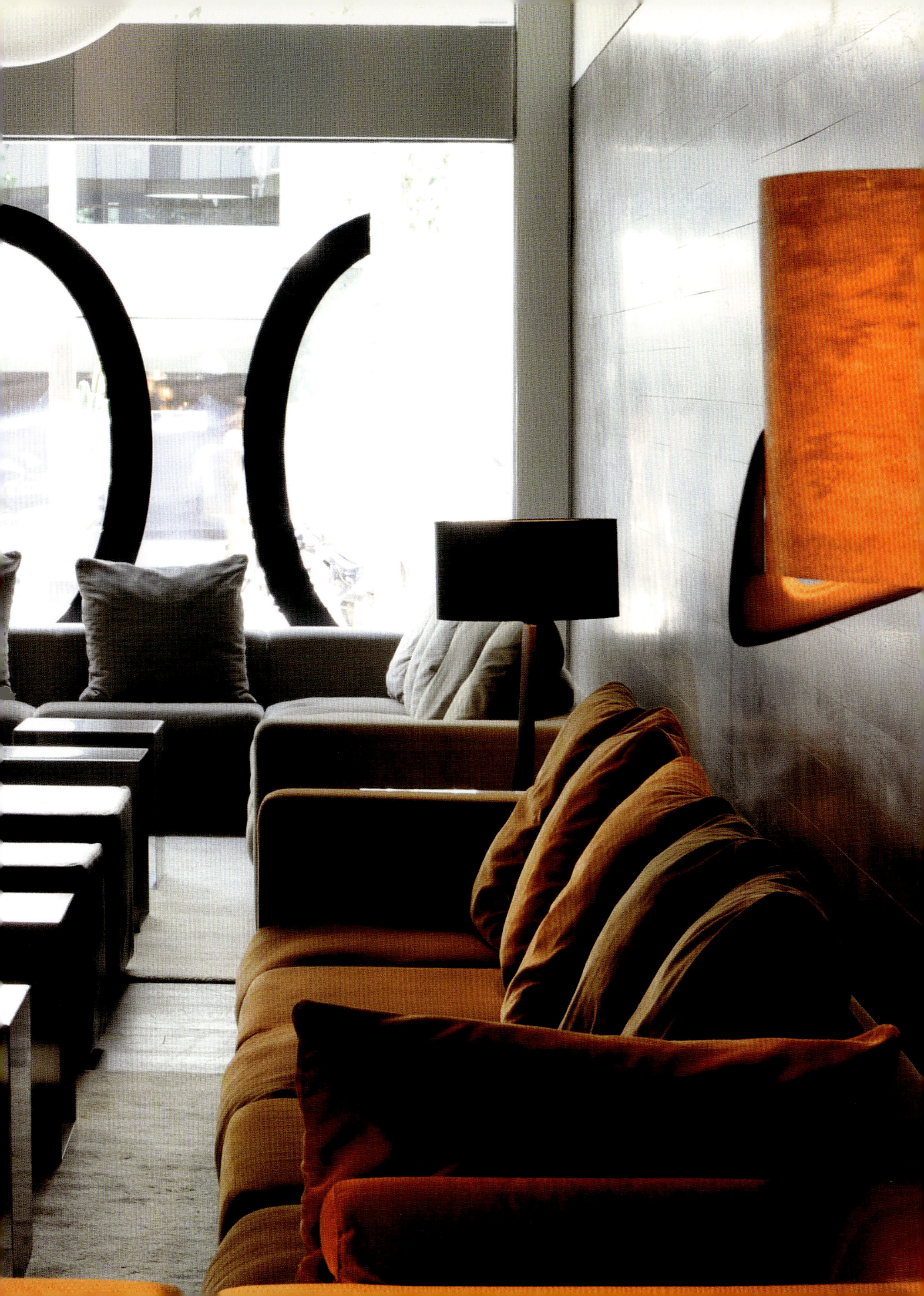

)OMMM

HOTEL OMM

163

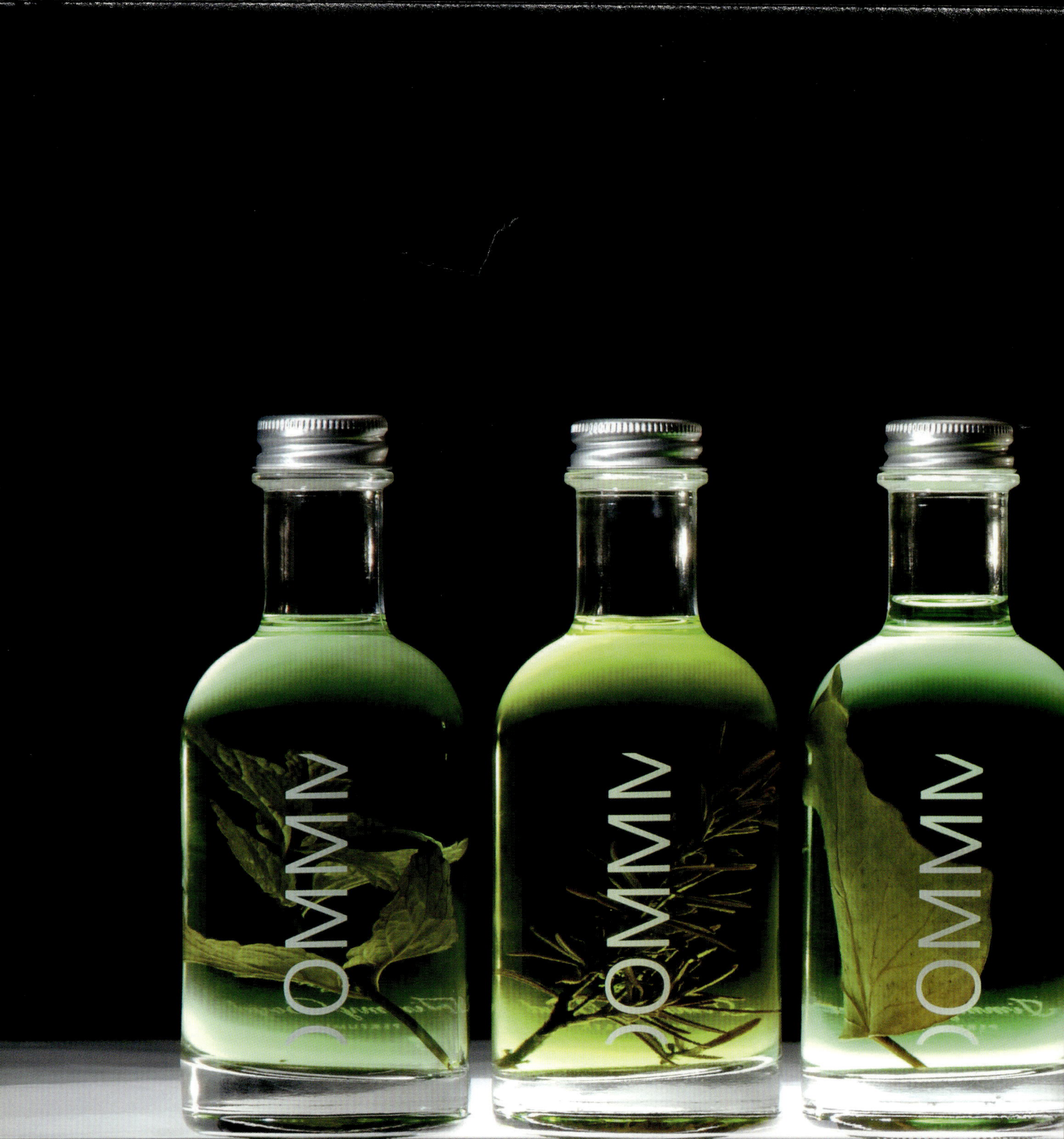

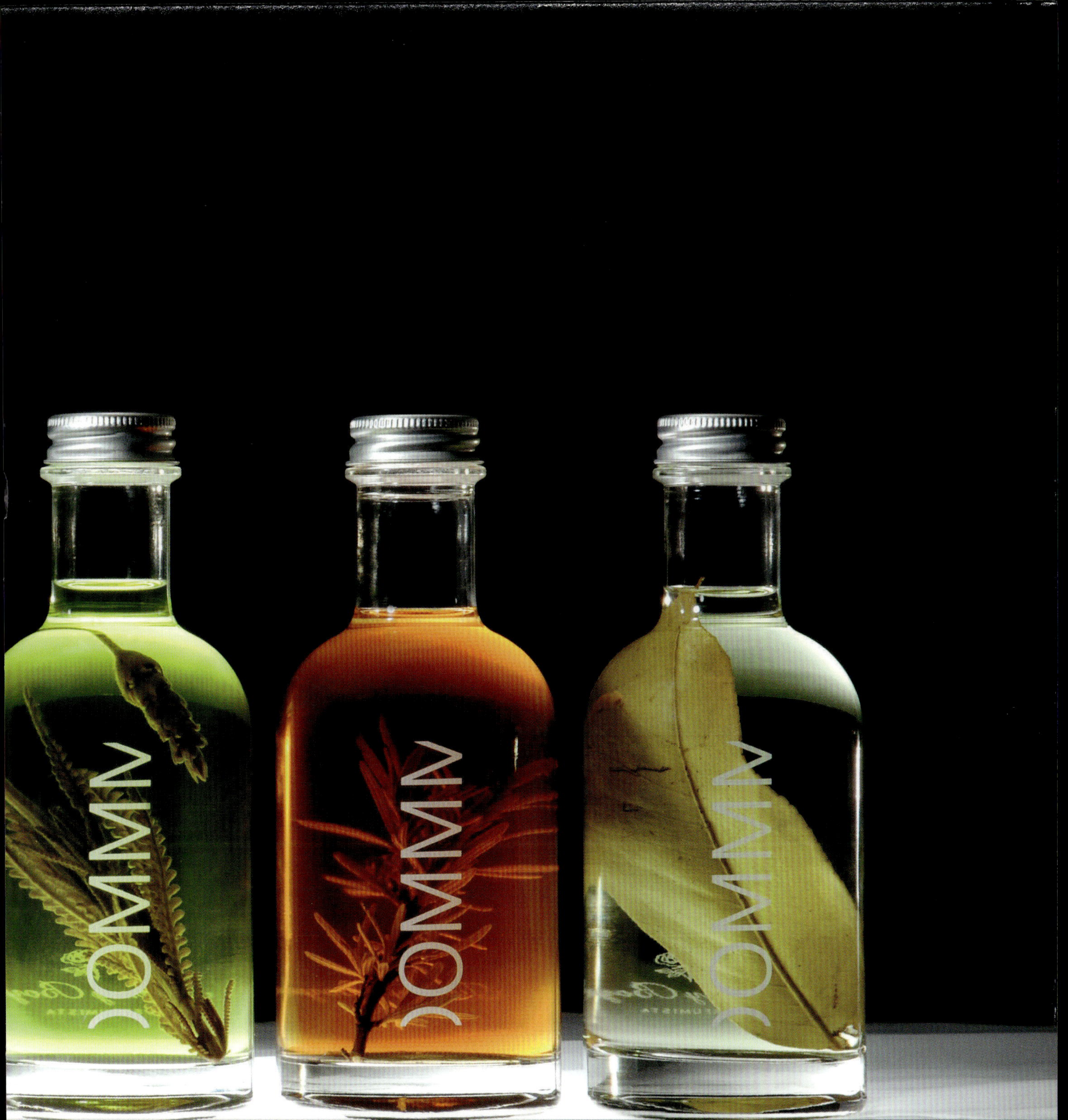

EUROPE | STOCKHOLM | ETT HEM

Ett Hem Stockholm, Sweden

ADDRESS | Sköldungagatan 2, Stockholm, Sweden
ROOMS | 12 Suites
OPENED | May 2012
ARCHITECT| Fredrik Dahlberg (original building 1910); Anders Landstrom (refurbishment)
INTERIOR DESIGN | StudioIlse
GRAPHIC DESIGN | Studio Frith

Ett Hem, meaning 'a home,' was first built in 1910 as a private residence. It has since been refurbished and, with the guidance of Ilse Crawford of StudioIlse, converted into an immaculate twelve guest room hotel.

Behind the security gated entrance, Ett Hem is a beautiful Arts & Crafts townhouse that comes complete with a glazed conservatory overlooking a courtyard garden, library, piano, several sitting rooms, kitchen and a marble hammam in the basement. The interiors are a blend of contemporary and vintage design in tactile materials (such as cane, brass, wood, leather and velvet), and each guest room features original artwork from the owner's private collection.

To ensure the hotel feels more like a home, Ett Hem's bar comes with an honesty policy; there is no dining menu, instead a 3-star Michelin chef prepares guests' food to order. The kitchen fridge is always stocked with food that guests are invited to help themselves to, and each room is furnished with full-size bathroom products, as well as perfume for guests' use during their stay.

The branding is sophisticated and subtle and utilizes a variety of embellishing techniques, including gold foil, to reflect the quality of the hotel itself. The overall experience feels more home than hotel, and once inside it is easy to imagine you are living in your own private castle.

'Behind the gated entrance, Ett Hem is a beautiful Arts & Craft townhouse. The interiors are a blend of contemporary and vintage design in tactile materials (such as cane, brass, wood, leather and velvet), and each guest room features original artwork from the owner's private collection.'

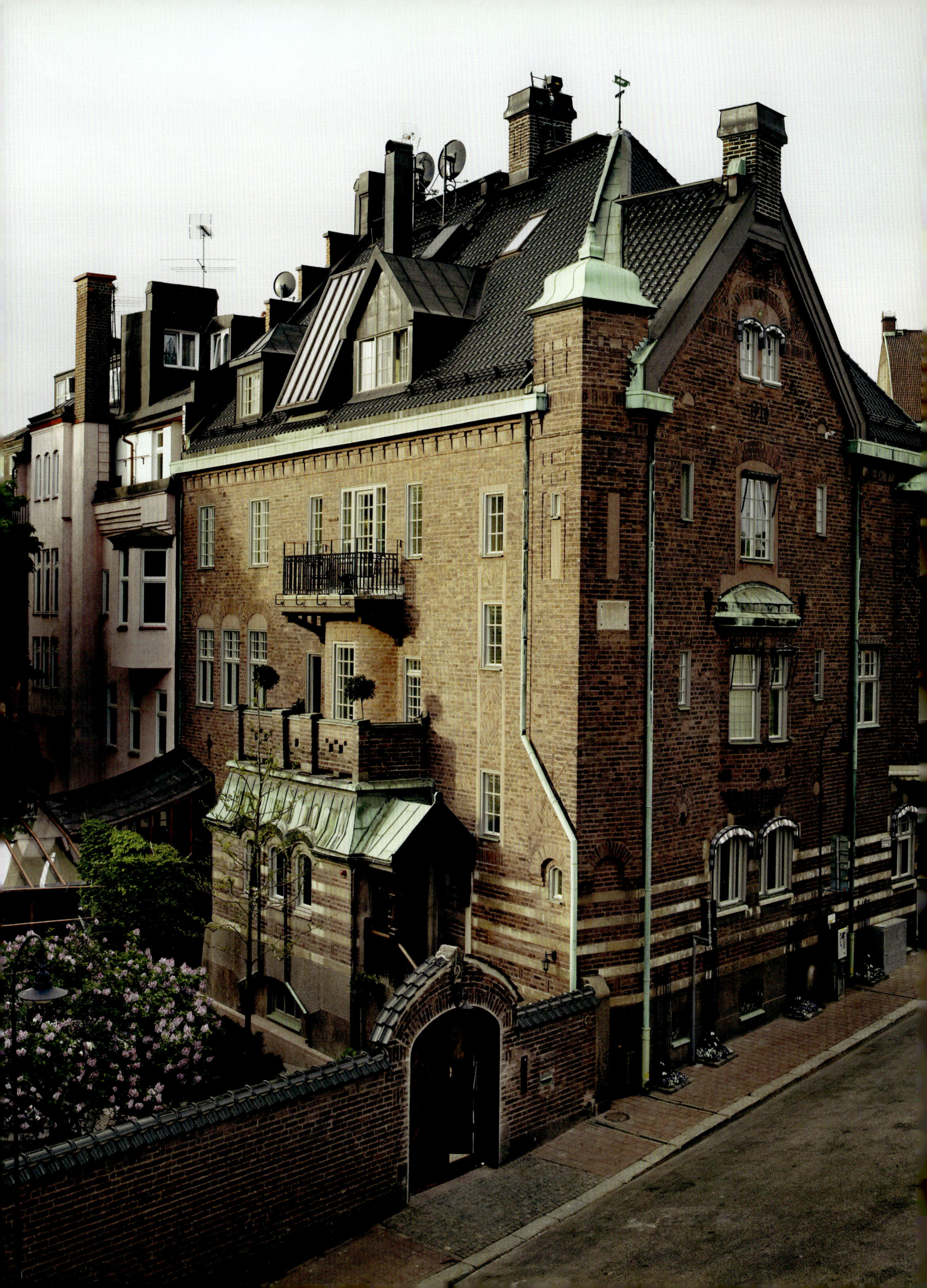

EUROPE | STOCKHOLM

The identity, created by Studio Frith, consists of a bespoke typeface in combination with four distinct and beautiful patterns. In a subtle manner, the identity has been cleverly applied to a range of materials, such as embossed onto leather folders, embroidered onto serviettes and towels, foiled onto bespoke bags and even debossed into every bar of soap. This attention to detail complements the elegance and sophistication of the hotel.

ETT HEM

EUROPE | STOCKHOLM

ETT HEM

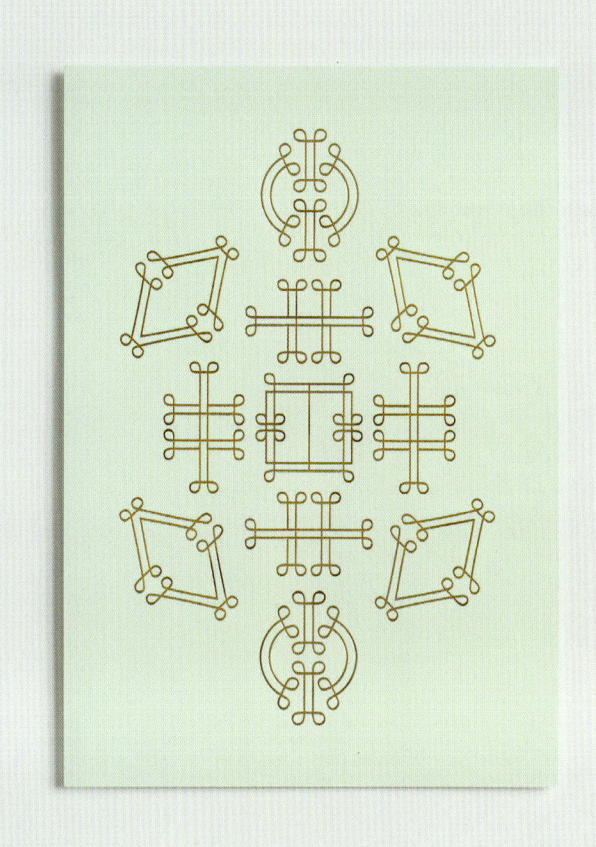

171

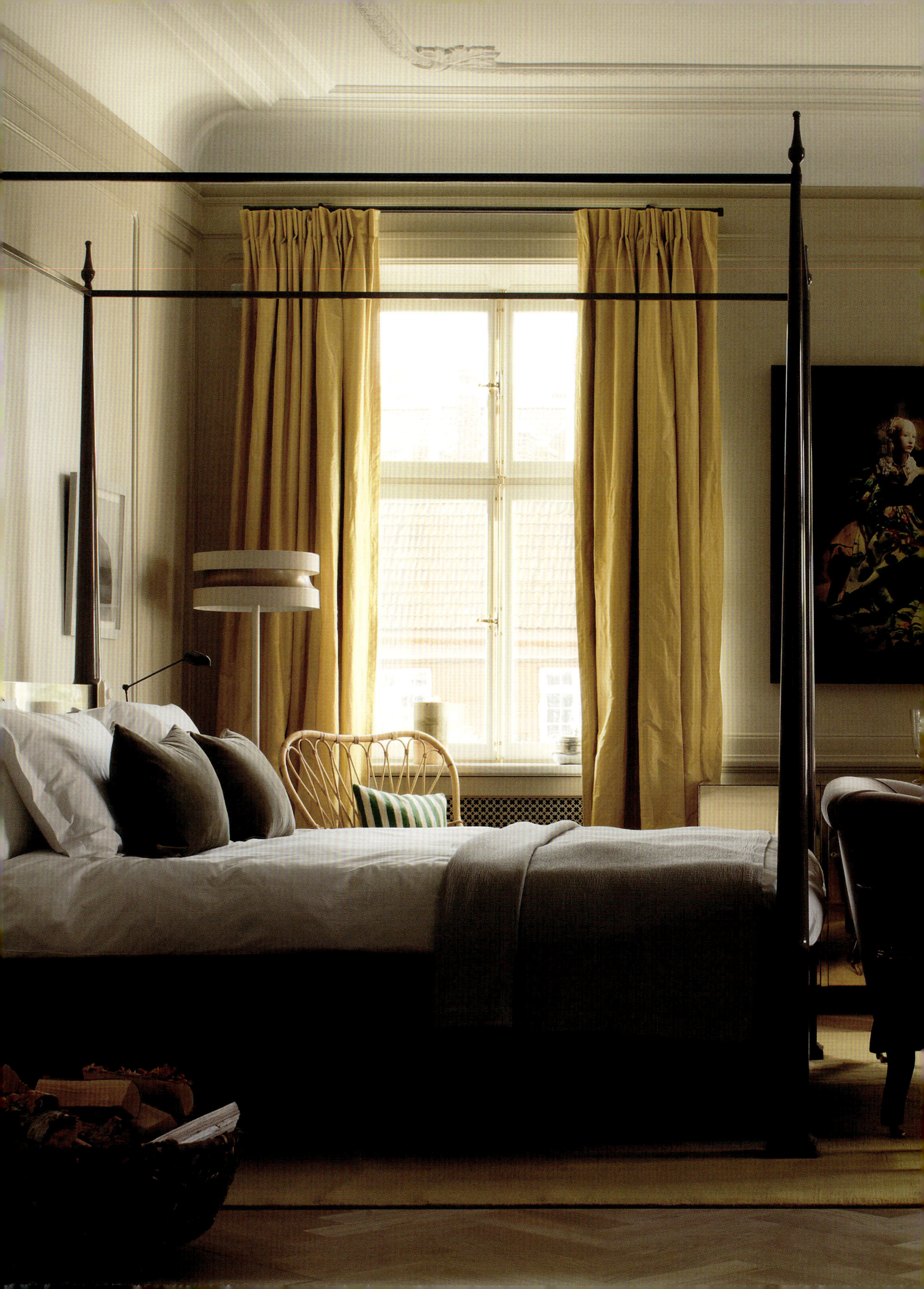

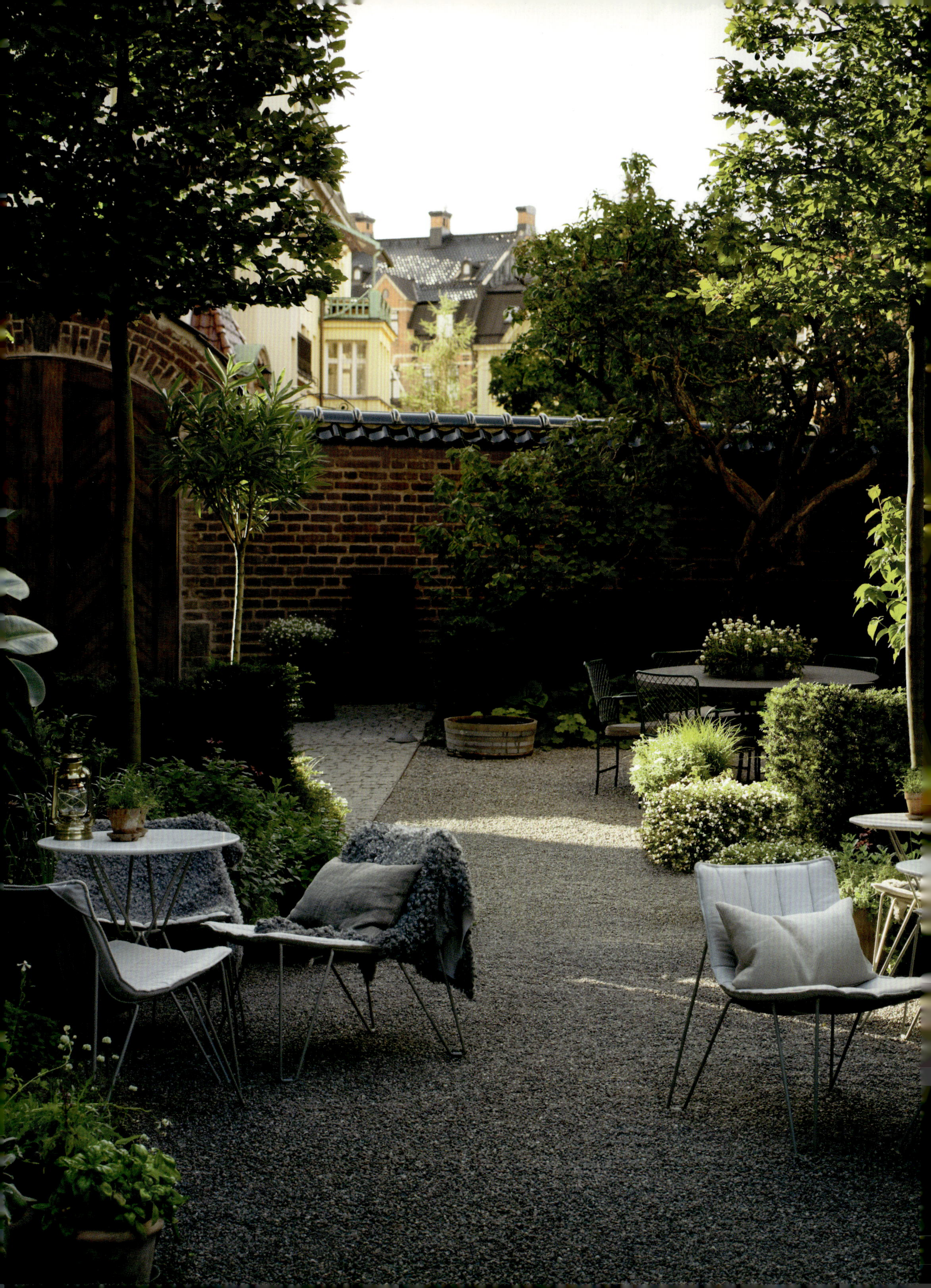

FRONT DESK
WAY TO THE LOBBY
ELEVATORS
WELCOME TO
SCANDIC GRAND CENTRAL
SGC
ENJOY YOUR STAY

Scandic Grand Central Stockholm, Sweden

ADDRESS | Kungsgatan 70, Stockholm, Sweden
ROOMS | 391
OPENED | 1 October 2011
INTERIOR DESIGN | Koncept Stockholm
GRAPHIC DESIGN | 25ah Design Studio

The Scandic Grand Central is influenced not only by the history of the building but also by the street life outside the hotel. The building was formerly known as 'The Lundberg Palace' and is situated in an old publishing/printing district in Stockholm.

The historical references surrounding the hotel are reflected not only in the interior design but also the identity and design collateral. Vintage frames, stage lighting, a photo booth and signage influenced by old street signs appear throughout the hotel. In a similar manner, all room numbers acknowledge the centuries old art form of letterpress.

The Scandic Grand Central not only embraces the history of the building but, through their branding, adds a modern interpretation to the experience. Photographs of local Scandinavian artists fill the lobby, and the custom designed carpet references the manhole covers found in the streets of Stockholm. There is also a gallery of love locks where guests are invited to collaborate creatively with the hotel.

This hotel not only pays homage to the neighbourhood but engages with their guests to create an experience that continues after the time comes to check-out.

> *'The Scandic Grand Central identity is based on three distinct, yet individual letters that create the primary brandmark and pay homage to centuries old art form of letterpress.'*

EUROPE | STOCKHOLM

'The urban theatre is the storyline that inspired the design,' says Ann Marie Ekroth from Koncept Stockholm. The late 19th century city palace collides with materials inspired by everyday street life, and together they create a unique and inviting atmosphere.

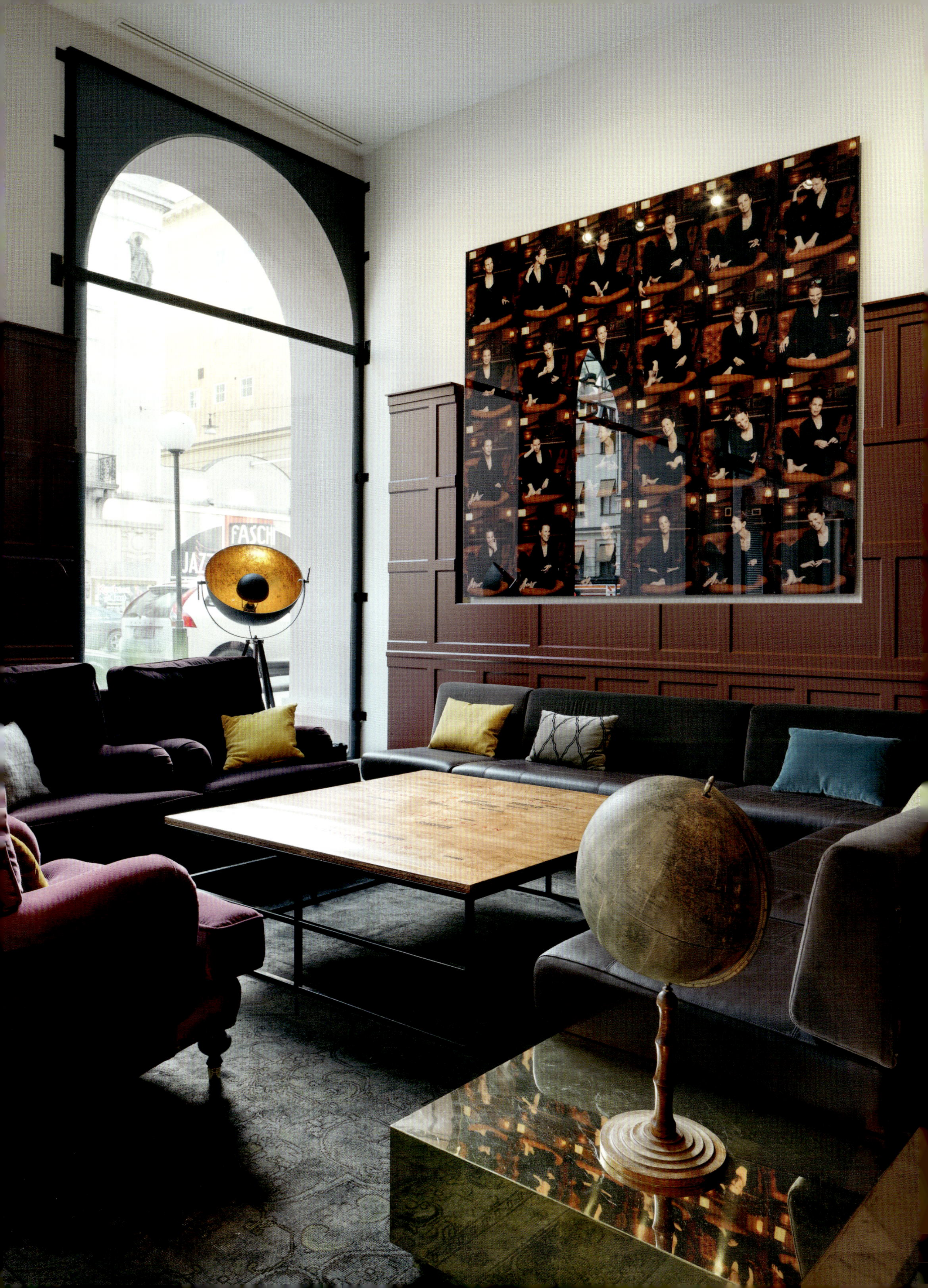
FASCH
JAZ

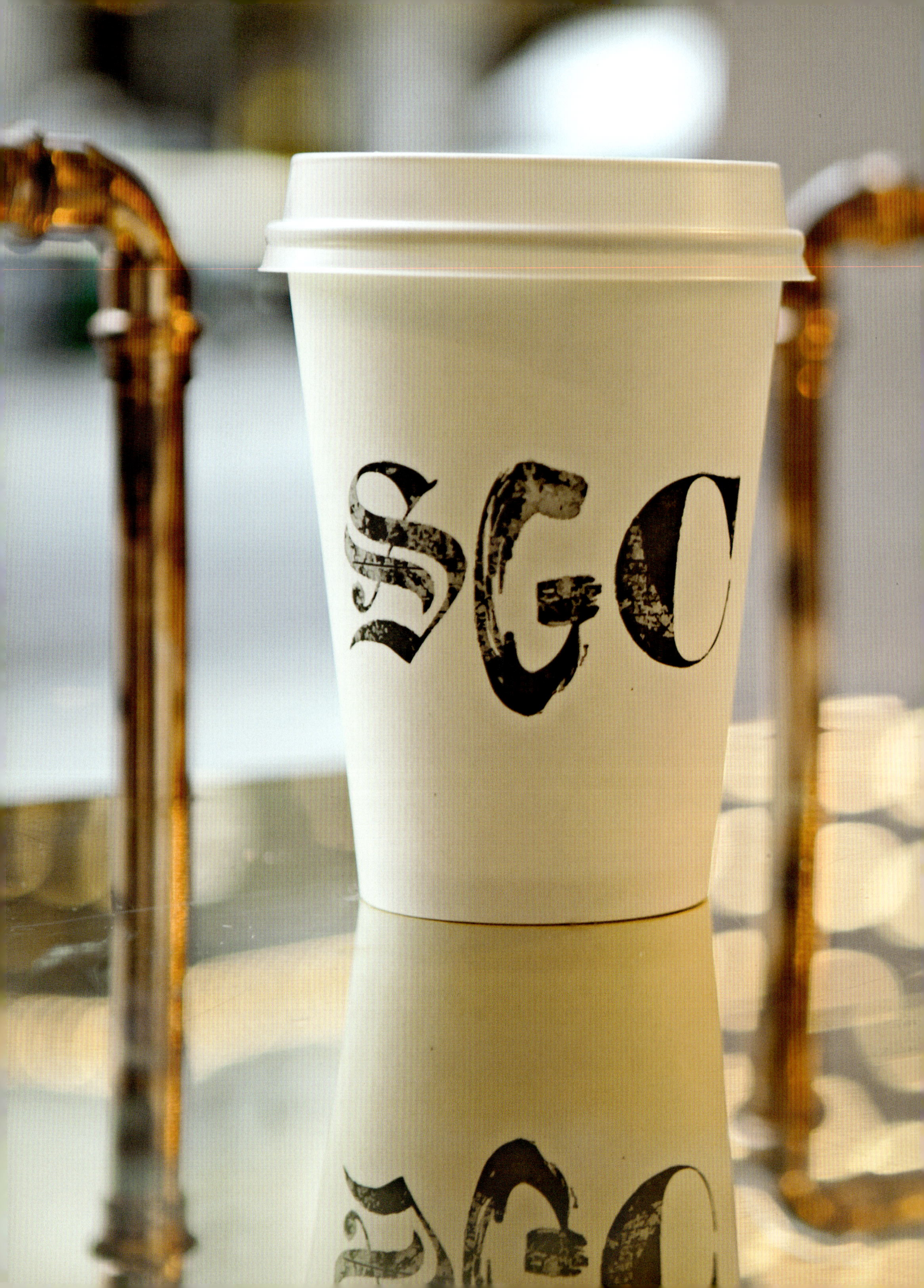
SGC

SCANDIC GRAND CENTRAL

Within the Scandic Grand Central, there is a cohesive melding between interior and graphic design elements used to unify the guest experience.

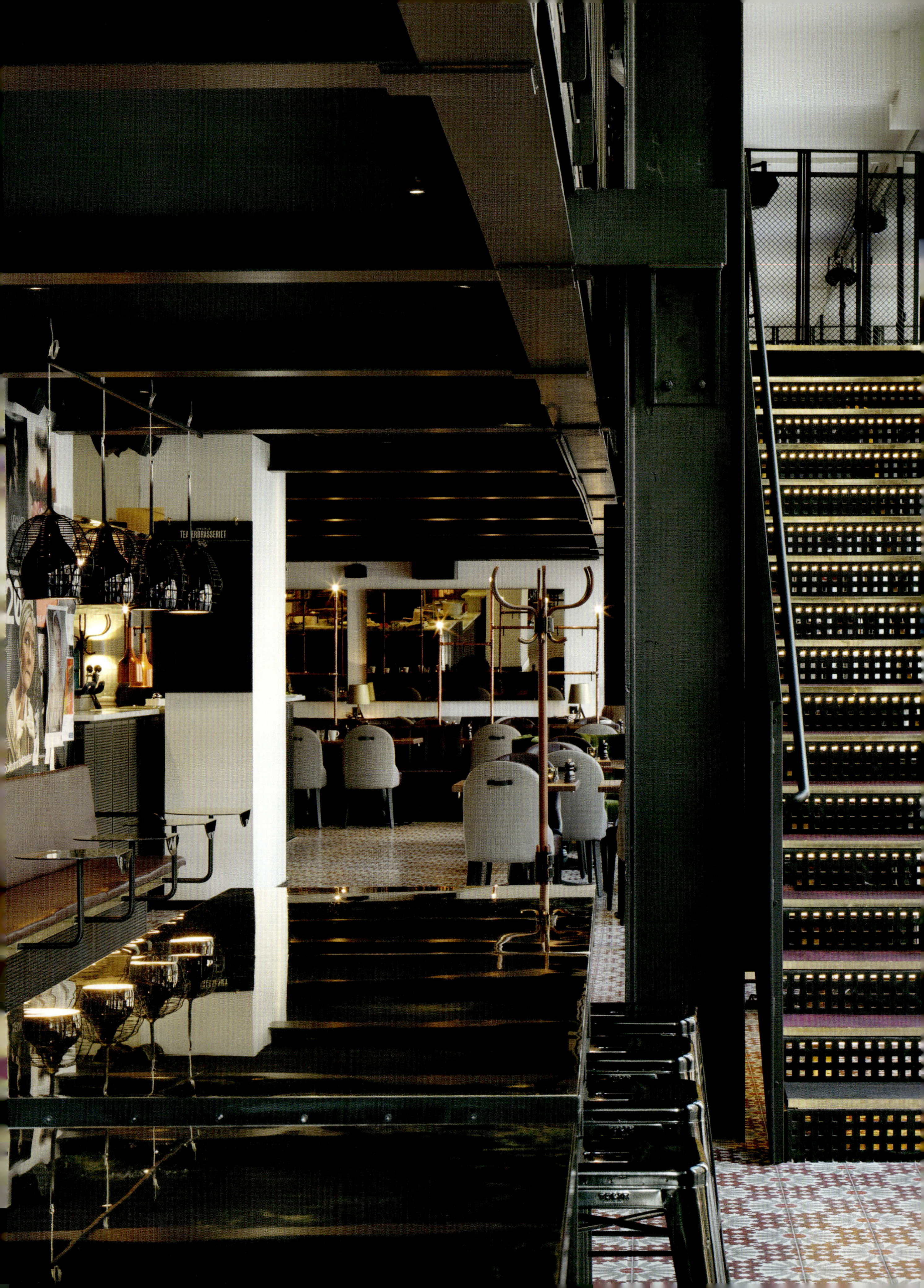

4093

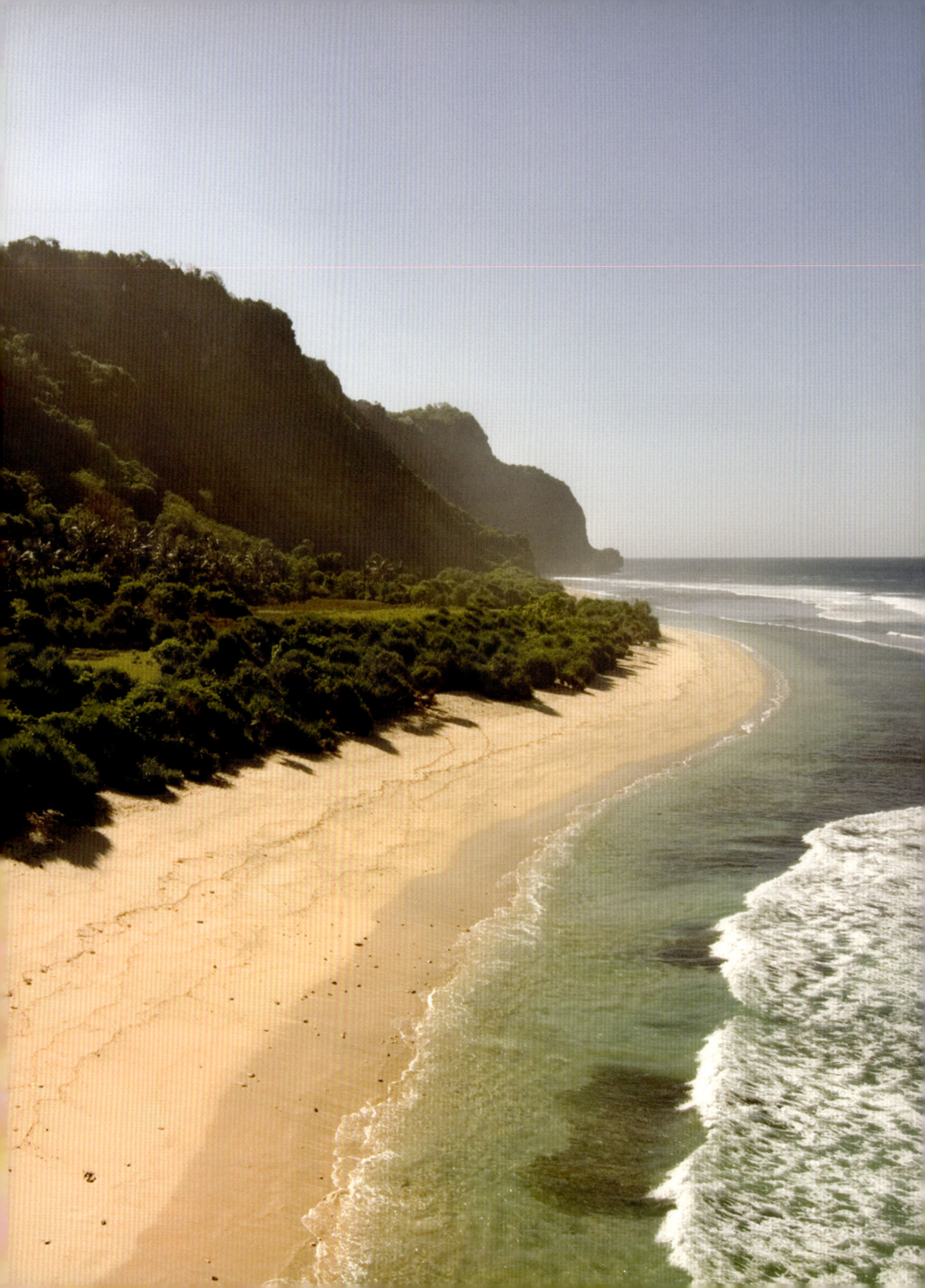

Asia

'I need something truly beautiful
to look at in hotel rooms.'

— Vivien Leigh

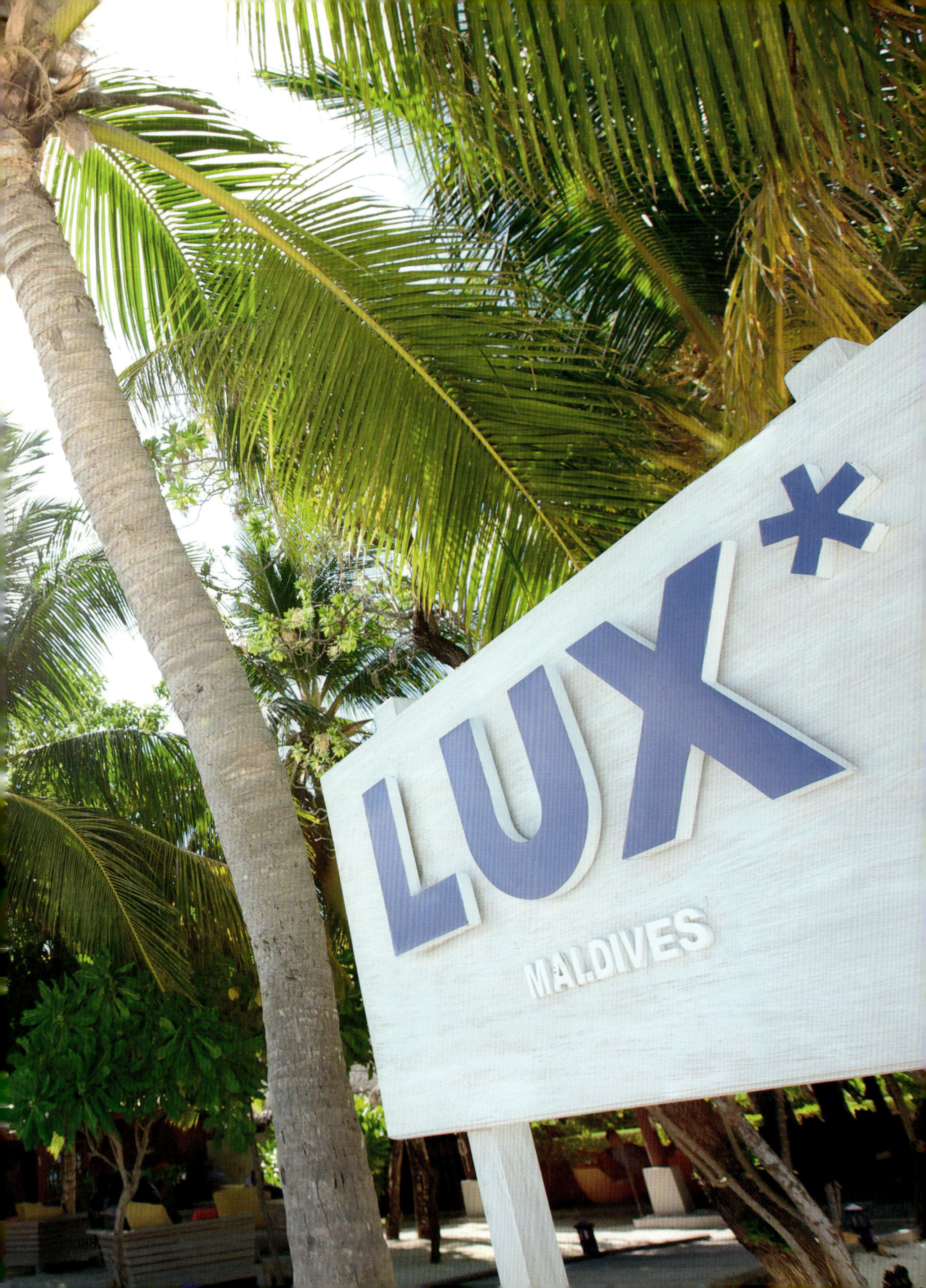
LUX*
MALDIVES

LUX* Maldives, Indian Ocean

ADDRESS | South Atoll, Dhidhoofinolhu, Maldives
ROOMS | 193 Pavilions, Suites and Villas
OPENED | 2012
ARCHITECT | GX Associates
INTERIOR DESIGN | V K Design Ltd
GRAPHIC DESIGN | & Smith

LUX* Maldives is situated on the island of Dhidhoofinolhu, the largest of the Maldives islands, with 4km of beaches and charming villas that celebrate the authentic energy of island life. The resort enjoys a relaxed atmosphere that is sophisticated yet playful.

The LUX* brand doesn't stand for luxury — it promises light. A lighter experience, free from formalities and pretensions. The hotel explains the asterisk in the identity as merely a tool to draw people's attention to the concept of 'Lighter, Brighter,' a phrase which is often paired with the logo.

The hotel embraces the energy, colour and taste of island life and allows guests to immerse themselves in the multi-sensory experience of the Indian Ocean island.

Reflecting these notions, &Smith have utilized a tropical colour palette with different colour combinations to distinguish between the current six LUX* resorts and hotels. With a vast array of collateral, from bathroom amenities, oils, and water, to a complimentary journal for every guest, the branding is modern, bold and playful.

> 'The LUX* brand celebrates the energy, colour and taste of island life while encouraging guests to immerse themselves in the experience.'

ASIA | MALDIVES

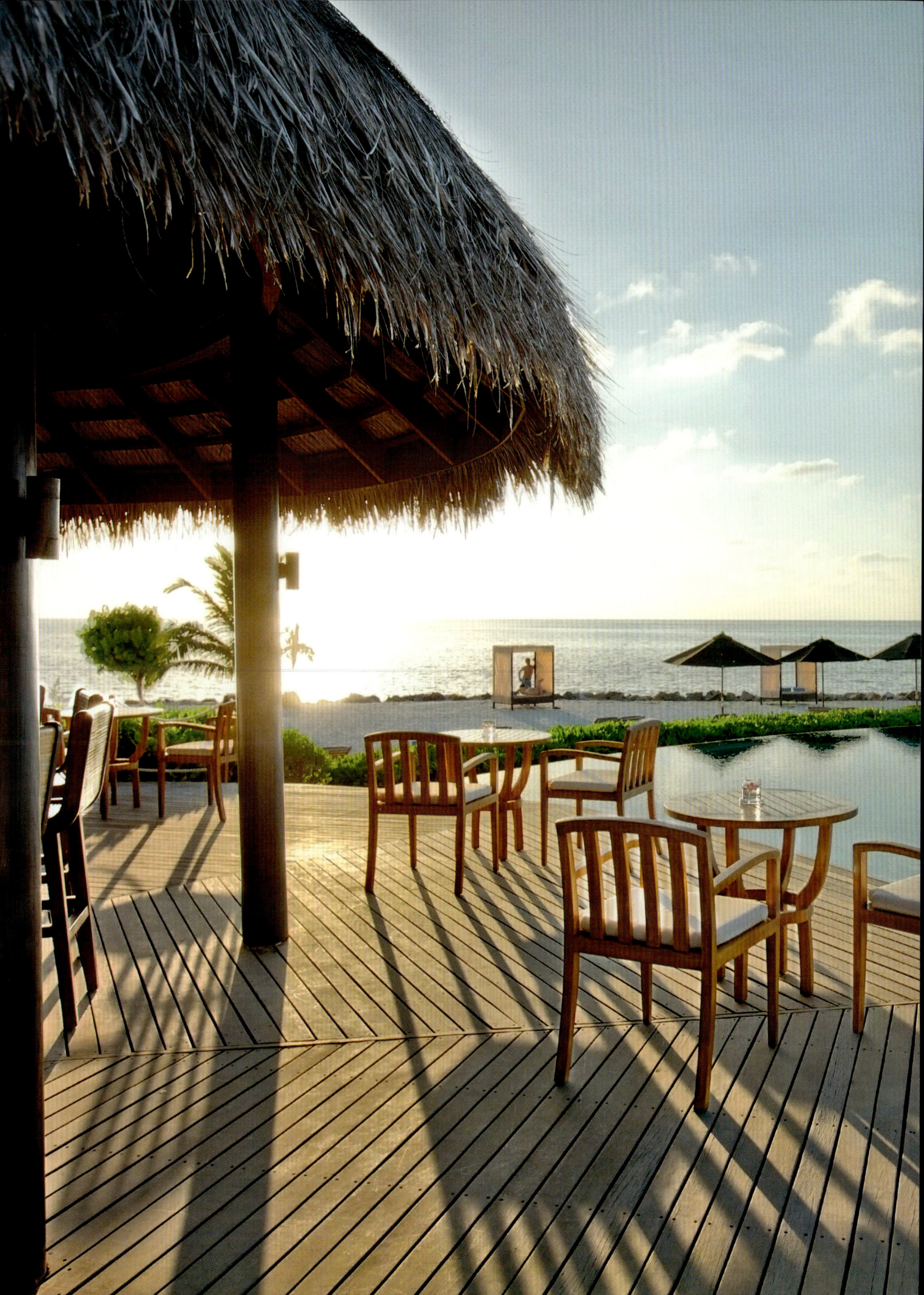

LUX*
RESORTS

PHILOSOPHY

WHAT'S YOUR PICTURE OF A DREAM HOLIDAY –
SWIMMING IN THE SEA OF SAMENESS OR, GIVEN THE CHANCE,
WOULD YOU LIKE TO CELEBRATE LIFE A LITTLE MORE RICHLY?

LYING ON A BEACH DAY AFTER DAY,
OR A RICH TABLEAU OF EXPERIENCES WITH
MEMORIES THAT LAST LONG BEYOND THE TAN?

FOR PEOPLE WHO WISH TO ESCAPE FROM CLUTTER AND COMPLICATION,
THE SIMPLE INSPIRATION OF OUR 1,804 TEAM MEMBERS IS YOUR TIME.
IT'S THE ONE, TRUE LUXURY AND ONE WE SHOULD ALL SPEND WISELY.

LUX* DOESN'T IMPRESS WITH PRETENTIOUS WINES AND CITY CUISINE.
WE'VE NO TIME FOR MEDIOCRE COFFEE AND EXPENSIVE PHONE CALLS.
AND WE DON'T IMPORT FANCY MARQUES OF WATER JUST FOR THE MARK-UP.

WE'VE CUT THE EXCESSES TO CREATE A SIMPLER AND MORE LIGHT-HEARTED VACATION.
UNCONVENTIONAL AND EXHILARATING, IT'S AN AWARD-WINNING CONCEPT:

START THE DAY WITH ORGANIC COFFEE, FRESHLY-ROASTED ON THE ISLAND
MANAGE YOUR LIFESTYLE THROUGH THE LUX* ME APPROACH TO WELLBEING
ENJOY REFRESHING WATER THAT DOESN'T COST THE EARTH, LITERALLY
INDULGE IN ICE CREAM, BURSTING WITH FRUIT FLAVOURS, FROM RETRO PARLOURS
FIND A MESSAGE IN A BOTTLE AND YOU'RE SURE OF A BIG SURPRISE
OPEN THE SECRET BAR BUT DON'T FORGET TO SIGN THE BOOK
DINE AL FRESCO AT THE POP-UP ISLAND KITCHEN
AND BE SURE TO CATCH A BEACHSIDE SCREENING BEFORE HEADING TO BED –
CINEMA PARADISO, ISLAND STYLE.

A LUX* RESORT IS A PLACE WHERE EACH MOMENT MATTERS.
IT'S WHERE THE ORDINARY IS DONE EXTRAORDINARILY.
IT'S A REST FROM WHICH YOU RETURN, BOTH INVIGORATED AND INSPIRED.

THERE ARE MANY REASONS TO GO LUX* BUT REMEMBER...
SOME DREAMS REALLY DO COME TRUE.

*LIGHTER. BRIGHTER.

LUX* MALDIVES

'Vibrant and distinctive, the identity reflects a lively, spontaneous brand seeking to avoid the predictable patterns associated with luxury travel. A monolithic logotype is supported by a broad colour palette and candid photography.'

— & Smith

WELCOME
BIENVENUE
Pascal Bertrand
LUX*
ISLAND RESORTS
ROOM DIRECTORY
LUX*
GRAND GAUBE
LET THE SHOW BEGIN...
LUX*
ISLAND RESORTS
FIRST SIGHT
THE SOUND OF LUX*
LUX*
ISLAND RESORTS
LUX*
BELLE MARE, MAURITIUS
GÉRALDINE
MAÏTA
MAÏTA
LUX*
ISLAND RESORTS
SHUTTLE

ISLAND LIGHT COLLECTION

Resort boutiques are often more airport kiosk than island couture. All change! The Island Light Collection is a tempting chest of locally-sourced treasures.

CAFÉ LUX* 'ISLAND BLEND'

FRESCOBOL BEACH BATS

PINK PIGEON RUM

LUX* JOURNAL

LUX* ME AROMATHERAPY OILS

SLEEP TIGHT

SCRUCAP AND POPCAP

MEN'S SHIRTS

YOGA COLLECTION

14/ WE CAN'T ALWAYS PROMISE CLEAR SKIES ABOVE THE INDIAN OCEAN BUT, WITH YOUR HELP, WE CAN GUARANTEE A CLEAR CONSCIENCE.

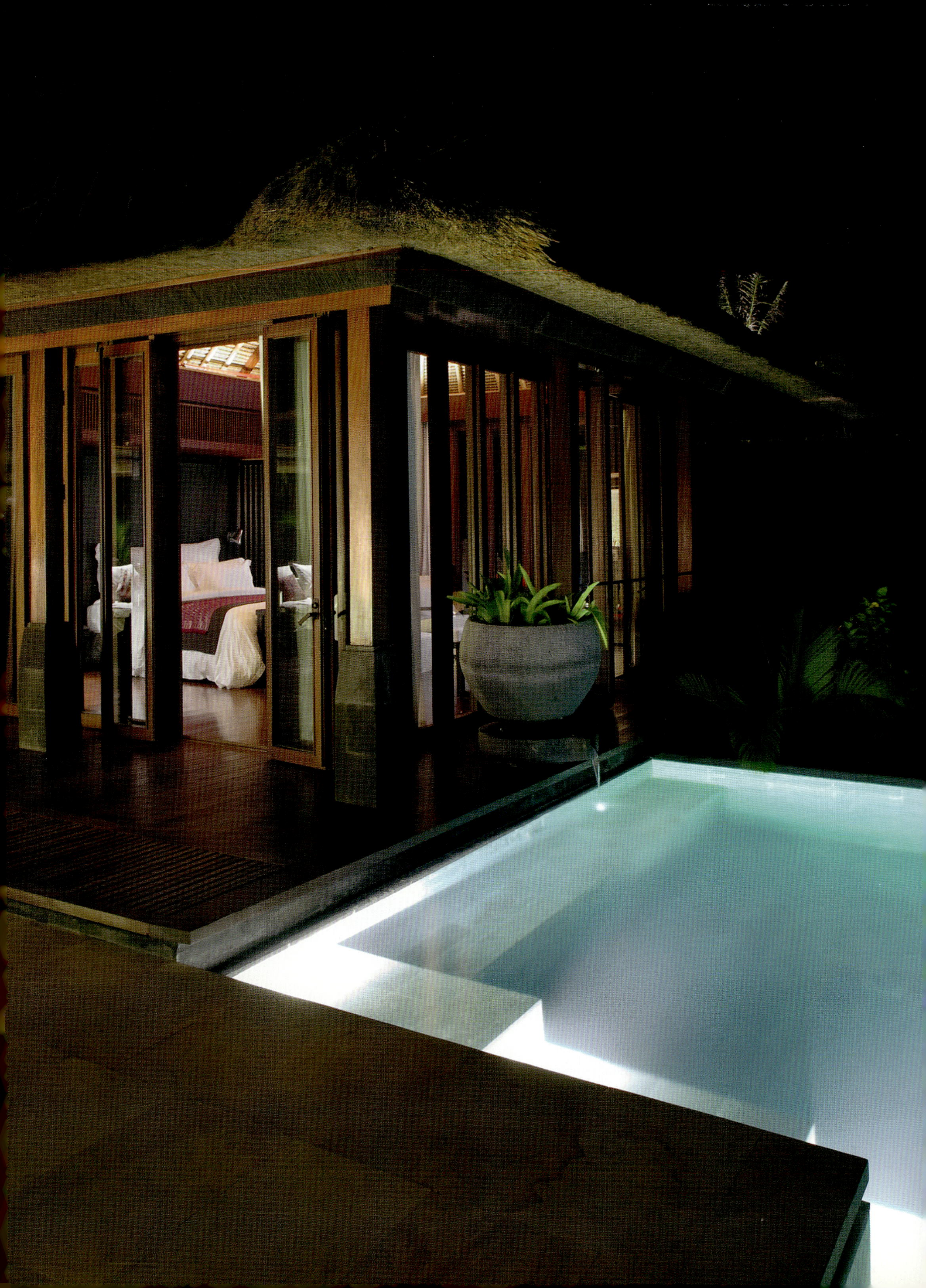

ASIA | BALI | BULGARI RESORT BALI

Bulgari Resort Bali, Indonesia

ADDRESS | Jalan Goa Lempeh, Banjar Dinas Kangin, Uluwatu, Bali, Indonesia
ROOMS | 59 villas and 5 mansions
OPENED | 23 September 2006
ARCHITECT | Antonio Citterio and Partners
INTERIOR DESIGN | Antonio Citterio and Partners
GRAPHIC DESIGN | Bulgari internal design team (stationery)

The Bulgari Resort Bali is uniquely positioned at more than 150 metres above sea level to offer unrivalled views of the Indian Ocean. The hotel combines traditional Balinese characteristics with the established, distinctive and contemporary Italian Bulgari style.

In conjunction to its unique location, the hotel provides an exclusive setting for guests who seek not only luxury but also privacy. The facilities and personalised services have all been crafted with the same attention to quality that distinguishes all Bulgari creations.

The interiors make heavy use of Bangkiray, a tawny type of Mahogany wood from Java, which sets the colour tone across structures, fittings, floors and details. This mellow tone, combined with the hand-crafted local artefacts that appear throughout the premises, give the resort a timeless elegance that reflects the jeweller's brand.

The hotel's stationery suite, comprising of textured stock along with the established Bulgari logo, is simple yet modern. A Balinese symbol has also been incorporated in order to distinguish the location and show respect to the traditional culture. The symbol, known as the 'Sekar Agung,' means 'great flower,' and refers to a special cake used in Suci Saji offerings to show great devotion and gratitude to the divine.

'The Bulgari Resort Bali combines traditional Balinese characteristics with the established, distinctive and contemporary Italian Bulgari style.'

ASIA | BALI

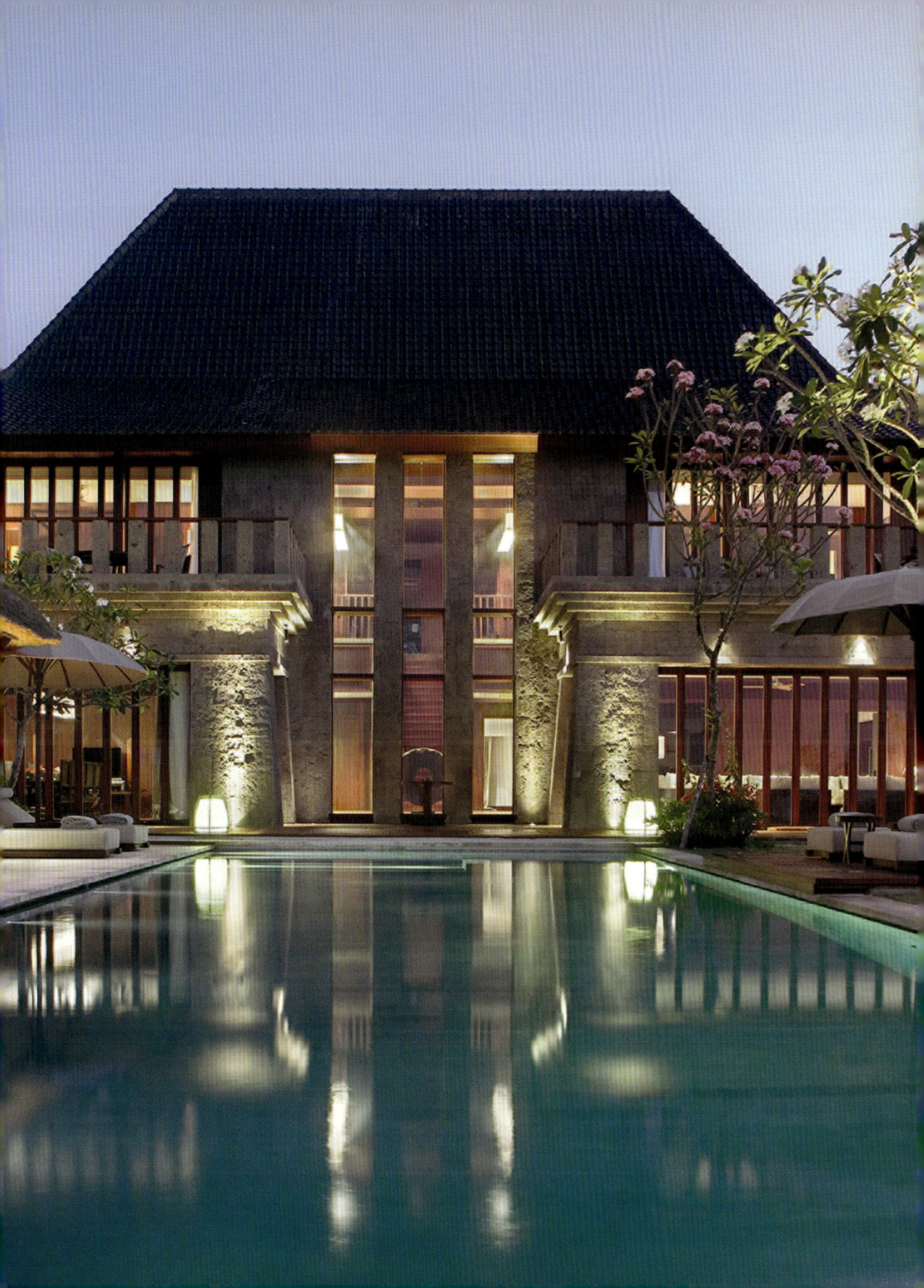

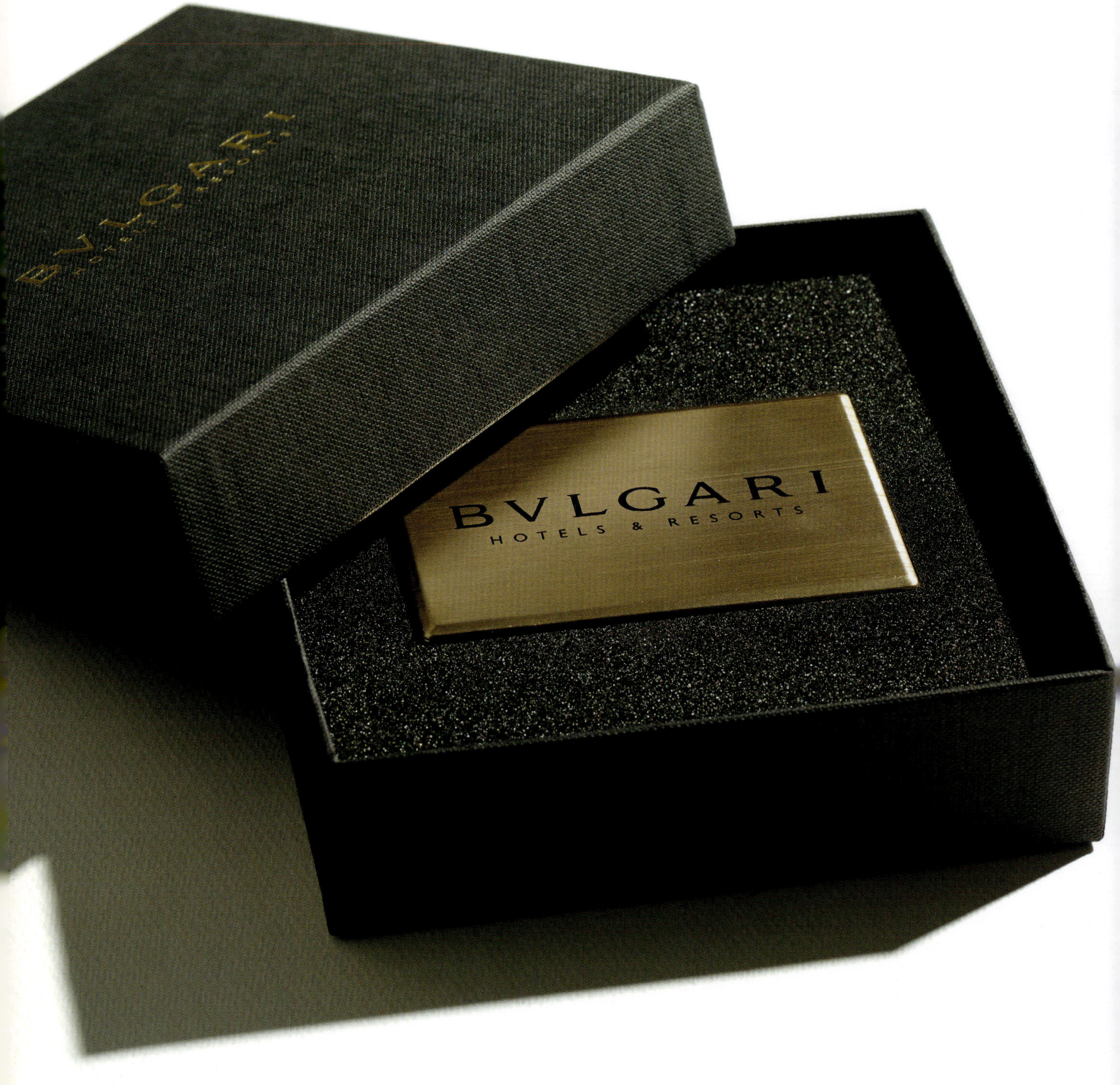
BVLGARI
HOTELS & RESORTS
BVLGARI
HOTELS & RESORTS

BVLGARI
RESORT BALI

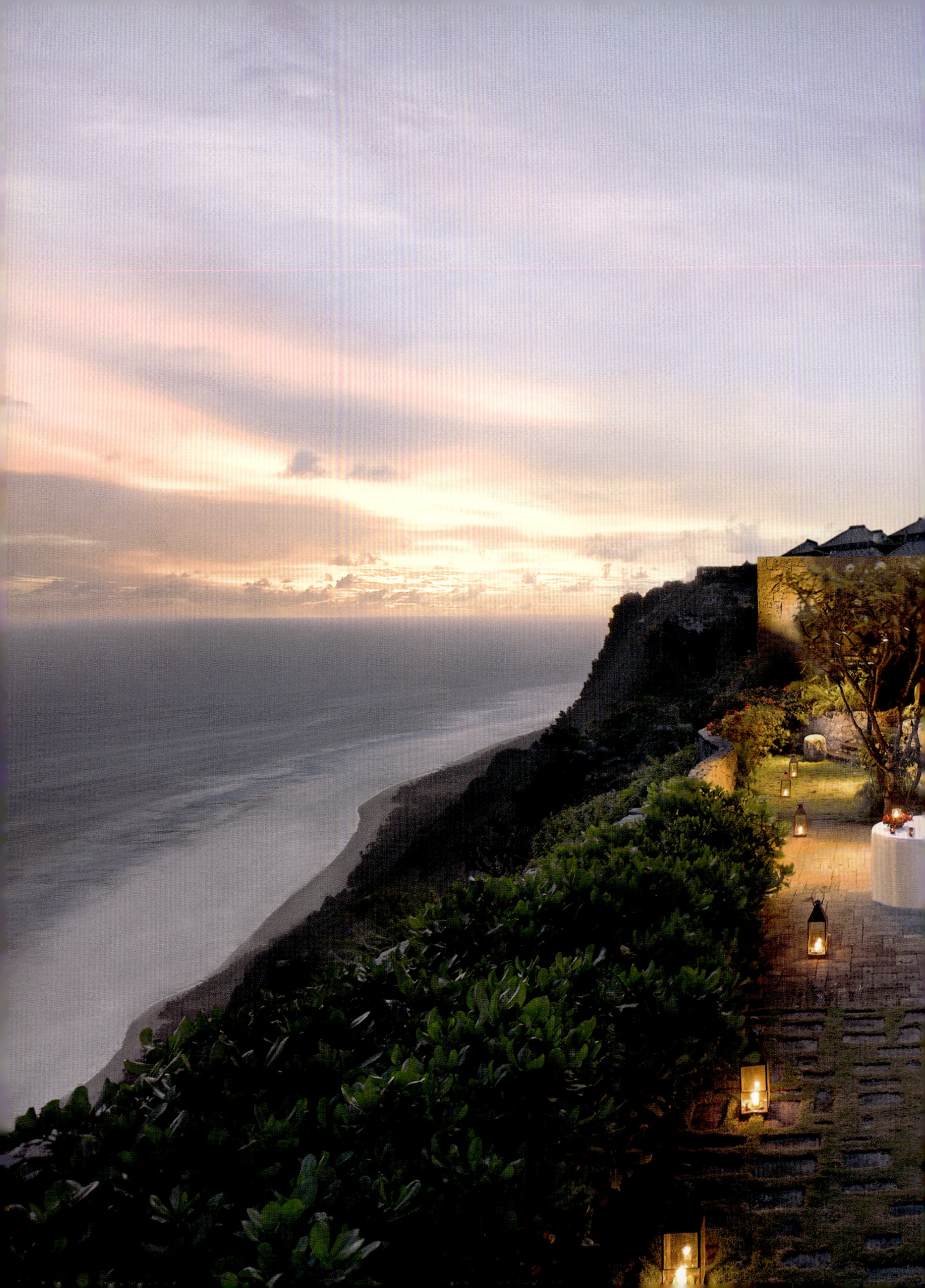

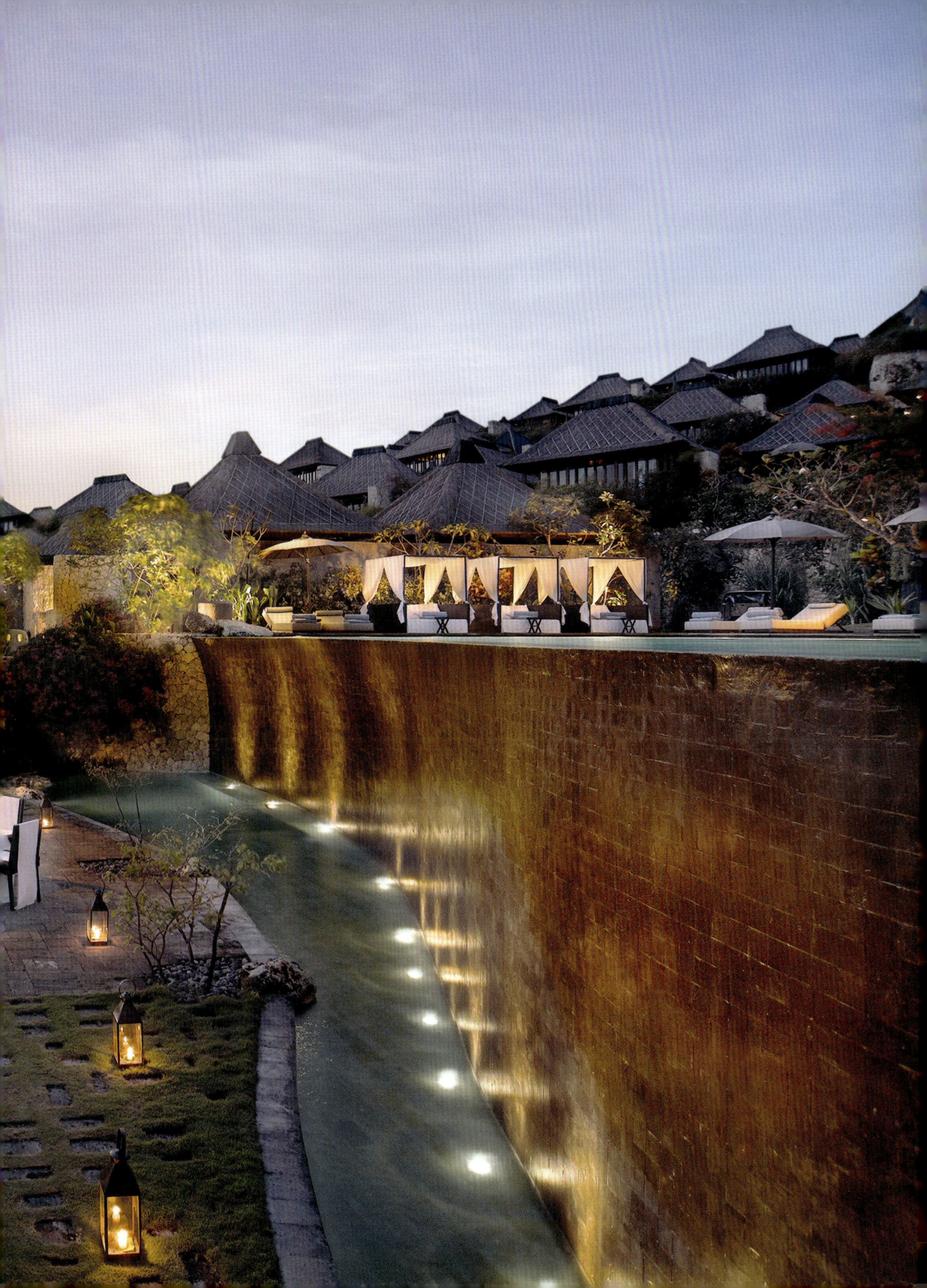

ASIA | KYOTO | NINE HOURS

nine hours hotel Kyoto, Japan

ADDRESS | 588 Teianmaeno-cho, Shijyo, Teramachi-dori, Shimogyo-ku, Kyoto, Japan
ROOMS | 125 over 9 floors
OPENED | December 2009
INTERIOR DESIGN | Nakamura Design Office
CREATIVE DIRECTION | Fumie Shibata
SIGNAGE & GRAPHIC DESIGN | Masaaki Hiromura

The nine hours capsule hotel epitomises minimalism. There is no meaningless decoration — the design is based on the notion that simple equals satisfying. Therefore, a minimal colour palette of predominantly white interiors interspersed with black iconography encapsulates this hotel.

This iconography creates the wayfinding within the hotel (colour coded according to gender — red for female and black for male) and provides visual interest to an otherwise blank canvas. The graphic elements, designed by Masaaki Hiromura, demonstrate how signage systems can be an important and integrated feature within hotel interiors.

As the name suggests, nine hours places a distinct emphasis on the value of time. The premise is based upon the notion that 'resetting your day, from one day to the next, needs three basic actions: take a shower, sleep and get yourself dressed.' The hotel has translated these actions to an equation of time — one hour + seven hours + one hour. For this reason, the hotel is perfect for travellers who require a short stay — ideally nine hours.

'As the name suggests, there is a distinct focus here on the 'value of time.' The concept is based on the premise that 'resetting your day, from one day to the next, needs three basic actions: take a shower, sleep and get yourself dressed.''

9h
nine hours

ASIA | KYOTO

In addition to the 24 hour check-in service, the hotel provides guests with the basic necessities for an overnight stay – shampoo and conditioner, toothbrush and toothpaste, disposable slippers along with lounge wear. Guests can then retreat into their own capsule which comes complete with an adjustable sleep ambient control system. Set the alarm and be woken through the modulation of light – this is where technology meets nature.

1 + 7 + 1 = 9ʰ

Shower   Sleep   Rest   9 hours

NINE HOURS

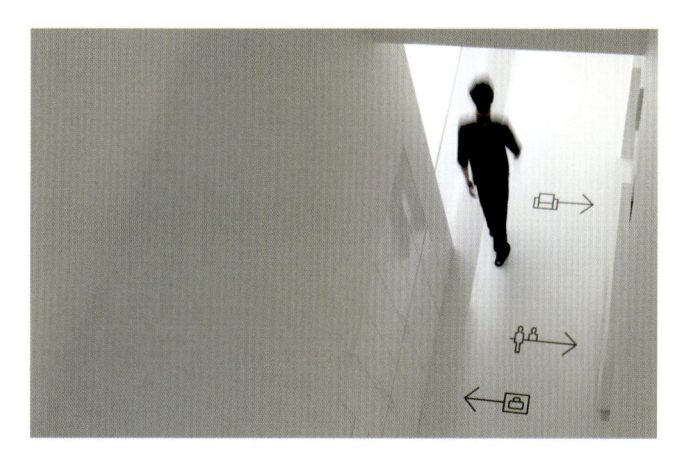

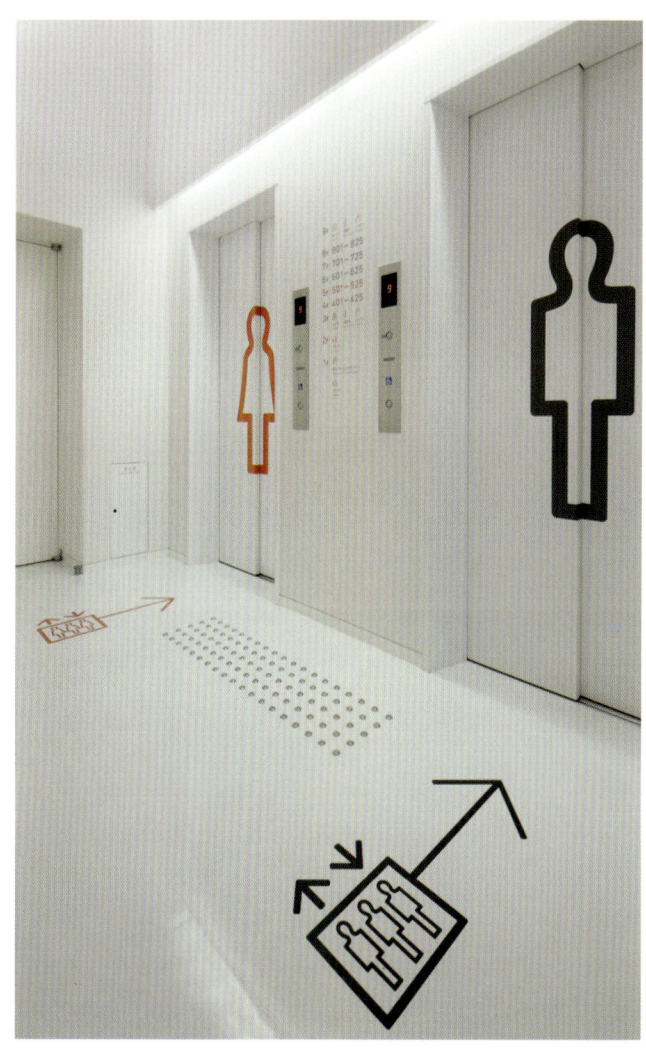

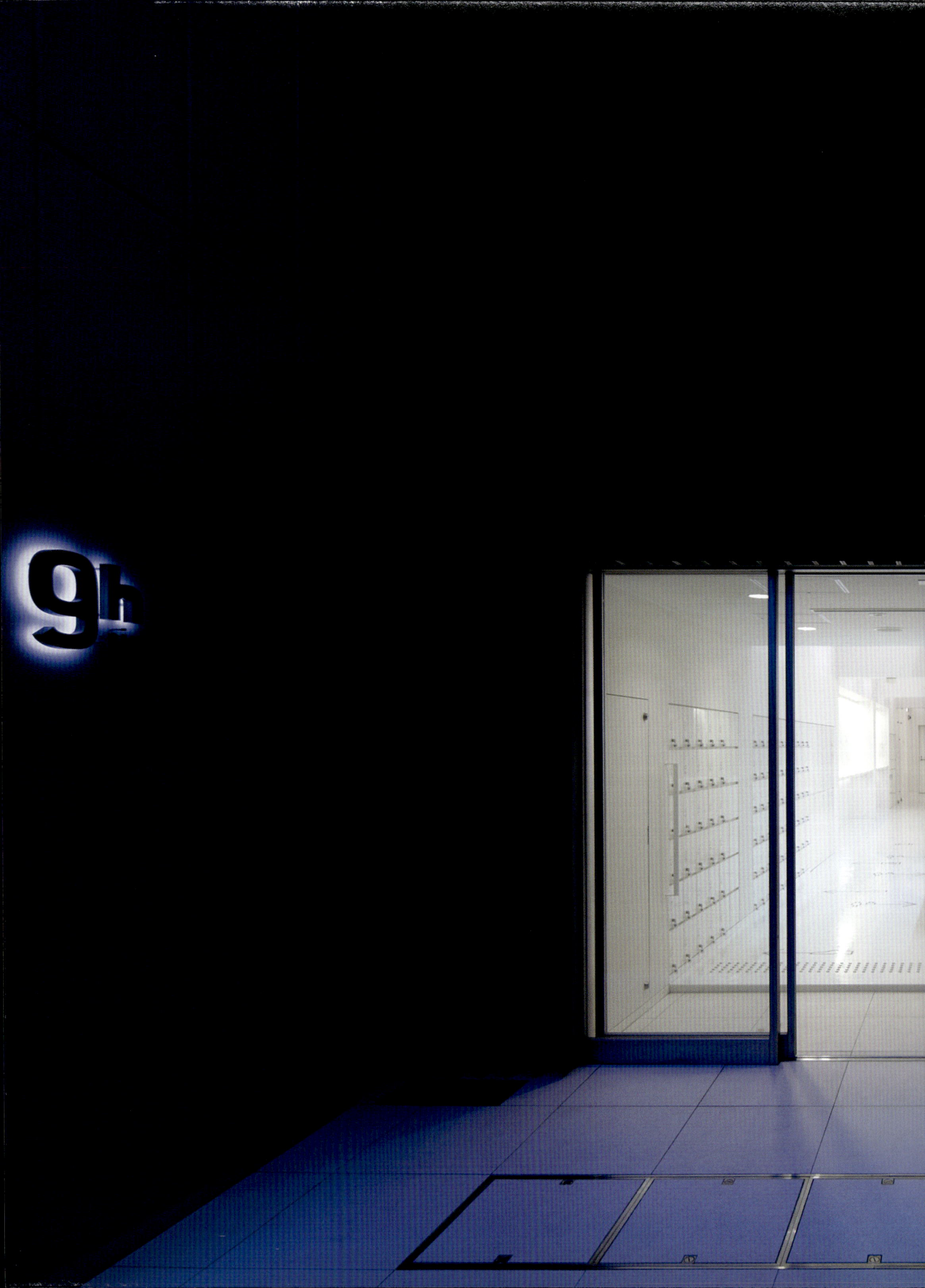
9h

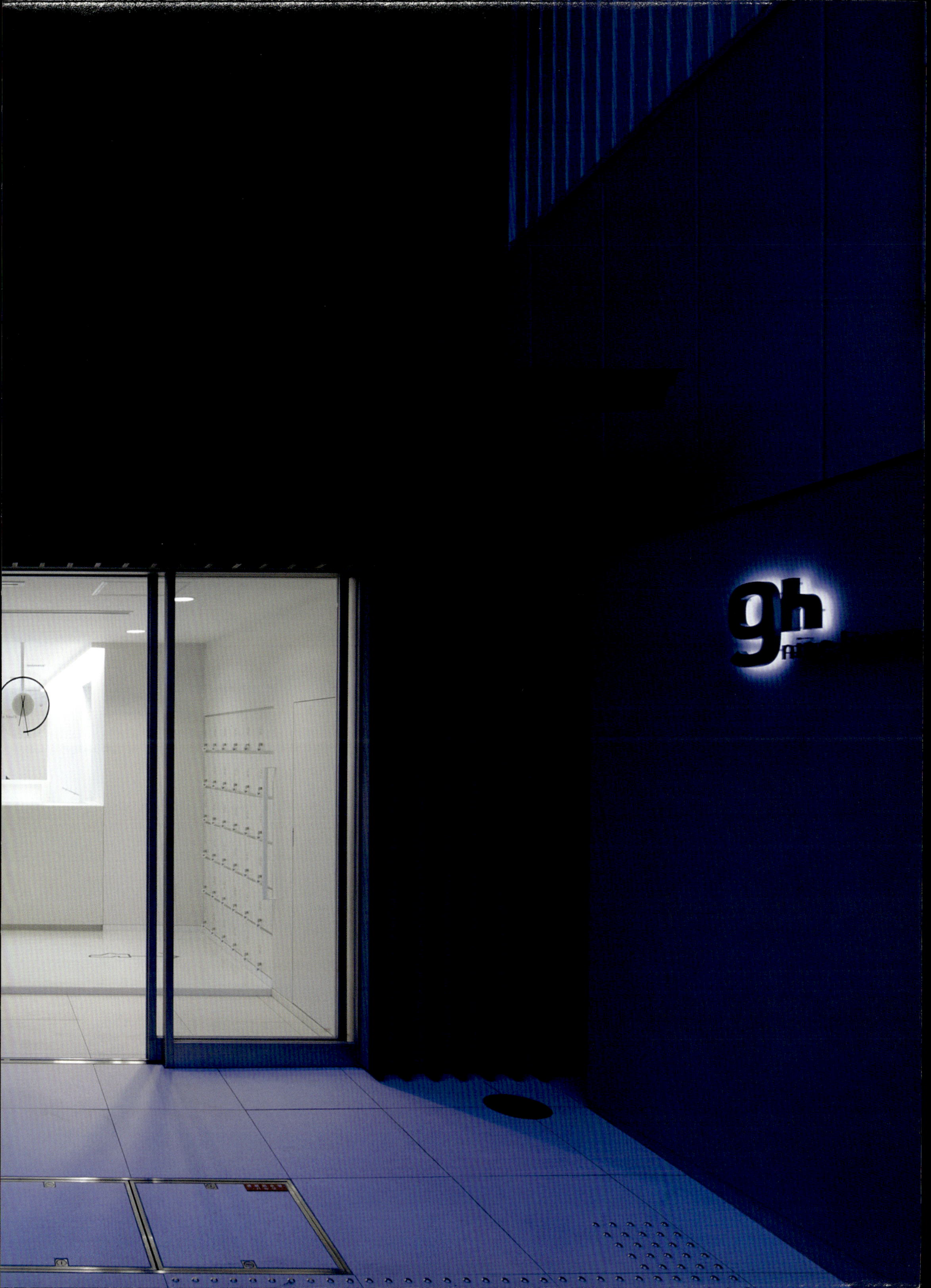
gh

074
080
086
091
097
092
098
075
081
087
093
099
100
094
088
082
101
095
gh

NINE HOURS

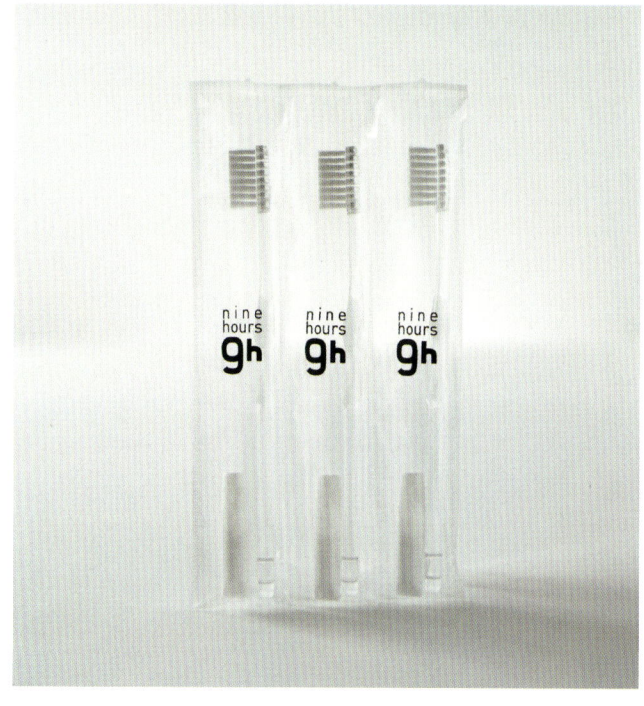

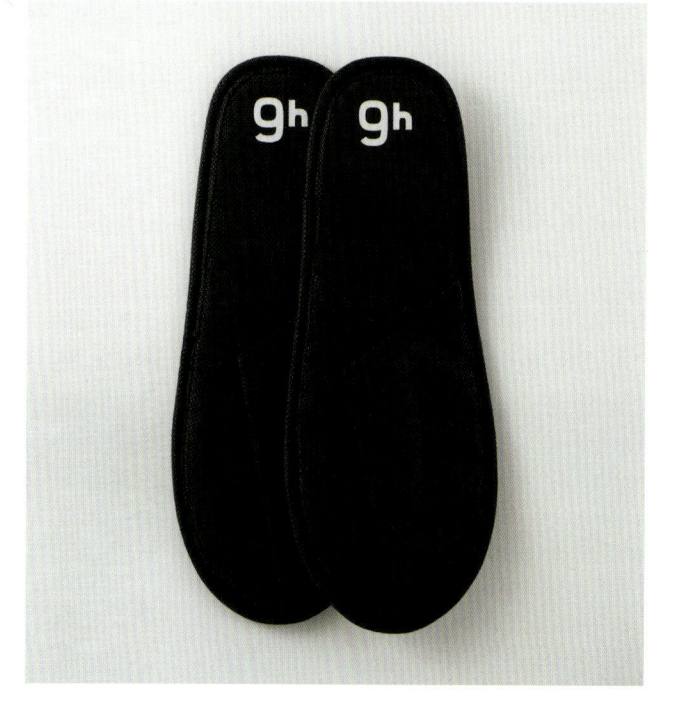

Wanderlust Hotel Singapore, South East Asia

ADDRESS | 2 Dickson Road, Singapore, South East Asia
ROOMS | 29 rooms
OPENED | August 2010
ARCHITECT | DP Architects
INTERIOR DESIGN | Asylum, :phunk Studio, DP Architects, fFurious
GRAPHIC DESIGN | Foreign Policy Design Group

Wanderlust, located in Singapore's Little India, is an experimental hotel that offers guests an escape from reality. Housed in a heritage-listed former school, each of the four floors were handed over to different design firms (specifically with no interior design or hotel experience) to create individual and quirky rooms for guests to experience.

As such, each floor is designed around a theme chosen by the individual studios. The lobby, designed by Asylum, represents 'Industrial Glam.' Level two, designed by :phunk Studio, is based upon Pantone (a standardized colour reproduction system used worldwide) and features rooms rendered in different hues that come with neon signs and song titles such as, 'Yellow Submarine' and 'Purple Rain.' Level three, based around black and white, created by DP Architects, takes inspiration from a mixture of origami and pop art. Level four, designed by fFurious, takes on more of a whimsical stage set around 'creature comforts' with varying themes.

With such an eclectic mix of interiors, it is no wonder that the hotel was created with adventurous travellers in mind, and the branding and associated collateral also reflect this theme. The experience of a journey begins straight after you check-in and receive your itinerary. Wanderlust is true to its definition and allows guests to explore different places and travel — all within the same hotel.

'Wanderlust (noun) — an irresistibly strong desire or an impulse to travel far away and explore different places.'

wanderlust

ASIA | SINGAPORE

BY AIR MAIL
PAR AVION
THAILAND
RATCHA ANACHAK THAI
BONJOUR
FRANCE PARIS
WELCOME TO SINGAPORE
欢迎来到新加坡

BAGGAGE
64
wanderlust
ECHOLAC
wanderlust
CHECKED BAGGAGE
LUGGAGE NO
64

WANDERLUST HOTEL

'The airmail tricolor band is synonymous with travelling and correspondence — the conveyance of the emotions and thoughts kindled during a journey via mail. The custom made logotype expresses the feeling of dreaminess, fantasy and the discovery of the surreal landscape of a new world. The dash lines evoke the impulse to join the lines, as with the impulse to travel.'

— Foreign Policy Design Group

CHECKED BAGGAGE
LUGGAGE NO
ROOM NO
wanderlust
SIN
wanderlust
boarding pass
BAGGAGE
ROOM NO
BAGGAGE CLAIM
wanderlust
wanderlust

W9494
ROOM RATES
JAPAN
PASSPORT
SINGAPORE
ITINERARY
wanderlust
CHECKED BAGGAGE
BAGGAGE CLAIM
ROOM NO.
LUGGAGE NO.
wanderlust
Arrival

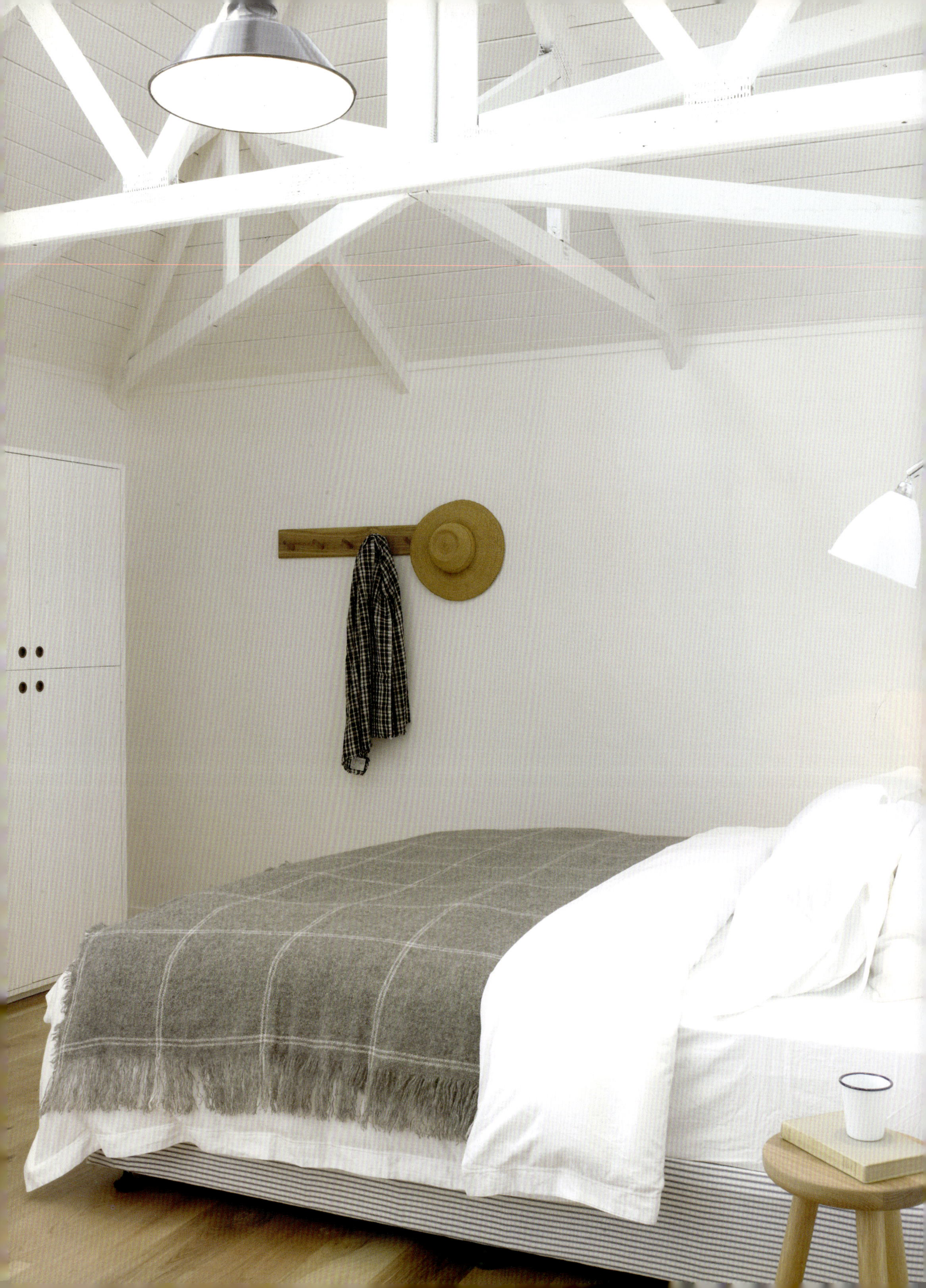

Oceania

'You are where you sleep.'

— Ian Schrager

QT Hotel Sydney, Australia

ADDRESS | 49 Market Street, Sydney, New South Wales, Australia
ROOMS | 200 guest rooms
OPENED | 17th September 2012
ARCHITECT | Crawford H Mackellar (original building 1912)
INTERIOR DESIGN | Nic Graham (public areas designer and stylist); Shelly Indyk (guest rooms designer and stylist)
GRAPHIC DESIGN | Fabio Ongarato Design

The QT Sydney is the melding of two of Sydney's most iconic heritage buildings — the Gowings Department Store and the State Theatre Building. The façade of the hotel has been restored to its former glory, while inside a mix of old world glamour has been integrated with new technology, distinctive art mediums and cutting edge emerging artists.

This hotel is a collaboration between art consultants, graphic designers, architects, stylists and even costume designers to ensure the experience engages with guests moments upon entering. The branding, applied across an extensive range of collateral, enhances the experience with a clever combination of language displayed with a neon effect mixed with a seductive series of collages.

The design team have played to the obvious eccentricities of the original historic buildings to create vibrant and edgy spaces. Once inside this 200 guest room hotel, an eclectic mix of quirky artefacts from around the world have been combined to create a distinct hotel experience.

A distinctive colour combination of Yves Klein blue, magenta and citron — along with the black and white used throughout — cleverly distinguishes this hotel from others. Complete with a curated art experience featuring unique installations, the QT Sydney combines a hotel experience with a sense of play.

'The façade of the hotel has been restored to its former glory, while inside a mix of old world glamour has been integrated with new technology, distinctive art mediums and cutting edge emerging artists.'

STATE

STATE

MERRY CHRISTMAS &
HAPPY HOLIDAYS
FROM ALL OF US AT
THE STATE THEATRE

GOWINGS

OCEANIA | AUSTRALIA

'The QT Sydney branding is a highly visual and photographic set of seductive images that are used independently as well as collaged together. The key creative themes are a mix of Art Deco, Innuendo, Surrealism, Voyeurism, Opulence, Noir and Intrigue — all captured within the space through portals, film loops, reflections and fragmentations, exotica, the celebrity, neon and light.'

— Fabio Ongarato Design

spa Q

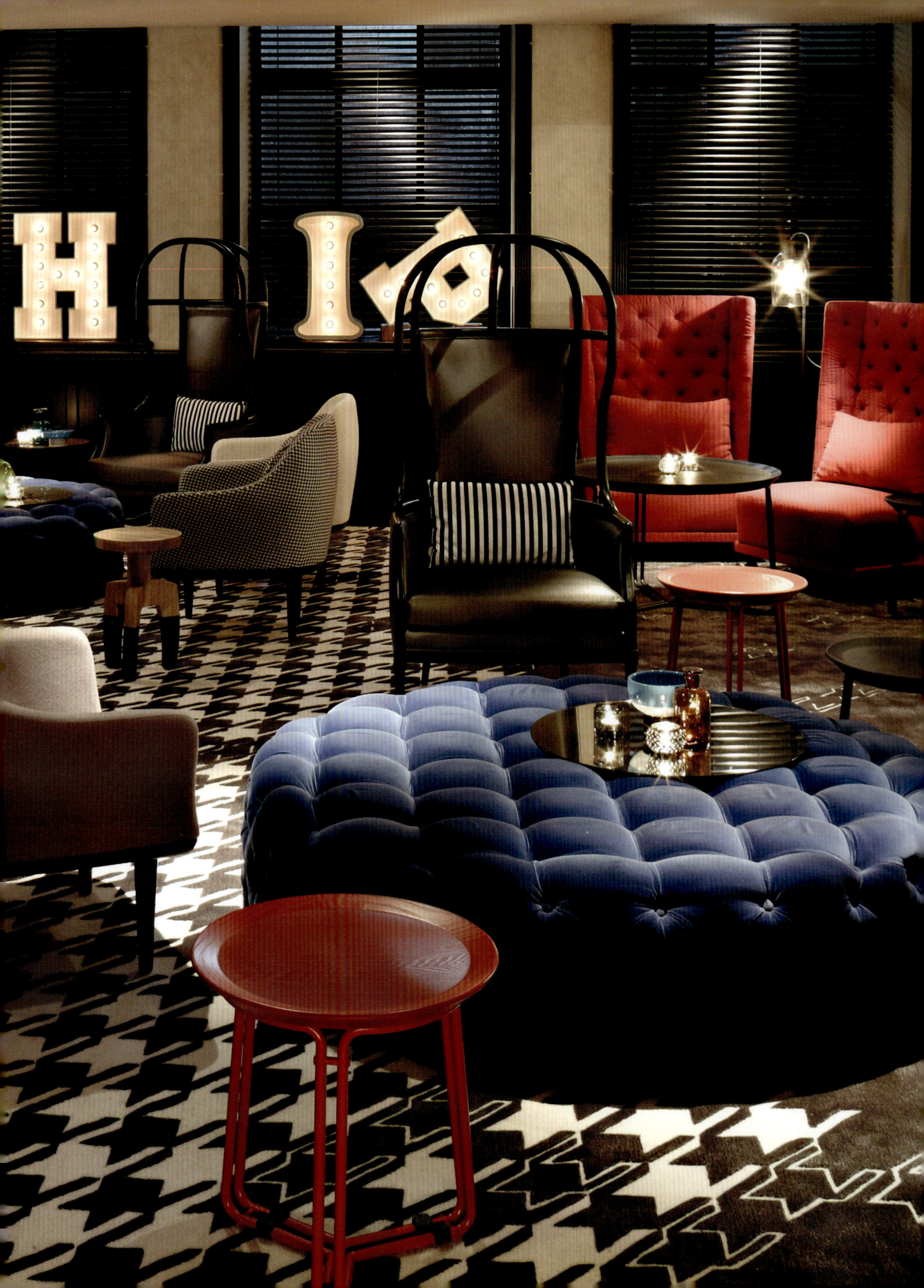
H
I

QT SYDNEY

223

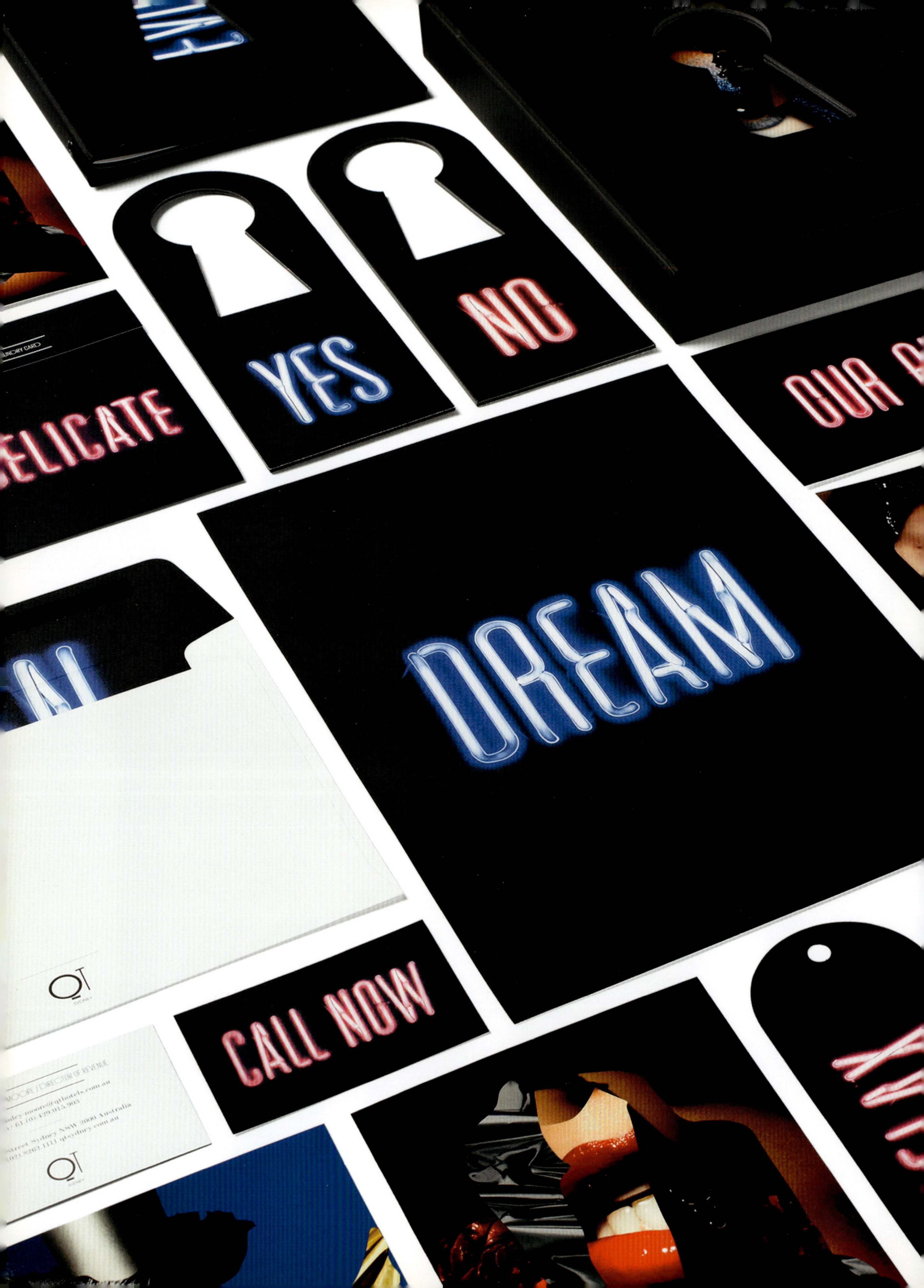
NO
YES
DREAM
CALL NOW

LOST FOR WOR
INDULGE
BOTTOMS UP
COVER UP
VALET TICKET
QT HOTEL
qtsydney.com.au
49 Market Street Sydney
+61 (02) 8262 0000

FIND YOUR INNER MUSE

OCEANIA | AUSTRALIA | ART SERIES HOTEL GROUP

Art Series Hotel Group Australia

ADDRESS | 6 boutique hotels across Australia
ROOMS | Dependent upon location
OPENED | 2009
ARCHITECT | Dependent upon hotel
INTERIOR DESIGN | Dependent upon hotel
GRAPHIC DESIGN | Toben

The Art Series Hotel Group launched in 2009 and contains a collection of hotels, along with Art Series Residences, in various locations around Australia. As the name suggests, each hotel is named after a famous Australian artist whose artwork is then featured throughout the hotel. In conjunction with their accommodation offering, this art inspired experience is completed with dedicated art channels, art libraries, art tours and art supplies for guests' use.

The hotels currently exist in six locations and are dedicated to their individual artist: The Cullen — modern artist Adam Cullen; The Olsen — landscape artist Dr John Olsen; The Blackman — figurative painter Charles Blackman; The Watson — Indigenous artist Tommy Watson; The Larwill Studio — figurative expressionist David Larwill and The Schaller Studio — contemporary artist Mark Schaller. At each hotel, the branding adopts its own individual style with the creative input of the artist. The Art Series Hotel Group is the master brand that exists in unison with the individual hotels.

Based on this, the identity for the Art Series Hotel Group remains predominantly black and white but utilizes the individual artist's work and style to create a distinct and unique look for each hotel. A combination of two typefaces (sans serif and serif), along with a series of appealing language (with selected underlined words) gives the Art Series Hotel Group a distinct look while remaining contemporary.

'As the name suggests, each hotel is named after a famous Australian artist whose artwork is featured throughout the hotel. This art-inspired experience is completed with dedicated art channels, art libraries, art tours and art supplies for guests' use.'

OCEANIA | AUSTRALIA

ART SERIES HOTEL GROUP

229

OCEANIA | AUSTRALIA

ART SERIES HOTEL GROUP

A **ROLL** **OF** THE **DICE**...

EXPLORE OUR LOCAL GEMS
Hire a bicycle, scooter or smart car.

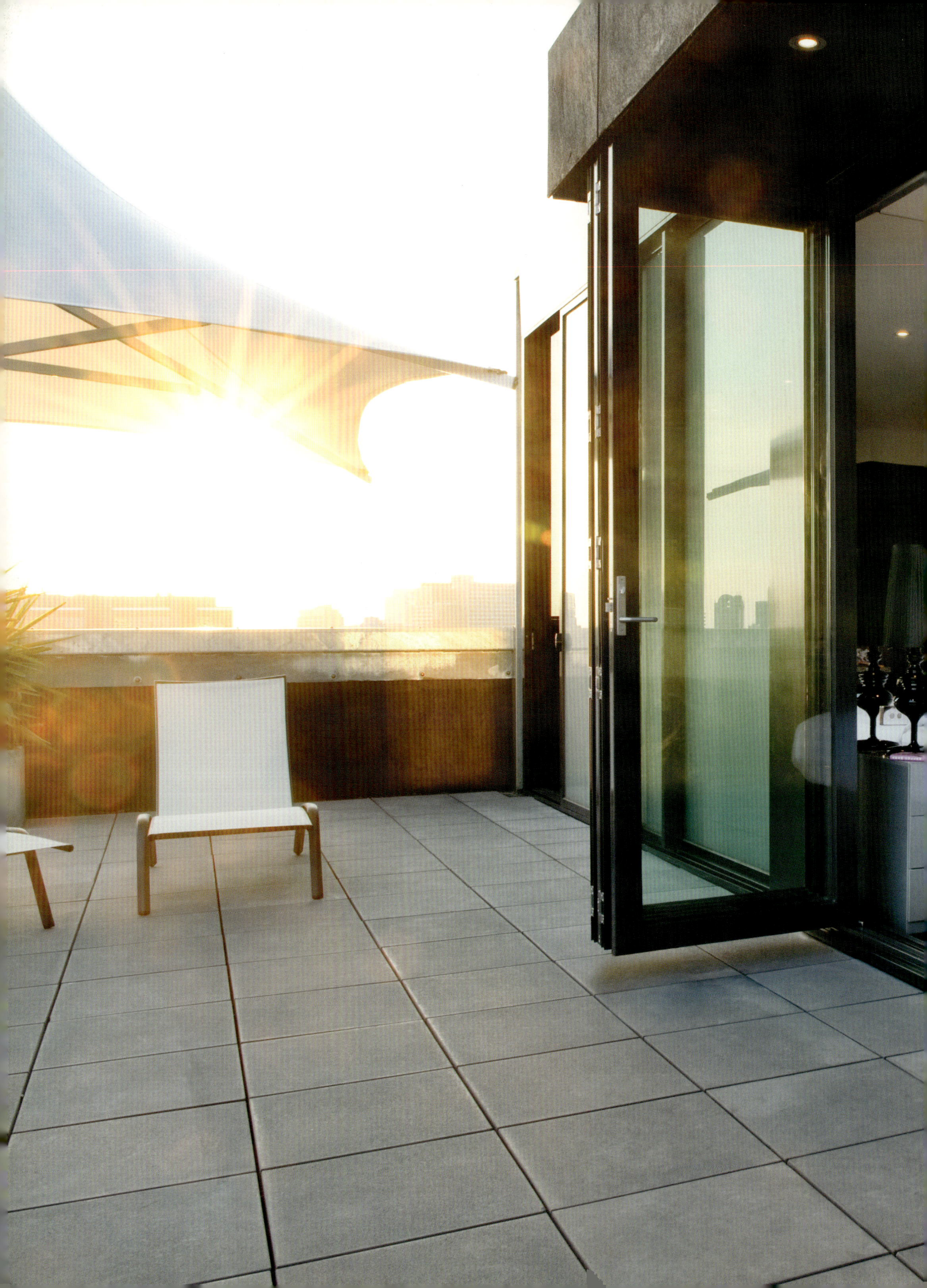

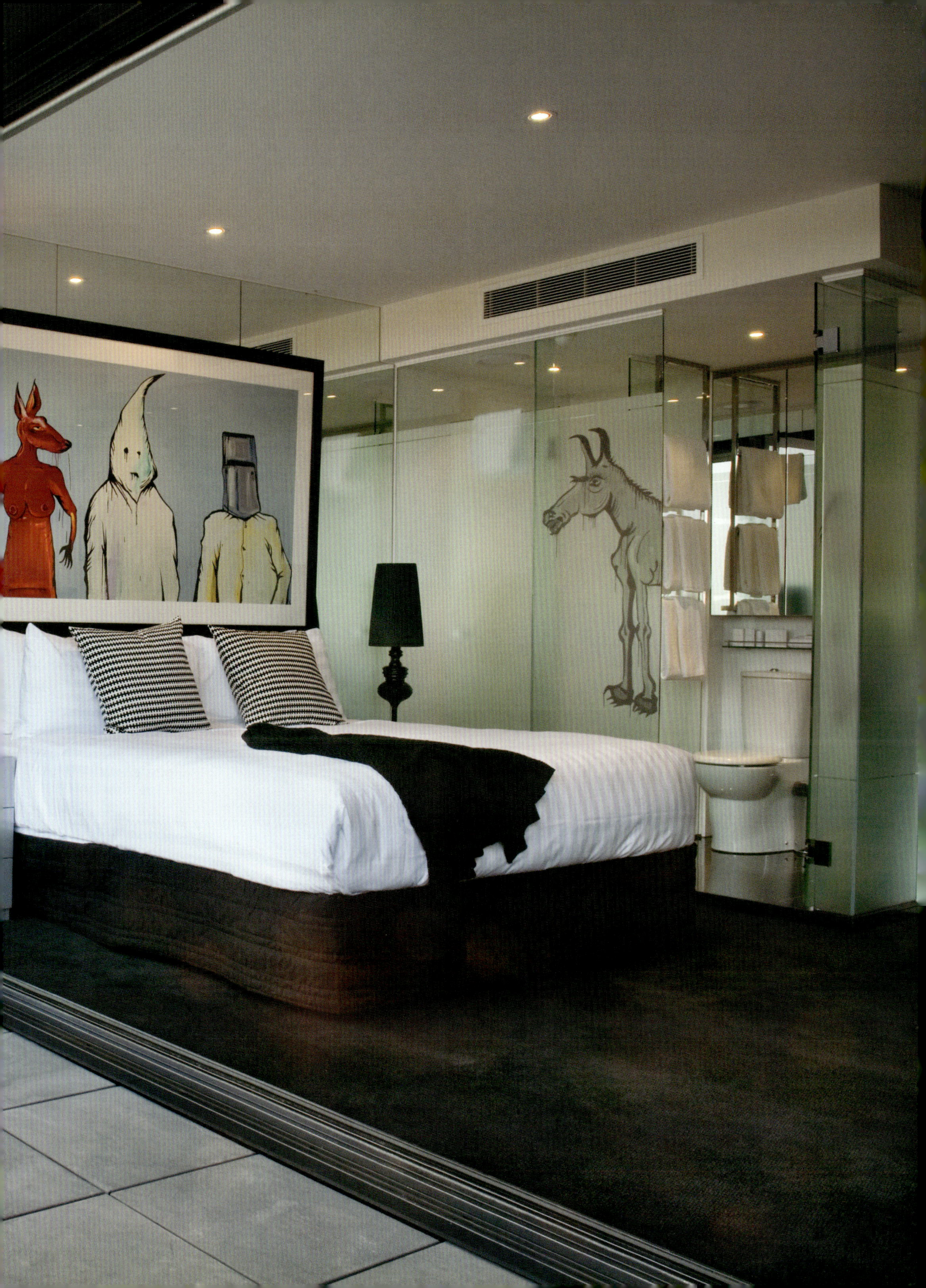

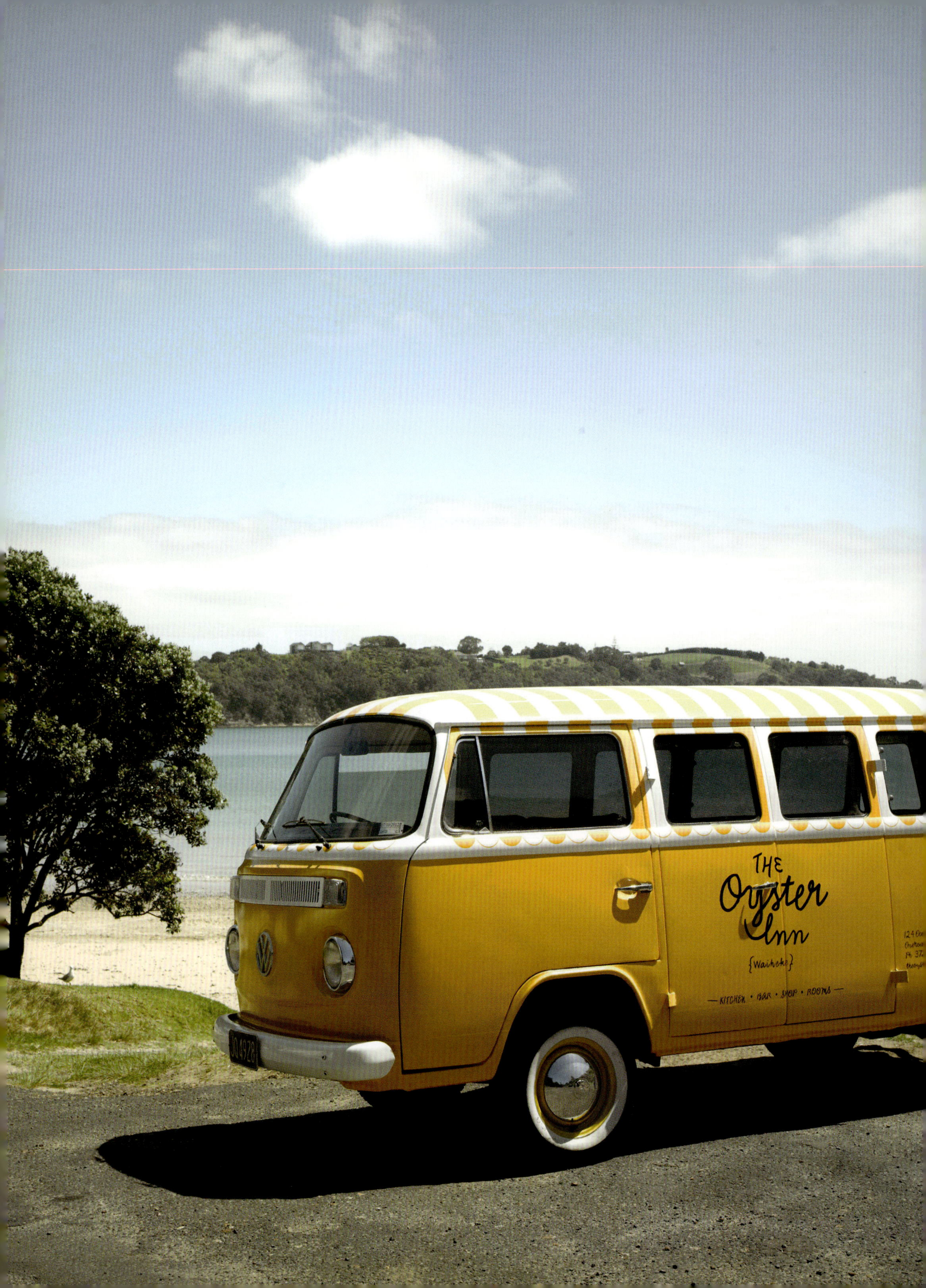
THE Oyster Inn
{Waiheke}
KITCHEN · BAR · SHOP · ROOMS

OCEANIA | WAIHEKE | THE OYSTER INN

The Oyster Inn Waiheke, New Zealand

ADDRESS | 124 Ocean View Road, Oneroa, Waiheke Island, New Zealand
ROOMS | 3
OPENED | November 2012
INTERIOR DESIGN | Katie Lockhart
GRAPHIC DESIGN | Special Group, New Zealand

The Oyster Inn is a boutique offering that includes kitchen, bar, shop and only three immaculately decorated hotel rooms. The local owners, Andrew Glenn and Jonathan Rutherfurd, returned to New Zealand from years abroad and created a hotel that feels both unique and familiar — almost as though it has always been there. A high level of personal service is the key offering at the inn, particularly since the number of rooms available is so small.

The branding itself, designed by Special Group, was created to inspire guests to feel as if the innkeepers undertook the design themselves. In reality, the authenticity of this well-crafted identity is based upon each element being painted by a traditional sign writer, digitally captured, crafted and then incorporated into the branding experience.

The bright and friendly colour of yellow, combined with crisp white (inspired by the building's iconic yellow striped awning) truly encapsulates the relaxed feel of Waiheke Island.

Along with traditional stationery, the branding also extends to their own 1970s VW Combi Van, providing an additional experience for guests arriving by ferry to be transported to the Inn. The Inn's store goes on to offer guests the perfect island experience with custom branded beach towels, sunscreen lotion and, for your feet, yellow Havaianas.

'Inspired by the building's iconic yellow striped awning, the identity created by Special Group, truly encapsulates the relaxed feel of Waiheke Island.'

OCEANIA | WAIHEKE

The Oyster Inn
{Waiheke}

OCEANIA | WAIHEKE

EXIT

THE Oyster Inn
THE Oyster Inn
THE Oyster Inn
THE Oyster Inn

THE SHOP

*

at the beach,
back in 5

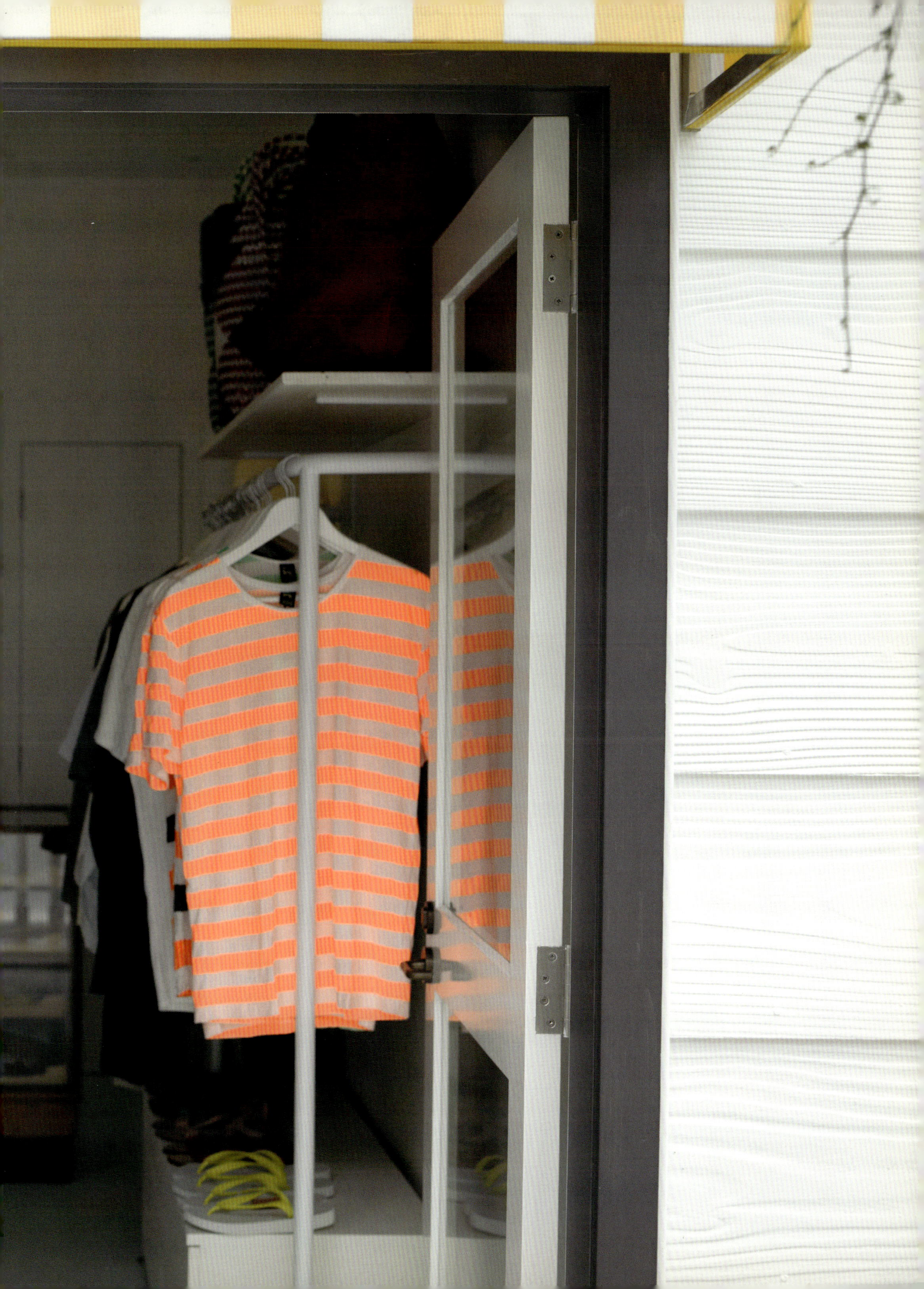

Photography Credits

Every reasonable effort has been made to acknowledge the ownership of copyright images included in this publication. Any errors that may have inadvertently occurred will be corrected in subsequent editions, provided proper notification is sent to the publisher.

Cover image: Courtesy of the Wythe Hotel.
Back image: Courtesy of Hotel Daniel.
Front and back endpapers: Courtesy of Dan Funderburgh.

p10: Courtesy of Grupo Habita; p12: Logo created by be-poles; pp14-15: Photo by Benoit Linero; pp16-17: Courtesy of be-poles; pp18-19: Photo by Benoit Linero; pp21-25: Courtesy of Grupo Habita; p26: Photo by Catherine Harvey; p27: Courtesy of Grupo Habita; p28: Courtesy of The Standard, High Line; pp30-33: Photo by Maikka Trupp; p34: Courtesy of KesselsKramer; p35: Courtesy of The Standard, High Line; p36: Photo by Adrian Gaut; p38: Photo by Adrian Gaut; p39: Courtesy of Derick Holt; p40: (top) Photo by Adrian Gaut (bottom) Courtesy of Derick Holt; pp41-43: Photo by Adrian Gaut; pp45-47: Courtesy of Palihouse, except p47 (bottom right) Photo by Maikka Trupp; p48: Photo by Maikka Trupp; pp49-51: Courtesy of Palihouse; p52: Courtesy of Joie de Vivre Hotels; p54: Photo by Maikka Trupp; p55: (top left and right) Photo by Maikka Trupp; p55: (bottom) Courtesy of Joie de Vivre Hotels; pp56-57: Courtesy of Joie de Vivre Hotels; p58: Photo by Catherine Harvey; p59: Courtesy of Joie de Vivre Hotels; p60: Photo by Nikolas Koenig; p62: Courtesy of KesselsKramer; p64: Courtesy of KesselsKramer, Photo by Freudenthal/Verhagen; p65: Logo designed by KesselsKramer, Courtesy of citizenM; p66: Courtesy of KesselsKramer; p67: Courtesy of citizenM; pp68-69: Courtesy of KesselsKramer, photographed by Freudenthal/Verhagen; p71: Courtesy of Claridge's Hotel; p72-73: Courtesy of Claridge's Hotel; pp74-75: Courtesy of Construct London; pp76-77: Courtesy of Claridge's Hotel; p79: Photo by Amy Murrell; p80: Photo by Amy Murrell; pp81-83: Courtesy of Goosebumps Brand Consultancy; pp84-85: Photo by Amy Murrell; p87: Photo by Nikolas Koenig; p88: Photo by Maikka Trupp; p89: Photo by Nikolas Koenig; pp90-91: Photo by Maikka Trupp; pp92-93: Photo by Nikolas Koenig; pp94-101: ©Hotel Wiesler; pp103-109: ©Hotel Daniel Vienna; pp110-117: Courtesy of Mama Shelter; p119: Photo by Michael Tewes; p120: (top) Photo by Michael Tewes, (bottom left and right) Photo by Maikka Trupp; p121: (top and middle left) Photo by Michael Tewes, (bottom left) Photo by Thomas Bach, (bottom right) Photo by Maikka Trupp, pp122-123: Photo by Thomas Bach; p124: Photos by Michael Tewes; p125: Photo by Thomas Bach; pp126-133: All interior imagery courtesy of Studio Aisslinger/Michelberger Hotel, Design by Azar Kazimir/Ulrike Ziggel, courtesy of Michelberger Hotel; pp135-136: Courtesy of The Exchange Hotel; p137: (top left and right) Courtesy of The Exchange Hotel, (bottom left and right) Photo by Catherine Harvey; pp138-141: Courtesy of The Exchange Hotel; pp143-144: Courtesy of The Student Hotel; p145: (top) Photo by Kasia Gatkowska, (bottom) Courtesy of The Student Hotel; p146: Courtesy of The Student Hotel; p147: Photo by Maikka Trupp; pp148-149: Courtesy of The Student Hotel; p150: Photo by Marcel Lelienhof; pp152-153: Photo by Square, Courtesy of The Thief; pp154-155: Photo by Studio Dreyer Hensley; p156: Photo by Studio Dreyer Hensley; p157: (top and bottom left) Photo by Studio Dreyer Hensley, (bottom right) Photo by Square; pp158-165: Courtesy of Hotel OMM, p167: Photograph by Magnus Mårding; p168: Photo and design by Studio Frith; p169: (top) Photo by Magnus Mårding, (bottom) Photo and design by Studio Frith; pp170-171: Photo and design by Studio Frith; pp172-173: Photo by Magnus Mårding; p174: Courtesy of Koncept Stockholm; p176: Courtesy of Koncept Stockholm; p177: Photo by Patrik Lindell, Courtesy of Koncept Stockholm; pp178-179: Courtesy of Koncept Stockholm; p180: Photo by Patrik Lindell, courtesy of Koncept Stockholm; p181: Courtesy of Koncept Stockholm; p182: Courtesy of Bulgari Resort Bali; p184: Courtesy of Lux Resorts and Hotels; p186: Courtesy of & Smith; pp187-188: Courtesy of Lux Resorts and Hotels (top, image left and right); p189: Courtesy of & Smith (middle, right); pp190-191: Courtesy of & Smith; p192: Courtesy of Bulgari Resort Bali; p194: Photo by Maikka Trupp; p195: Courtesy of Bulgari Resort Bali; p196: Photo by Maikka Trupp; pp197-199: Courtesy of Bulgari Resort Bali; pp201-207: Courtesy of Nacasa & Partners; pp209-215: Courtesy of Foreign Policy Design Group; p220: Courtesy of The Oyster Inn; pp219-221: Courtesy of QT Sydney; pp222-225: Photo by Todd Barry and Peter Bennetts, Courtesy of Fabio Ongarato Design; p226: Courtesy of Art Series Hotel Group; p228: Photo by Maikka Trupp; pp229-230: Courtesy of Art Series Hotel Group; p231: Photo by Maikka Trupp; pp232-233: Courtesy of Art Series Hotel Group; p234: Photo by Mark Smith; pp236-237: Design by Heath Lowe and Emma Kaniuk, Special Group, Photo by Tony Brownjohn; p238: Photo by Mark Smith; p239: (top left) Photo by Duncan Innes, (top right, bottom left and right) Photo by Mark Smith; pp240-241: Photo by Mark Smith; p244: Photo by Kate Ballis.

Acknowledgements

The idea for this book has consumed me for more than seven years. During this time, I have kept a close eye on the hotel industry and waited for what I believed was the right time to begin the process of creation. Firstly, therefore, I would like to thank Mo Cohen, David Lopes, Rick Markell, Amy Detrich and the team at Gingko Press for believing in my idea and allowing me the creative freedom to design and write this book over the past years.

In order to ensure the authenticity of this book, I spent countless hours researching and traveling to the majority of the hotels within to experience them for myself. This was no small feat, and I would like to thank all of the hotels who welcomed me, provided the time to talk with me and ensured that I had all the relevant information.

The creation of a hotel brand and the entire hotel experience is the combined effort of many people — from the owners, architects, builders, interior designers, graphic designers, marketing and PR, right down to all the employees who operate the hotels on a day-to-day basis. In particular, the branding for any hotel relies on the vision of a designer (or team of designers) to create an identity that will come to reflect the entire experience.

For these reasons, I wish to express my sincerest gratitude to the people behind each hotel who I have had the pleasure of meeting and/or corresponding with for their contribution. In no particular order this includes: Siri Løining Kolderup, Dominic Gorham, Azize Ayhan, Jacqueline Jacoel, Axel Kårfors, Ann-Marie Ekroth, Reynald Phillippe, Danya Guillén, Rafael Micha, Lucia Montemayor, Daniela Maerky, Eliane Cho, Moya Hewitt, Kirsten Leigh Pratt, Adrienne Der, Derick Holt, Brittany Ellish, Stephanie Poquette, Emily Childers, Marina Köstl, Ulrike Leonhartsberger, Jérémie Trigano, Jason Gregory, Eef Vicca, Azar Kazimir, Leah Lee, Bruno Marti, Suki Verwiel, Suzanne Oxenaar, Renate Schepen, Frank Uffen, Darla van Hoorn, Charlie MacGregor, Nathalie Hoffard, Michaela Ingels, Benedict Kingsmill, Rebecca Brennan, Lily Dodwell-Hill, Judith Fereday, Robin Chadha, Dave Bell, Amy Van Der Veer, Jeroen van Zijp, Paula Fitzherbert, Tom Thrussell, Ivan Poljak, Clementina Milá, Mar Pérez, Frith Kerr, Bryony Quinn, Jeanette Mix, Filippa Henningsson, Mae Noor, Angga Adhitya Syailendra, Ricky Utomo, Miho Endo, Géraldine Perrier, Marjovic Sorabally, Aimee Emerson, Mark Liebermann, Stephen Howard, Beckie Mitchell, Celia Doyle, Andrew Glenn, Georgia Fendley, Emma Kaniuk, Michael Tavani, Caroline Sloan, Seagren Doran and Nicola Amos.

I would also like to thank Maikka Trupp, who kindly provided her time and photographic expertise for capturing the additional imagery this book required. Following this, my sincerest thank you to Dan Funderburgh for the endpapers and Kate Ballis for photographing myself.

On a personal note, I would like to dedicate this book to my husband Daniel Withington and our beautiful daughter Ruby — my love and dedication to both of you is endless. In addition, I would like to thank Matthew Moloney for without your support over the years, I wouldn't be where I am today.

And finally, I would like to thank Steven Heller who kindly agreed to write the foreword. I have admired you from afar for many years throughout my design career and I have learned a great deal from your words. Most importantly, you have given me the confidence to not only have an opinion but also a voice.

Author

Catherine Harvey is a graphic designer and writer with over ten years experience working in Asia, Europe and Australia.

Her interest in branded experiences, design trends, and branding strategy, along with an inexplicable obsession with hotels, has driven her to travel extensively to stay with the most creative hotel brands in the world.

Catherine holds a Bachelor of Design (BVisComm) from Monash University and is currently completing her Masters of Entrepreneurship & Innovation.